ORIGINAL SPIN

ORIGINAL SPIN

Misadventures in Cricket

VIC MARKS

First published in Great Britain in 2019 by Allen & Unwin

Allen & Unwin
c/o Atlantic Books
Ormond House
26–27 Boswell Street
London WC1N 3JZ

Phone: 020 7269 1610
Fax: 020 7430 0916
Email: UK@allenandunwin.com
Web: www.allenandunwin.com/uk

A CIP catalogue record for this book is available
from the British Library.

Internal design by Patty Rennie

Hardback ISBN 978 1 91163 019 7
E-Book ISBN 978 1 76063 548 0

Printed in the UK by TJ International, Padstow, Cornwall

1 3 5 7 9 10 8 6 4 2

For the Crackington Crew

CONTENTS

ONE

TAUNTON 1974

'WELL, WE'RE NOT GOING to get into the team ahead of him.' Peter Roebuck and I stared at one another and simultaneously came to the same conclusion.

It was April 1974 at the County Ground and the Somerset players were having their first middle practice. A gangling pace bowler from Burnham-on-Sea, Bob Clapp, who would one day become a far better teacher, raced in and hurled the ball down as fast as he could. The delivery was not too bad, a fraction short perhaps and a little wide. There was the crack of willow on leather and the ball disappeared to the cover point boundary at staggering speed. A square cut of awesome power and certainty. Clapp looked a little puzzled and crestfallen. Meanwhile the batsman made ready for the second delivery of his practice session, although it took some time for the first one to be retrieved from beyond the greyhound track that encircled the playing area. Isaac Vivian Alexander Richards had arrived in Taunton.

Richards was barely known outside Antigua and Lansdown in Bath, where he had played a season of club cricket in 1973. That state of affairs would not last for long. Those who had played with or against Richards at Lansdown had soon recognized something special. Within a decade it was tricky to argue with the assertion that here was the best batsman of his era. I never bothered to try. He was the best.

Maybe it was Richards' exploits for Lansdown the previous summer that allowed him to change in the main dressing room of the old pavilion when he first reported as a Somerset cricketer in that spring of 1974. There he found himself alongside three giants of the county game: Brian Close, an exile from Yorkshire having been controversially sacked in 1970, was the captain of the club; Tom Cartwright, once of Warwickshire and an exquisite bowling machine, was now Somerset's player/coach; and in his last season as a professional there was 'Gentleman' Jim Parks, who had spent most of his career caressing the ball up and down the slope at Hove.

There were also some old Somerset stalwarts sitting under their usual pegs in that homely dressing room (well, there were a couple of sofas and an old gas fire in between the cricket bags) in the bucolic figures of Mervyn Kitchen and Graham Burgess, and some young ones, too – namely a pair of athletic blonds from Weston-Super-Mare, Brian Rose and Peter Denning. To augment the locals there was an assortment of cricketers from elsewhere: within the last few years Derek Taylor, the wicketkeeper, had come from Surrey; fast bowler Hallam Moseley from Barbados; left-arm spinner Dennis Breakwell from Northampton; and from Sussex Allan Jones, who would end up bowling fast for a good percentage of the clubs on the county circuit before sending batsmen on their way with his right index finger as an umpire.

At the back of the pavilion was a little alleyway beyond which was a dingy stone-floored room, which in later years would serve far more appropriately as modest toilets for gentlemen spectators.

There was one tiny, thin window near the ceiling, a couple of benches and a few pegs on the wall. This was where the new recruits to Somerset were housed since there was not enough room in the main dressing room for the entire staff. That room no longer exists; it was demolished to make way for the suave, state-of-the-art Somerset Pavilion in 2015. There were no preservation orders to overcome in that process.

Back in the winter of 1973 the chairman of cricket, Roy Kerslake, who had captained Somerset in 1968, had successfully advocated a youth policy to the committee. Hence there were five newcomers in addition to Richards: Phil Slocombe, another batsman from Weston-Super-Mare; John Hook, a tall, gentle, prematurely deaf off-spinner, who was also from Weston; Roebuck and Marks, who had both been enlisted as batsmen (I'll explain later) and a young man from Yeovil named Ian Botham. We were the occupants of the makeshift dressing room. All of us were eighteen years old though Botham seemed to have lived a bit longer – or at least more vigorously – than the rest. He tended to dominate proceedings even then, especially in our claustrophobic dressing room.

In that cubby hole a pattern emerged in those first few weeks. Ian rubbed along happily with Peter Roebuck, who was a very bright, Cambridge University-bound Dylan fan with huge feet, far more prepared to lower the drawbridge as a teenager than in later life. Ian and I were two South Somerset boys – I had grown up on a farm near Yeovil – and we got on perfectly well. Fairly early on in our relationship I learnt the necessity of identifying some form of escape route late in the evening when in Ian's company. In Somerset I did not have to use it very often since I always had a forty-minute drive back home; hence the nocturnal haunts available in Taunton were never my specialist subject. By and large it always seemed wiser to avoid a serious argument with the young Botham if at all possible, a philosophy I maintained in later life.

Ian did not take so easily to Phil Slocombe; he sensed too many airs and graces, real or imagined. The point to remember, given how Somerset would disintegrate a dozen years later, was that Roebuck and Botham were once in the same camp, both intrigued by their obvious differences and enjoying one another's company for the best part of a decade. They would argue merrily about most things and they would even write a book together, *It Sort of Clicks*, a task that, unsurprisingly, fell largely – no, entirely – upon the shoulders of Roebuck.

Slocombe, Roebuck and I had all come to the fore as cricketers by excelling to various degrees at local independent schools. Phil and Pete had played together, not necessarily in perfect harmony, at Millfield while I had been at Blundell's School in Tiverton just across the border in Devon. Along the way we had all played cricket for the county in the school holidays – sometimes in youth sides run chaotically by the old Somerset cricketer Bill Andrews, who, according to the title of his autobiography, possessed the hand that bowled Bradman (for 202) – and later for the second team. That has been a pattern repeated frequently with the Somerset sides of the twenty-first century (minus the endearing, larger-than-life Andrews). Whatever the merits of the system, James Hildreth, Arul Suppiah, Jos Buttler, Craig Kieswetter, the Overton twins, Tom Abell, Dom Bess, Eddie Byrom, George Bartlett and Tom Banton have all progressed in a similar manner, though, as Jack Leach has demonstrated, other routes are still possible.

Meanwhile Ian had spent two years on the Lord's groundstaff, a more fertile training ground then than it is now when every county boasts its own academy. That was a hard, boisterous, old-fashioned school, which may have suited him well. Botham had probably become more streetwise and more confident – not that he has ever been lacking in these departments – after spending two teenage summers in London rather than Yeovil.

Richards' path to Somerset had been more unorthodox. In early 1973 Len Creed, a mischievous Bath bookmaker, was visiting Antigua with a touring side, the Mendip Acorns. In his wallet he had a cutting from *The Cricketer* magazine in which Colin Cowdrey had noted, 'There was a chap called Vivian Richards who looked promising.' Creed met Richards, watched him score a brisk 30 and was impressed. He phoned the club's chairman, their former captain Colin Atkinson, because he had decided that he wanted to bring Richards back to Somerset. Atkinson was understandably reluctant to agree to this since it would involve the club in a risky outlay of cash on the recommendation of just one man. Then Creed suggested that he would bring Richards over to England himself to play for Lansdown CC, on the understanding that Somerset would cover the expenses incurred if the young batsman proved good enough to be granted a contract having served his qualification year. Atkinson thought this was a much better idea.

So, upon the hunch of a Bath bookmaker, never previously renowned for his cricketing nous, Somerset hit upon a jewel. Creed could dine out on the tale for the rest of his life – no one could ever begrudge him that – and for one season Lansdown CC became one of the most feared clubs in the county. Such a glorious sequence of events would not have been possible in 2019. Now it is necessary for an overseas signing to have played the requisite number of international matches in the previous year for him to be allowed into county cricket. A bookmaker's hunch would not be enough.

This was an interesting time to join Somerset. Yet my first day as a professional cricketer was a bit of a disappointment. I arrived wide-eyed, eager for the fray and scrupulously punctual after the drive from home in a fifteen-year-old black VW beetle with no fuel gauge and orange indicators that protruded from the side of the car like arrows when they deigned to work. It was raining at Taunton, but there was never any intention among the players to leap straight into the nets to hone the strokes that we had been working on in the indoor net sessions, on Thursday nights throughout the winter, under the omniscient eye of Tom Cartwright.

There were more important matters to discuss as we huddled around the gas fire in the main dressing room. 'This petrol money is bloody diabolical,' said Merv Kitchen, 'and you couldn't feed a mouse on our meal money.' Of course such crucial minutiae had not crossed my mind as I contemplated the season ahead but it'd be the duty of our player's representative, Derek Taylor, to go off to see the secretary, Jimmy James, to haggle for a more reasonable rate. It was not quite the big, happy family I had envisaged. Throughout that period the players had absolute faith in Kerslake, the cricket chairman, but that confidence did not necessarily extend to every member of the committee – and there were plenty of them.

Once the rain stopped we did something rather modern. We played football. In 2019 England do that for about fifteen minutes before every day's play and I can understand why, despite the risk of the odd embarrassing injury. It cheers everyone up. Just about every cricketer thinks he is a very fine footballer and there were times at Somerset when the despair among those not selected for the football team for those end-of-season benefit games was far more obvious than when they were omitted from a County Championship match at Derby.

When today's England team play football before the start of a Test match there are understandable restrictions, rigorously applied. It is a two-touch game with a lot of noise but no tackling. At the County Ground in 1974 there was also plenty of noise but no tackling ban. The matches were often extremely competitive and the tackles reflected the influence of Norman Hunter of Leeds United and Ron Harris of Chelsea; arguments raged and decisions were fiercely disputed. Sometimes these games would end abruptly as they overheated. 'Come on,' said Kitchen to his faithful dog, Thumper, who often came to pre-season training with him, 'we're buggering off now.' That meant the game was over because it was Merv's ball.

At some point we would disappear down the road to Wellington Sports Centre for a few days of fitness training. We dutifully donned a motley range of tracksuits (there were no sponsors for them in 1974), ran up and down hills and were detailed to complete devious training circuits. It was not that scientific. Even D. B. Close, who was forty-three, would do some press-ups. To be more precise, he would do two: one for the BBC cameras and one for those of HTV, which was the local ITV station.

Soon the cricket took over. I remember being in the twelve travelling to Warwickshire for a warm-up match and nervously discovering that the room list read 'Parks and Marks'. I was twelfth man and when Close asked me to sandpaper his bat while the side was out in the field I set to work with a zealous determination to impress my old, new captain. I found the Stuart Surridge bat bearing the initials DB and I cleaned it up meticulously. There was not a blemish to be seen. My pride was soon dented when the team returned to the dressing room and a puzzled Dennis Breakwell picked up his bat to find it mysteriously spotless.

In that first summer I was never entirely sure that Close could tell all of the newcomers apart. For some reason it did not take him long to work out which one was Botham, who would end up playing in sixteen of the twenty Championship matches. After that he might have been guessing whether it was 'Pete lad', 'Phil lad' or 'Vic lad'. When carrying out the twelfth man duties we all happily made Close his pots of tea upon which he seemed to survive throughout a day of county cricket. I was not quite so adept at placing bets on his behalf down at the bookies, which may have saved him a bit of money.

Despite an injury to Cartwright, from which he never really recovered, Somerset had a successful season. Viv Richards made his mark in his first game for the club against Glamorgan at Swansea in the Benson & Hedges (B&H) Cup on 27 April. He hit 81 not out with thirteen fours and one six to win the match. Close apparently delivered the immortal words, 'You'll do for me, lad'. It was all too much for Len Creed, who was in tears.

Soon it was evident that Richards was touched with genius and destined for a long international career. It was never so obvious with Ian. We watched eagerly when he played in the first team in the knowledge that anything might happen. If he succeeded that cheered us all up because here was a positive sign: if Ian, our peer, could hold his own, then perhaps we could as well at some point in the not too distant future. Ian was captivating, but one of England's greatest all-rounders, a future knight of the realm? There was more chance of a band comprised of furry creatures of dubious provenance making the top ten in the hit parade (mind you, that happened to the Wombles in 1974).

However, on 12 June at Taunton in front of 6,500 spectators Botham's performance suggested that, like Richards, he had something special. This was the B&H quarter-final against Hampshire. I watched almost every ball of that match. I had been stationed along with Roebuck inside the old, brown scoreboard almost opposite the pavilion. It was our job to operate it by pulling levers left and right and then leaning out of the window to plonk a few figures on the outside. We had a direct telephone line to the scorer just in case we occasionally lost track of the score, but with two alert young men who would soon be Oxbridge undergraduates, what could possibly go wrong?

When Hampshire batted Botham yielded 33 runs from his eleven overs and took two wickets, Peter Sainsbury and, rather more memorably, Barry Richards, who at the time was arguably the best batsman in county cricket, if not the world. However, the most instructive recollection is the manner of Richards' dismissal. He was bowled by Botham yet he was very reluctant to leave the crease because he thought that our wicketkeeper, Derek Taylor, whose twin brother, Mike, was playing for Hampshire, had inadvertently knocked off the bails. So here is evidence that in 1974 Botham bowled at little more than medium pace. The wicketkeeper – and Taylor was especially adept at this against seamers – stood up to the stumps to him most of the time. Over the next few years, encouraged by Close and tutored by Cartwright, Botham added pace in abundance. But at the start he propelled gentle away-swingers.

Hampshire scored 182, which looked more than enough when Hallam Moseley joined Botham at the crease with Somerset languishing at 113–8. I now know exactly what would have been happening in the press box. Everyone, recognizing a Hampshire victory as a foregone conclusion, would have been writing up feverishly to meet their paper's deadline and to get the job done as quickly as possible.

Andy Roberts, Viv's mate from Antigua and the most fearsome bowler on the circuit, was recalled. Yet with Moseley surpassing all expectations alongside Botham the score reached 150. Roberts now bounced Botham and the ball hit him in the face, loosening some teeth and spilling some blood. Another bouncer and the Somerset faithful were jeering Roberts angrily. Then Botham clipped a delivery from Mike Taylor for six, just clearing Roberts on the boundary. Now the crowd sensed an impossible victory while those in the press box began to anticipate an inconvenient rewrite. Botham hit another six and when Moseley was lbw to Roberts only seven more runs were required.

By now there was chaos inside the scoreboard as Roebuck and I lost control, whether it was through excitement or sheer incompetence I can't quite recall. We completely miscalculated how many overs had been bowled and were corrected by the shouts of thousands in the crowd. There was no guarantee that the score was right either. The telephone was ringing incessantly.

It was just as tense out in the middle. Last man Bob Clapp was neither the best of batsmen nor the fastest of runners. Somehow, amid a flurry of dust generated by a desperate dive he survived a run-out appeal and then, from the last ball of the penultimate over, Botham unveiled a flowing cover drive that sped to the boundary. The match was won though I'm not so sure that the scoreboard ever registered the victory. Here was a vivid reminder not to underestimate the young Botham.

After that we did not see Botham in the second team again. In August Roebuck played two games in the senior side, while the rest of us from the outhouse were exclusively in the second XI, playing against Minor County sides or in the newly formed, Under 25 forty-over competition among the counties. Roy Kerslake or Peter

Robinson, who would be employed by the club for four decades as player, assistant groundsman, coach and security officer, would usually captain the team. There would be the occasional, inevitable mishap. Early on there was an administrative/selectorial cock-up, which saw us turn up for an Under 25 match without a wicket-keeper. After a desperate process of elimination I was given the gloves – further confirmation that my bowling was an irrelevance at this stage of my career. Unlike Taylor I stood back to Botham and Richards and also, for the last over of the match, the off-breaks of Kerslake.

Robinson as captain was canny and occasionally carping as befits an old pro; Kerslake was cavalier as befits an old amateur, refusing to let any two-day game fizzle out into a dull draw by making some preposterously generous declarations. He would often claim afterwards: 'Oh, I thought stumps was six-thirty rather than seven.' In their differing ways they both kept a kindly eye upon us from Truro to Macclesfield. So did Tom Cartwright who put his heart and soul into the nurture of Somerset's new, young players. He was tough, stubborn, occasionally severe yet utterly devoted to us with an impish sense of humour, which surfaced with a mischievous chuckle. He knew the game inside out and he cared.

And so the season passed. In between working the scoreboard and shunting deckchairs around Bath and Weston for the festivals there, I scored enough runs to justify my contract without ever threatening to break into the first team. And I barely bowled a ball. At the weekends the club had arranged for Roebuck and me to turn out for Taunton CC, who played many of their games at the County Ground. There we were given every opportunity to bat up the order. They even gave me a bowl.

There could not have been a better way to spend the summer

of 1974 but at the time I did not appreciate how fortunate I was. Somehow I had ended up alongside a couple of youngsters, Viv and Ian, who would become two of the greatest cricketers of the twentieth century. In the same dressing room was Close, who would become an inspiration as well as a constant source of merriment – almost always unwittingly – to those newcomers at Somerset. Botham and Richards, decades on, never stint in their admiration of their first captain and the impact he had on their careers. And there was the wisdom and warmth of Cartwright.

They will reappear, along with a few others who inhabited a Somerset dressing room that was seldom dull as I meander around a life, which, to my amazement, has centred upon cricket for more than four decades. Sometimes it seems I have not travelled far even though the game has taken me to Vancouver, Suva, Chittagong and Hinckley. I've graduated from playing cricket to writing and talking about it. When I first joined the press corps I may have annoyed my new colleagues by suggesting that it was much tougher to play the game than report it. Three decades on I stick by that. After a bad day in the press box there are no figures of 0/100 next to your name. But a few positive reviews of what follows would be handy.

At this point I'm not precisely sure what will follow. It takes some of the spice out of writing if you know exactly what you are going to say. However, do not anticipate passages specifically designed for lucrative serializations in the national press. There may be a few insights into some of the foremost cricketing characters of the last four decades; don't expect too many revelations.

But you might be interested to learn about some of the following: how my first Test appearance triggered a decade or more of hostility between the great cricketing nations of England and Pakistan; Botham's peculiar addiction on the 1982/3 tour of Australia (calm down, I'm talking cribbage here); memories of the 'sex, drugs and rock and roll' tour of 1983/4 (but if I can remember that infamous trip could I really have been there?); Christopher Martin-Jenkins shopping in Marks and Spencer's; my time at Oxford with Tony Blair and Theresa May – though there is no guarantee that I actually met them; drinking with Tavaré, driving with Roebuck; Henry Blofeld unplugged...

So please plough on.

TWO

ON THE FARM

IN OUR HOUSE THE telephone was situated in a draughty, windowless hall, which did not encourage long conversations. It was the sort of phone that was inconvenient for those with farmer's fingers – like my father – since the holes on the dial were so small. It was sombre black and would now serve as a handy prop for an Agatha Christie play, especially since the home number possessed just three digits: Chiselborough 223.

Just before the Christmas of 1973 I received two calls on that phone and they were very welcome ones, which were to have a major impact on the rest of my life. The first came from Roy Kerslake, the cricket chairman at Somerset CCC, offering me a contract with the county for the 1974 season, which was worth £15 a week from April to September. The second informed me that I had been offered a place at St John's College, Oxford, to read Classics – or Literae Humaniores as they liked to call it.

The philistine truth is that I was more excited by the first offer than the second partly because I understood its implications more easily. I had been down to the indoor nets at Taunton several times and had played some games for Somerset's second XI. So I had a rough idea of how it all worked. Moreover I had been infatuated by the game of cricket for as long as I could remember and I knew that I was quite good at it. So this was unadulterated good news. There would be no haggling over pay.

I was far less sure about what going to Oxford would entail. None of my immediate family and none of my cousins had been to university. To say that I was infatuated by the study of Latin and Greek would, to put it mildly, be stretching the truth to breaking point, as would the notion that I was peculiarly gifted at those subjects. One headmaster's report hinted at that; perhaps Clive Gimson was lamenting my lack of curiosity and creativity when he concluded that 'we need Athenians not Spartans', an observation that would have meant absolutely nothing to my father and mother.

I had been sent away to public school at Blundell's in Tiverton on the eastern fringes of Devon and there it was assumed that you would proceed to university if at all possible. So I automatically kept following that path. It was a surprise that it took me to Oxford. I subsequently came to realize that the ratio of applicants to places was far more favourable for those intending to read Classics than almost any other subject. Perhaps my cricketing prowess helped a bit – I had played for England Schools XIs – but if that were the case this was an advantage that very soon disappeared for those hoping to go to Oxford, not entirely because of the decision to offer me a place, I hope.

I had no real idea what awaited me at Oxford although I did know that the university cricket team played first-class matches against the counties. So that offer, while more intimidating than the one from Somerset, was good news as well. The masters at Blundell's, no doubt hiding their astonishment adroitly, kept telling me so.

Just about everyone in my family was a farmer with the exception of one uncle, who had diversified; he was a butcher. We lived as long-term tenants in a grand-looking Elizabethan farmhouse in the little village of Middle Chinnock in south Somerset. It was an old-fashioned mixed farm with the dairy herd being the main source of income.

My father was a gentle soul, who did not say much and who pined for a quiet life. There was a warmth about him, most easily sensed by children, including my two daughters, who liked to cuddle up to him in the all too brief time that they knew him. My mother was a hands-on farmer's wife, who kept the account books meticulously and calculated the farmworkers' wages each week as well as rearing calves and orphaned lambs, and looking after the chickens. She made most of the big decisions. In between all that she would, increasingly often, ferry me around the county to play in some cricket match somewhere that seemed, to me at least, of vital importance.

She was a tough, determined woman, who was averse to any waste or extravagance, qualities that eventually enabled the farm to prosper. But occasionally she surprised me. Well into her seventies and long since widowed she announced that she was going to the Caribbean while England were on tour there, with me following in their wake in the press pack. She had been invited to accompany the mother of the man who had bought our old farmhouse, which was just up the road from her cottage. Before that expedition her travels had barely taken her out of the country. So I have a clear memory on that tour to the West Indies of flying over to Tobago from Trinidad to visit her and going for a ride with her fellow holidaymakers in a Mini Moke. We started driving down an overgrown lane in a deserted part of the island and suddenly were confronted by a mighty bullock in the middle of the track, which showed no sign of letting us pass. Most of us were still staring at the animal as my mother resignedly clambered out of the Mini Moke with her stick, advanced on the bullock and expertly shooed it out of the way. She was always the farmer's daughter/wife; she was the one in our party who knew best how to deal with the problem without any fuss. And so she did.

I have a brother, John, and a sister, Sue, twelve and eight years older than me respectively, the offspring of my father's first marriage, which ended tragically when his wife died at the time of my sister's birth. Somewhere I have a team photo from the farm. There was old Joe, the carter, who still looked after the two carthorses that were now in retirement partly because of their age but also due to the advent of a couple of Massey Fergusons. Charlie was the shepherd and Fred the handyman, who was especially skilled at laying hedges. None of this trio knew how to drive but Lionel, a Lancastrian who always wore a beret, did. Which probably explains why he was the tractor driver. Lionel had other useful qualities: he could play cricket.

In the back row, where the newcomers always reside in any team photo, was 'young' Arthur, who was Joe's son and the cowman. Now he could drive brilliantly. He could reverse tractors and trailers bearing hay and straw in the confined space of the covered yard, through gates and around pillars, as if there were no obstacles there at all, a skill I never threatened to master. As all these farmworkers reached retirement age they were never replaced. Finally there were John and my father. They could play cricket as well.

We played on the lawn at the back of the house, which was just long enough to provide a realistic pitch. I did more batting than bowling – as least that is what my brother keeps telling me.

John, Lionel and my dad could all bowl, though in his time my father may have had the odd square-leg umpire peering hard at his action. From the age of six one of them sometimes bowled at me after work in the summer and I loved that.

I'm sure the topography of our lawn dictated how I batted in the years to come. There was a greenhouse at mid-wicket and a privet hedge, about two or three feet high, beyond a path on the offside. So it was dangerous to hit anything to mid-wicket or there would be the grim tinkle of broken glass; but there were no such hazards on the offside.

So it may not be so surprising that I developed an inside-out swing of the bat that had a tendency to send the ball square on the offside, where the hedge was. But I was never so adept at hitting the ball smoothly through the onside, where the greenhouse was situated. We obviously needed more hedges for me to become a batsman of classical orthodoxy.

I can't recall seeing my dad play – except in one father's match at school – but I've glimpsed scorebooks of North Perrott Cricket Club, where he used to turn out occasionally. His innings look as if they must have been brief but eventful: 6, 4, 6 and out. My brother played some games for that club as well and so did I in my teens. Now that a plush new pavilion has been built Somerset second XI often have a fixture there. It is a lovely ground.

Later on my brother helped to re-form the cricket club in the village of Middle Chinnock. He prepared the pitches, found the players – mostly local youngsters – and captained the side. Along with his friend Henry Simon, a lively opening bowler and auctioneer, and their guitars he would sometimes sing in the pub afterwards. They would do the same each New Year's Eve in a pub in the depths of south Somerset when I was allowed to go along with them despite my tender years, usually without mishap. Wherever they played they always seemed to start with 'Sloop John B' and finish with 'Hi Ho Silver Lining', songs which have served them well over half a century.

John is still preparing the pitch in his seventies and, occasionally, still singing. He is another gentle soul, though much more gregarious than my father ever was. He does not relish confrontation either, which makes the fact that he once sent off one of his own team for boorish behaviour all the more admirable. In some ways that's as impressive as anything I ever managed on a cricket field.

One match in 1988 at Middle Chinnock was played in the best of spirits when we were on opposite sides. It was my benefit year, and Somerset with Martin Crowe and the rest of the first XI were all there for the game against the village. John and I were the captains and we both opened the batting and the bowling for our teams and thoroughly enjoyed ourselves. I can't speak for the other twenty players involved.

Away from the back lawn there might be mini-Test matches up at the vicarage with Andy and Phil Nichols, the vicar's sons. There it was necessary for the bowler's run-up to start on the other side of the road before progressing up the steps and into their back yard just before the delivery stride. Fortunately there was barely any traffic in the village to disturb the bowler's rhythm.

In more solitary games with a tennis ball in my own back yard I would try to ape the great players I had glimpsed on television. The greatest was Garry Sobers so, despite being right-handed, I often bowled left-arm spin and pace to invisible batsmen, doing my best to emulate Sobers' action in the process. Over twenty years later towards the end of a Test match in Faisalabad I bowled left-arm spin again. Unfortunately the batsman was not so invisible; it was Zaheer Abbas, who ruthlessly sidled down the pitch to hit a respectable, though very slow, delivery through the covers for four. In county cricket I tried the same ploy, more seriously – and more desperately – against Les Taylor, Leicestershire's number eleven. I didn't get him out either.

Sometimes, I'm often reminded, I would take an old stick and then pick up a little stone from the driveway that I'd toss in the air and try to hit – I think Don Bradman's youthful practice routine was a bit more scientific. So my enthusiasm for cricket must have been obvious from an early age. Miss Casson, a chiropodist from Lancashire, who lived in one of the farm cottages, gave me my first *Wisden*, the 1962 edition, and she continued that tradition for several years, for which I was very grateful. Hence I've always been well versed in the 1961 Australian tour of England when captain Richie Benaud contrived one of the most improbable Ashes victories in Manchester, a game that probably curtailed Brian Close's Test career. In the second innings Close was one of Benaud's six victims, caught on the leg-side boundary. My impression is that Close was always an easy scapegoat; he did not play again for England for another two years. It may not have been a great shot but surely the defeat was not all his fault – Peter May was bowled for a duck, sweeping. I was later intrigued to hear that when Benaud, the victorious captain, returned to the dressing room he just burst out laughing at Australia's great escape alongside his old mate, Neil Harvey. I could name both sides of the 1961 series now. By contrast the 1960 season is a blank.

Occasionally my father took me down to Taunton to watch Somerset. I saw Australians young and old, Bill Alley and Greg Chappell, and was mesmerized by their batting; the only autographs to survive were those of Fred Rumsey, one of the architects of the Professional Cricketers' Association (PCA), and Peter Robinson. Yeovil was nearer to the farm and there in 1969 I witnessed Brian Langford bowl eight overs, all maidens, in the newly formed John Player League in which there were forty overs per side. Most of his deliveries were to Essex's Brian Ward, who in his own mind heroically fended off Langford's off-breaks on a helpful pitch. Keith Boyce, a formidable hitter from Barbados, faced one ball from Langford and swung with great intent. A single ensued and a leg bye was signalled. Whisper it softly but some say there was a hint of an inside edge.

One other oddity of that match was that it marked the last appearance of Doug Insole in county cricket. He had retired six years earlier but in that era clubs like Essex and Somerset had threadbare staffs. An injury crisis had left Essex short of manpower. So Insole undertook the tortuous journey down to the south-west to make up the eleven on that Sunday afternoon. This might have worked out well for Essex since the one thing that Insole, the batsman, could do better than most was to sweep off-spinners like Langford. After his selfless response to this call-to arms Insole was run out without facing.

In the mid-sixties Somerset had one of the better sides in their history and they progressed to the final of the Gillette Cup at Lord's in 1967. To my unfettered delight my father acquired two tickets for the match against Kent. There were only 5,250 available for Somerset and the club secretary, Richard Robinson, reckoned he could have sold three times this miserly allocation.

I had hardly been to London before, let alone Lord's. I remember going once with my parents because we had to trek to Harrods to buy the school uniform for a pretentious local prep school, which, unsurprisingly, soon went bust. Running ahead on the underground the doors shut automatically and I was separated from my parents, which was momentarily alarming. We managed to reunite at the next station so no obvious traumas ensued, though it seems I still remember this mishap over a half a century later.

So the trip to Lord's for the final was quite an expedition. We were in the grandstand by 10.30 and looked over towards the Tavern where the most boisterous of Somerset's supporters were stationed. To satisfy the stereotypers they were clad in smocks and sucking straws. They also had a pact to down a pint of scrumpy every time Somerset took a wicket. In the morning they stayed thirsty. At lunch Kent had lost just one batsman, Mike Denness. But after the break and a session of almost complete abstinence nine Kent wickets fell in 90 minutes. No doubt those in the Tavern rose to the challenge. By then even sober Somerset supporters thought there was a good chance of the club's first ever trophy. But a target of 194 in sixty overs, not such a bad score in 1967 yet a trifling one today, was too much. It had been a brilliant, captivating, exhausting day marred only by the result and the fact that we left our sandwich bag at St John's Wood tube station.

My only other visit to Lord's before I played there was in 1968 when I was taken to the second day of the Test against Australia by Bruce Broker, the master in charge of cricket at my prep school. After the demise of the school at East Coker just down the road (with its uniform from Harrods), I was sent to St Dunstan's School in Burnham-on-Sea as a boarder at the age of nine.

Initially I was bewildered and distressed that I had to stay away from home. But I was soon enjoying the experience not least because there were so many sporting opportunities and some very good sportsmen at the school. Here I first met up with Jeremy Lloyds, who would also go on to Blundell's. With the odd interruption I was his scrum-half for the best part of a decade and we would play cricket together at Somerset before he joined Gloucestershire in 1985. Charles Kent, 'Crash Ball Charlie', who won five England caps in the centre, was two years older. I would follow his path from Burnham to Blundell's to Oxford.

At Lord's with Mr Broker, a stern English teacher when he was not running the cricket and football, I was enthralled again. In the morning we watched Geoff Boycott and Colin Milburn bat with the latter to the fore. There was the mighty frame of Milburn attacking Graham McKenzie and Neil Hawke before hitting the first ball of the day from Bob Cowper, a modest off-spinner, way up into the grandstand, threatening the tranquillity of Old Father Time in the process. Oddly it was the delicacy of Milburn's batting, despite his massive frame, that was most striking; he never seemed to be trying to hit the ball hard. Boycott was almost as enchanting. The next time I saw him batting at Lord's was in my debut for England in a one-day international (ODI) against the West Indies in 1980 – when he won the man of the match award even though he was no longer around to collect it.

At thirteen I arrived at Blundell's with the reassuring knowledge that there would be a few fellow pupils – like Jerry Lloyds – that I would recognise. It was a good, friendly school with a rounded, unstuffy outlook, which valued sporting achievement as well as many other activities beyond the classroom, and that suited me well. It is still a good school though this distant assessment may be coloured by the fact that it currently employs my daughter and son-in-law. I enjoyed the majority of my time there and was happy to be asked back to Speech Day a few years ago, albeit at very short notice because The Stig from *Top Gear*, an old boy, was suddenly unavailable. This allowed me to ask the gathering of parents, pupils and staff, 'How can you be so sure that I'm not The Stig?'

Back in 1968 it was no coincidence that I was directed to Francis House, whose housemaster, Chris Reichwald, was the master in charge of cricket. This particular house seems to specialize in producing off-spinning all-rounders. Roger Davis, a regular in Glamorgan's Championship winning side of 1969, was in Francis House; so too were Lloyds and Marks and more recently Dom Bess, who made such spectacular progress as a Somerset cricketer in 2016 and 2017 and who became an England one in 2018. Hugh Morris, the other notable old Blundellian cricketer of recent times, was in a different house but then he was always a useless off-spinner.

Reichwald was an old school housemaster in the best sense and he was much respected. He had won the Military Cross in the war when serving in the Queen's Royal Regiment in Italy and North Africa. His right leg was severely shattered by a shell, which eventually caused him to be invalided out of the Army. He was six and a half feet tall and walked with a pronounced limp for the rest of his life, but he would never let this stop him playing cricket or rugby fives and drinking Bass.

He ran the house by the book though he seldom sought out any trouble, not that he was ever particularly adept at creeping up on anyone committing indiscretions. Because of his limp and the hard stone floors of Francis House his arrival on the boys' side of the house could be identified from a distance. The distinctive 'clip clop' of his steps way up the corridor was reminiscent of the crocodile that swallowed a clock in *Peter Pan* and proved a most reliable early warning system. Reichwald taught modern languages very efficiently, though there were suggestions that when he went on holiday to France the locals had a bit of bother deciphering what he was talking about.

He was more fluent when speaking of cricket or fives. For two of the four years that I was in the first XI at Blundell's Chris kept an eye on me – especially so in my first season when I was tiny and struggling to hit the ball off the square but still capable of staying in for a long time. As a housemaster he did the same, overseeing my academic progress, which was not quite so obvious. Reichwald also ensured that in the winter I would play the far more civilized game of rugby fives rather than squash.

I once defeated Alastair Hignell at fives in the semi-final of the national Under 19 competition, a triumph that exhausted me so much that I was a spent force in the final. For those unfamiliar with fives you will have to make do with this definition from an old Oxford friend, John Claughton: 'a game played by few, watched by none and conducted in a court like a rhinoceros enclosure at a zoo'. In fact it's squash with gloves rather than a racket. Hignell gained easy revenge on the rugby field. To my horror I found myself opposing him at scrum-half when he was at Denstone College and I waved him through several times. Forty-five years on I would still encounter one master from Blundell's, Paddy Armstrong, who would recall my 'quick hands' on the rugby field and my cowardice, which he politely described as an 'enhanced instinct for survival'.

I was better at cricket. Twice I played for an Under 15 Public Schools XI, which was run by Hubert Doggart, an England Test cricketer of the fifties and subsequently a headmaster, against the English Schools Cricket Association (ESCA). I failed miserably in Norwich in 1970 but scored a few runs in Liverpool the following year when opening the batting with my captain, Peter Roebuck. We won the match there partly because the selection of our opposition side may have been flawed.

The ESCA side was chosen after teams from the North, South, East and West had played in a quadrangular tournament earlier in the week. In their wisdom the selectors invited one of the cricketers from the West, Ian Botham, to be their thirteenth man. This was not an invitation that the young Botham was inclined to accept and he immediately returned to Yeovil in high dudgeon, though he may have put it less delicately.

A couple of years later I was selected for ESCA sides to play against touring teams from overseas, one from India and another from the West Indies. The only Test cricketer from that Indian team was the captain and wicketkeeper, Bharat Reddy; the West Indies side contained Jeffrey Dujon, then just a batsman, and Wayne Daniel. None of us had ever encountered anyone who could bowl as fast as Daniel; nor were we accustomed to dealing with bouncers. We all put on our new ESCA caps for extra protection.

England's side contained some fine batsmen: Nigel Briers was the captain. Paul Parker and Hignell scored some runs and fielded brilliantly but the best player was Chris Tavaré with his free-flowing front-foot drives on either side of the wicket. He would become a good friend and colleague at university and beyond; he was there when I first met my wife, Anna; indeed he was partially responsible for that meeting – on a punt, as it happens. He also has the distinction, for want of a better word, of playing in my first and last first-class match.

In my last two summers at Blundell's John Patrick, who had played cricket with the Nawab of Pataudi at Winchester College as well as in the odd game at Oxford, had taken over from Reichwald as master-in-charge of cricket. Earlier in my schooldays I had been taught English by John for a brief period, a subject he taught pragmatically. Our written work always needed to be adorned with a few incisive lines from the literature we were studying. When I wrote the required definitive essay on *Othello*, for example, there would be John's curt assessment at the bottom. 'Not too bad… but where are the quotes?' – a refrain that I subsequently heard from a succession of sports editors a few decades later.

John was a swarthy man, capable of biting sarcasm when riled or let down, but very soon he became a guide and mentor to whom I was devoted. During the winter John and his great friend Paddy Armstrong would organize football matches with a few staff and boys forming a team to play against local villages on Sunday mornings (at the time Blundell's was resolutely a rugby school). So Jerry Lloyds was no longer Barry John but Martin Chivers whenever I tried to manoeuvre the ball in his direction.

The cricket was an altogether more serious matter. John's commitment when running the team was absolute; he would give up every spare moment for that extra practice if he thought it necessary. He did not much like losing. Despite my mild exterior neither did I and in my last year I was his captain, a role that I soon realised was a source of enjoyment and much-needed confidence. We lost just one game in what now seems a golden summer. John and I talked of cricket, of our cricketers and many other things, and we shared a similar sense of humour. We became great friends.

The following year on 10 October 1974, on my second day as an Oxford undergraduate, I had the bleakest phone call from Jerry Lloyds. He said that John had died suddenly from a heart attack after playing squash in Devon two days earlier. I was devastated. I could talk to John more easily than just about anyone else. He was the first person, to whom I was close, who had died. In my dreams he was still alive and I was talking to him about everything.

Just over two weeks later I went back to Blundell's for John's memorial service in the school chapel. There was Sally, John's wife, defiant in a bright red dress alongside their two young children, whom I used to babysit. The organ pumped out 'The King of Love, My Shepherd Is'. Why? Because it was one of John's quiz questions. It is the hymn that contains three Test cricketers in the first line. Years later Anna and I chose it for our wedding, not so much for the Test cricketers but in memory of John.

He would have been intrigued and maybe a little surprised at what became of me. Progressing to be a county cricketer may not have startled him too much, but he might have been mildly astonished that I became a Test cricketer, a national cricket correspondent and broadcaster though any praise would have been artfully coded. He did not gush. But how he might have relished a post-mortem on those experiences; how I would have enjoyed that too.

At the end of the day of the memorial service at Blundell's Sally gave me two treasured gifts, John's Oxford University Cricket Club (OUCC) tie and the tie of Vincent's Club, which is the sporting club at the university. I still wear the Vincent's tie often. Back in 1974 it would not be long before I was entitled to wear both of them.

THREE

OXFORD

'I THINK I CAN bowl as well as the others,' I said to my Oxford University captain, Trevor Glover. This was a rare expression of self-confidence on my part, which Glover, a squat Lancastrian with a warm heart, a rugby blue and a pragmatic technique when opening the batting, took on board. Every captain craves as many options as possible in the field, and when playing for a university side against the professionals you can spend an awfully long time out there.

With increasing frequency Trevor tossed the ball in my direction and before too long I had acquired all-rounder status in the university side. Soon I sensed that those keeping an eye on my progress back at Somerset must have been intrigued that I was starting to bowl so many overs. This probably did not include Brian Close, whose eyes would more likely be fixed upon the runners and riders for the 2.30 at Catterick than the latest scorecard from the Parks, the home of Oxford University cricket, but Roy Kerslake and Tom Cartwright would have noticed. I suppose a couple of my Somerset colleagues might have done as well since at the end of May 1975, in the Parks, Dennis Breakwell and Hallam Moseley became my first first-class victims. I can't recall how Dennis, a left-hander, was bowled so he cannot have been undermined by a classical delivery that pitched on leg-stump before clipping his off-bail. I would have remembered that. So he probably made a mistake, which is the source of most wickets, by the way. I'm more certain that Hallam was cheerfully trying to hit me into the next county when his stumps were disturbed.

Learning to bowl seriously – I had delivered my off-breaks quite frequently at school but never at representative level and seldom for Somerset second XI in 1974 – was a very handy career move. It would help my passage into Somerset's first team and, more surprisingly, enable me to play for England. But none of us saw that coming in the Parks in the spring of 1975.

Getting into the Oxford side, although I would have fretted about this throughout the winter, had not been a problem. Like my fellow freshman, Chris Tavaré, I had a bit of pedigree with those appearances for England Under 19s plus a county contract. Moreover I always like to acknowledge the role of Andrew Wingfield Digby in boosting my confidence at those pre-season nets.

I knew the name before I arrived at Oxford. Andrew was in his second stint at the university. In his first, when he read History, he had gained a cricket blue in 1972 and I must have logged that; he was back in 1975 reading Theology. I was intrigued to meet him and watch this senior citizen preparing for the summer ahead. As I remind Andrew as often as possible, I watched him batting and bowling in the nets at the Parks and soon concluded that it should not be so difficult to get into this university side after all. Hence my gratitude.

That may be unfair. Andrew took 96 wickets in his university career at 33 apiece. Among those victims were Colin Cowdrey and Viv Richards. It may have suited him that he played in the era before the speed gun. I imagine he exceeded 70 mph but not by much. As a courtesy our wicketkeeper, Paul Fisher, might stand back for a few overs whenever Andrew was given the new ball but soon he would be up to the stumps. Andrew was not the sort of opening bowler who hastened the evolution of the helmet.

Yet his system worked quite well; off an economical run-up Andrew was accurate; he bowled from very close to the stumps and he hit the seam more often than most. And he was unquenchably optimistic and competitive (I hesitate to repeat what an officer of the armed services called him upon being dismissed lbw after an inside edge and a most vociferous appeal from the bowler).

There were several pros who hated facing him as well – Brian Rose at Somerset was one – partly because of his lack of pace. Digby's batting was less reliable but he did produce the highest score of his career, 69, in my debut in first-class cricket. It was no wonder that he became one of Alan Gibson's 'characters' in his inimitable match reports for *The Times*. It was more surprising that he was appointed the England team's chaplain in the nineties until he was given the elbow by Raymond Illingworth, who had a more traditional view of how to deal with the frailties and needs of an England cricketer.

That debut in April 1975 was against Sussex, who were led by Tony Greig, one of the few England cricketers who had come out of the 1974/5 Ashes tour in credit. As I took guard there was John Snow, a hero of the 1970/1 tour of Australia, at the end of his mark. I was in dreamland. One might construe this debut as a triumph, the good news being that I top-scored for Oxford in that first innings. The bad news? I was out for 22.

Snow was wearing about five sweaters as he glided up to the

crease; his first ball thudded into my front pad but only after nicking the inside edge of the bat. Eventually – in fact, not very long after – I was caught by Snow off the bowling of John Spencer and in the second innings I departed in identical fashion for a duck. There may be a small minority out there who might like to note that this was the first known collusion of Marks and Spencer in the history of the game.

Oxford were thrashed in that match and the side would be weakened for the next one since Imran Khan had played in the fixture against Sussex but now, in his final year, he would withdraw to concentrate on his studies, returning for the end of season games and the Varsity match. At that stage of his career Imran was just discovering that he could bowl fast, a development that Alastair Hignell, now at Cambridge University, would witness at first hand at Lord's. Imran plonked Hignell on his backside a few times with hostile bouncers in that Varsity match. Of course Hignell always bounced back up again.

Captain the previous year, Imran was in a different class to the rest of us and he knew it. He could sometimes appear haughty, but in part that may have been due to shyness. He was encouraging to the likes of Tavaré and me since he could see that we were 'serious' cricketers and he was more relaxed in the company of the senior players but, when he took over the captaincy for one game just before the Varsity match, he was not so sensitive to some of the lesser ones, whom he ignored.

The other old man in the side was David Fursdon, a tall away-swing bowler in his final year, who would astound everybody, including himself, when he scored a century in the Varsity match, batting at number eight. When he reached 65 he confided to his partner, Wingfield Digby, that he was now in uncharted territory whatever the level of cricket. He kept going and finished with 112. As a consequence Oxford, who had been reduced to 57–6 on the first morning, were then able to declare at 256–9 and the match was eventually drawn.

David was also at St John's College. We had combined at the base of the scrum for the college side for which he was a roaming number eight, and his similarity to Mervyn Davies of Wales and the British Lions stretched to a shock of black hair, an occasional moustache and a white headband – but no further than that. David had an old Morris Minor 1000 Traveller, which he christened Ken after Ken Barrington since it would not go very fast but was very reliable. His bat was named Arthur (possibly in homage to Arthur Milton). He has, however, denied the suggestion that when he proposed to his wife-to-be, Catriona, while sitting in his car, he began with 'Arthur and I have something we'd like to ask you.' Yet here was a man, it eventually transpired, with serious connections. Fursdon shared a house in Oxford with another St John's student, Tony Blair, and he is currently the Lord Lieutenant of Devon. I remain more impressed by that century at Lord's.

David had paid me a visit in my first few days in college to make contact about winter nets with the university cricketers and to enlist me for the St John's rugby team. (I had politely declined Charles Kent's invitation for rugby trials with the Greyhounds, the university second XV, for reasons already explained.) So in that first winter I turned out for the college rugby side as well as the football team, which had the future Tory MP, Alastair Burt, alongside me patrolling the midfield. That was the easy bit.

The academic side was trickier. Like a number of students arriving at Oxford I looked at my new colleagues and concluded that they must all be incredibly clever and that I was out of my depth.

I should have noticed that there were a lot of other freshmen and women wandering around with similar misgivings. Moreover, studying Classics was not easy; the language skills required were formidable – or so it seemed to me.

My tutor was as we all assume Oxbridge tutors should be. Donald Russell was a small, shy, kindly man with no hair on top of his head but unruly wisps flying out from above his ears in all directions. He was a brilliant classicist yet those early tutorials with half a dozen colleagues had a surreal air to them. We might be studying a passage from Thucydides and there would be the deluded assumption that somehow we all effortlessly understood the chunks of Greek in front of us. In my case, and I was not alone here, this was some distance from the truth yet it was deemed far too menial to dwell upon the nuts and bolts of translation. We were supposed to be beyond that and capable of discussing the style and implications of the text. So this resulted in hours of desperate bluffing on my part, which I'm sure fooled nobody.

For Ancient History, a marginally more accessible subject for me, we visited A. N. Sherwin-White, who had been at St John's as an undergraduate in 1930 and had stayed there ever since apart from the war years. Essays had to be written but they would not necessarily be handed in. Instead we would be required to read them out loud to Sherwin-White and the other St John's classicists in attendance. This could be an embarrassing process, though it now occurs to me that it might have been good training for a novice cricket reporter at Derby in later years. There the process could be equally stressful. Having plucked up the courage to hire the only phone in the press box it was then time to read your match report in front of hardened local hacks, very slowly and very loudly, to a distant copytaker. 'Is there much more of this?' she might intervene helpfully from the other end of the line. Sherwin-White and a few fellow students were usually a sympathetic audience by comparison.

Lectures I had a few, but then again too few to mention. Russell would suggest some that might be worthwhile at the beginning of each term but there was no element of compulsion, no register of attendance. Gradually my appearances at lectures dwindled though I became quite committed to those in the Ashmolean Museum just around the corner from St John's, which related to Greek vase painting. The only problem here was that when the lecturer displayed the paintings on the slide projector she turned out all the lights.

It was much more rigorous and structured for the scientists, one of whom was Tavaré reading Zoology at St John's. We spent a lot of time together that first winter, much of it contemplating the summer ahead. We often used to meet in the Eagle and Child pub for a pint, the only difference being that Chris was usually celebrating the completion of his work while I was still seeking inspiration for mine. There we might sit underneath the plaque commemorating the regular presence of C. S. Lewis and J. R. R. Tolkien for literary meetings in the pub, where Lewis had distributed proofs of *The Lion, the Witch and the Wardrobe* in 1950. We talked more of trigger movements when facing fast bowling.

So I tiptoed into Oxford life slowly in that first winter. I could still be painfully shy in the company of either sex – in those days there only seemed to be two. I was more the farmer's son pitched into alien territory than the young Oxbridge gadabout. I never knew of the existence of the Bullingdon Club, though that was not and never has been a source of regret. To a great extent, too great probably, the cricket was my raison d'être and in that first season in the university side it went well. I relished the opportunity to play against the professionals and if ever I pulled back the curtains to spy rainclouds over Oxford I was desperately disappointed. Moreover the Parks, where no spectator could be charged until they sat on a bench at the boundary's edge, was a wonderful cricketing venue and so it remains.

I was comfortably the leading run-scorer for the university in the first-class matches, amazingly outstripping Tavaré along the way. Late in our season against Derbyshire I missed a Venkataravaghan full toss on 98 so there was no hundred in the major matches, but there was an unbeaten double century against the Army at Aldershot (sadly not first-class). My outscoring Tavaré that summer can be explained in part by our different attitudes to batting at the time. I reasoned that I was unlikely to prevail by attempting long, risk-free innings. So I remained aggressive in a 'gather ye rosebuds' kind of way and somehow that worked. Tavaré opted to play properly, trying to build an innings in the approved manner. It was not until the following summer that he stamped his undoubted class upon proceedings.

The Varsity match was drawn; Peter Roebuck more than matched Fursdon's remarkable century with a majestic innings of 158 for Cambridge. Roebuck's 'old leg clip' was working well and here was early evidence that he was much more than a tenacious blocker. I have always contended that Tavaré and Roebuck, who would both become renowned for their self-denial at the crease, were far more gifted than many realised; more significantly they were better than they themselves often thought. At certain stages of their careers both of these contrasting characters were reluctant to explore the limits of their batting ability.

After the Varsity match the officers for Oxford's next season were decided by the simple method of the players in the dressing room having a vote. I was chosen unanimously to be the captain for 1976 with Tavaré as the secretary. That boosted the confidence a bit. The university captain was supposed to run the show. The secretary would organize stuff and in Tavaré's case this would include arranging the annual netball match between OUCC and the Blues netball side. Notice how keen we were to sharpen our competitive instincts in the off-season even though we did not understand all the rules.

At some point Trevor Glover, our much respected, outgoing skipper, pulled me to one side and offered some advice. 'Pick your mates,' he said. 'You'll have a much better time if you do.' The unspoken implication was that the university side was not going to win many games come what may. It was good advice though curiously I would not follow it to the letter.

That era of university cricket may now seem like a relatively good vintage. Aside from Imran, there were a couple of future internationals at Oxford and others who would play some county cricket; at Cambridge there was Chris Aworth, Hignell, Roebuck and Paul Parker and there would soon be Nigel Popplewell, Ian Greig and Derek Pringle. Yet we never beat the counties – though there were some memorable one-day victories for the Combined side in the B&H Cup – and there was some speculation, even then, that the first-class status of Oxford and Cambridge cricket was at risk.

At the time we did not realize how fortunate we were. Soon Oxford and Cambridge universities would take a different stance towards extra-curricular activities. The old leeway for gifted sportsmen would soon vanish. The colleges now want students who will deliver 'firsts' to the extent that candidates with aspirations of playing cricket in the Parks are today often advised not to mention their sporting prowess in their applications. The yearning for sporting excellence at the university has all but disappeared. In the current climate it would be impossible for a student to spend so much time playing cricket for the university, no matter how good he is. Today nearly all of the Oxford side that plays against the counties are from Oxford Brookes rather than the old university. The imperative to get a good degree is now all-embracing. Five of the Oxford side that played in the Varsity match of 2018 got firsts; that was certainly not the case in 1976.

So the standard of university cricket has declined and so too has the fixture list. We were able to play against county sides regularly containing international players who were happy to come for a relaxing few days in Oxford – with every chance of boosting their averages in the process. Viv Richards, Zaheer Abbas, Mike Procter, Mike Brearley, Ray Illingworth, Ian Botham, Colin Croft and Sylvester Clarke were, routinely, our opponents and in combination with Cambridge we would have a fixture against the tourists most years. This was a magnificent training ground for young cricketers who aspired to play the game professionally – runs and wickets would be far more valued than any gleaned in second XI cricket – but this is no longer the case. I watched a bit of the 2018 Varsity match at the Parks, won by OUCC, which confirmed that the standard has dipped. We will probably never see any of the players involved in that match playing professional cricket (they all have to attend the university rather than Oxford Brookes to play in the Varsity match), but I was still struck by the zest and enjoyment of all those participating. For them the match against Cambridge remained of vital importance.

Mind you, the university side seldom won a game in the seventies. In our defence we would point out that the great Colin

Cowdrey had never played in a winning Oxford side against the counties either. Cowdrey was OUCC's president when I was there. He had played for the university from 1952 to 1954 and the story still doing the rounds twenty years later was that if there was no game at the Parks, he would frequently be asked to turn out elsewhere. On any one day he might receive three invitations to play. He would say yes to all of them and appear for the last team that had been in touch. Who knows how true that is? But the tale hints at his eagerness to please and a certain indecision, which surfaced throughout his career. Apparently he had to be persuaded by his teammates that the famous Garry Sobers' declaration in Trinidad in 1968 demanded that England go for the win, which they did successfully with Cowdrey at the crease. More seriously, those attributes may well have been present at Lord's throughout the infamous selection meeting for the tour party to South Africa later that year when Basil D'Oliveira was sensationally omitted. But no one knows for sure and there is not a witness left.

But as president of OUCC Cowdrey was an important ally, not just because he was a cricketing legend coming to the end of a most distinguished career. He devoted considerable time and energy to the post and, recognizing that our status was under threat, his presence and guidance was invaluable. Not that his advice was difficult to follow. He said that it was important that counties visiting the Parks should have a good time if we wanted to maintain our first-class status; we should extend a warm welcome, which meant that we would always invite the opposition for drinks after the day's play either in a nearby pub or up at Vincent's, Oxford's sporting club, which is just off the High Street. The professionals might be curious and happy to have a beer in different surroundings.

So that is what we did and some good nights ensued. Generally the county players accepted those invitations and how we enjoyed and appreciated their company. Tony Greig, for example, right at the start was happy to socialize; David Lloyd liked playing at the Parks, perhaps for the MCC as well as Lancashire. He would buy a great chunk of Cheshire cheese, a hunk of bread and a beer and disappear into the undergrowth or along the riverbanks of the Parks once he had been dismissed. Then he might well entertain and educate in the evening. It was fascinating to rub shoulders with Dennis Amiss one week, Eddie Barlow or Geoff Cook the next – and to listen to them.

On one occasion when we were playing Glamorgan I issued the standard invitation to Vincent's to their captain, Majid Khan, the great Pakistan Test cricketer and Imran's cousin, and he was happy to accept. As ever most of our players gathered at the club, eagerly awaiting the arrival of our opponents and after a while we began to wonder whether they would turn up. Eventually Majid appeared, but only Majid. 'Where are the others?' we asked. As if surprised by the question, he replied, 'Oh, I didn't invite them.'

Cowdrey had given a glowing reference to our coach and quite rightly so. The appointment of Arthur Milton was a minor stroke of genius (not mine but the work of Glover and Bob Reeves, a PE guru from Bristol University, who helped us in our pre-season preparations) from my first year onwards. Arthur was the last man to play football and cricket for England, a feat that will surely never be repeated. He had just retired after twenty-seven years as a pro-fessional cricketer for Gloucestershire, during which time he had also played for Arsenal and, briefly, Bristol City.

Oddly enough I had played against Arthur at Bath in 1974 when I was in Somerset's second XI and somehow, at the age of forty-six, he had an outing in Gloucestershire's second team. It puzzled me why one of his nicknames was 'Arthur Clothbat' – until he batted. The ball seemed to make the softest of sounds on his bat, a muffled plop before it rolled away between the fielders. Even then he scored runs effortlessly, still gliding between the wickets. He was one of the most gifted, least ambitious sportsmen of his time.

In 1975 Arthur's approach to coaching must have seemed outdated to the uninitiated. I don't think we ever saw him in a tracksuit. Even Trevor Bayliss, as low-key and laidback as they come, puts on a tracksuit every morning. Occasionally Arthur would take off his old Gloucestershire blazer and hit a few catches or demonstrate how to take them for he had always been a superb fielder. In fact his antennae would be alerted whenever he spotted a brilliant piece of fielding: 'I bet you he can play a bit,' he would say.

He was certainly not an interventionist coach. In fact he would never intervene at all unless invited. He recognized that most of the players in the team were playing for fun; the challenge of competing against the pros was always going to be uneven and he did not want to burden the students with a barrage of unwanted technical advice. Instead he would wait to be asked. So it was that in Arthur's first summer Wingfield Digby asked him whether he had any tips for his bowling. Apparently the gist of the answer from OUCC's new coach was, 'I have watched you closely. Do people really get out to your bowling? If they do I dare not say a thing. It's a mystery to me, but if it works I wouldn't care to interfere.' Then Wingfield Digby added, 'We never mentioned my bowling again.'

Others were more inquisitive. Chris Tavaré would have long chats with Arthur, some of which would be about batting. So too would John Claughton, who made a century on his debut for the university side in 1976 – he went on to play briefly for Warwickshire before embarking on the most distinguished of careers in teaching. And so would the Cambridge boys whenever we combined in the B&H Cup and, of course, Arthur was just as happy to talk cricket with them.

Obviously he knew the game inside out, but he was also wonderfully suited to the role of an avuncular guide to a motley collection of students in the Parks. He was very bright with a mischievous sense of humour; he would never hold court yet we hung on his every word; he would polish off the *Telegraph* crossword as well as plucking out a few fast greyhounds from the *Sporting Life* long before the toss had taken place. He had never been to university, but he would have liked that opportunity. In part that was denied him because he was such a gifted sportsman that he was inevitably propelled towards professional sport as a teenager and, in any case, the opportunity may not have been there. On many days we needed a sense of perspective about our predicament in the Parks and Arthur was the ideal man to provide it.

As captain I spent hours chatting to him, listening and learning and debating what might be our best team. He would always be there on the first morning when the captain is at his most pre-occupied; there would be decisions to make about the twelfth man or the toss. Before long I would earnestly grab Arthur for an early consultation and march him out to the pitch. 'Have a look at this, Art. What do you think we should do if I win the toss? Bat or bowl?' I needed his advice badly. Arthur would pause for a while and then say, 'I don't think it'll make much difference.' Do not take this as indifference on his part. He cared all right but he knew that we would be probably be outgunned however the coin rolled.

He never lost his temper with us. In part this was because he was the gentlest of men; he would also think this counterproductive.

We were young student amateurs, after all, up against the pros. But occasionally I did see him berate the umpire with well-delivered venom. Of course Arthur knew them all well and recognized that some of them liked a day off. So if he spied them giving a few 'university' lbws on the second afternoon in order to hasten the end of the game, he would give them no peace.

His mere presence in the Parks also bridged the gap between the professional cricketers and the students. All of our opponents, from Geoffrey Boycott downwards, looked up to Arthur and they wandered over for a chat and sometimes we would naturally join in. So we discovered the names were mortals after all; occasionally they, too, might miss a straight one.

It was the happiest of unions. I know Arthur enjoyed his time as our coach and mentor, and we all kept in touch sporadically afterwards. I remember him speaking at one of my benefit dinners in 1988 and can picture him getting up, holding the order of events programme in his hands presumably to shield his notes from the audience. 'We first met up at Oxford,' he said, 'and we both had hair then. And we were both reading Classics. His was Latin and Greek and mine was the Derby, Oaks and St Leger.' And off he went for an effortless, enchanting twenty-five minutes. As for those notes they did not exist; he just pretended to have some.

The core of that university side – Wingfield Digby, Claughton, Paul Fisher, Tavaré and myself – were all devoted to him. He was a key element in our enjoyment of university cricket and it was a special time for all of us even if we were not winning many games. In a fine biography of Arthur by Mike Vockins, the former secretary of Worcestershire CCC, Claughton recalls inviting Arthur and his wife, Joan, to lunch along with Paul Fisher thirty years after those Oxford days. By then Claughton and Fisher were long-established, successful headmasters at King Edward's Birmingham and Lough-borough Grammar School. 'Arthur and I were very close,' says Claughton, 'and I was honoured when Arthur came back and spent a day with me and my family. I really loved Arthur and treasured the fact he wanted to come and see Paul and me, and I'm really proud that my children met him'. Arthur would have enjoyed the day, too.

With Arthur on hand for guidance I enjoyed captaining the side more than I could have imagined. I was never inclined to employ the stick – I would not have been good at that in any case – and I am not sure I had many carrots to hand. But this was a dressing room full of contrasting characters, who were stimulated by one another's company. Even when we kept losing they were easy to captain. On-field decision-making was never a major problem and was aided by the fact that, by university standards, we had some decent bowlers.

David Gurr, tall with a whippy action, surprised a few pros. We even spotted the odd timid opening batsman rejecting that second run to wide third man in order to avoid facing him. He bowled some serious spells at Oxford, which prompted me to alert Somerset. David played there for a couple of years, initially with success, but then for no obvious technical reason he acquired the fast bowler's equivalent of the yips. The act of becoming a full-time professional seemed to coincide with his problems.

Richard Savage was an unusual, mercurial cricketer, who bowled fast off-breaks with the wicketkeeper standing back – as the great Don Shepherd of Glamorgan often used to do. He could be a handful when the ball was gripping and for a while he was on Warwickshire's books. He was full of ideas and quite an ideal-ist, and probably more suited to teaching than the county circuit.

Sadly I have not seen him for years but the woman he married keeps popping up on *Question Time* speaking more coherently than the others. Caroline Lucas at the time of writing is the country's solitary Green MP.

And then there was Andrew Wingfield Digby, a reliable old hand, who has retained his boyish enthusiasm for the game over five decades. He loved bowling and he's still doing it. I think he rated me as a captain and I think I know why. We were playing Glamorgan and Andrew was bowling from the Pavilion End at the Parks. Alan Lewis Jones, a left-handed opening batsman, was at the crease and suddenly he hit every ball of Andrew's over for four. The normally effervescent Digby was crestfallen and slunk off to long leg. Another over passed by, whereupon Andrew looked at me enquiringly. 'Have another one, Diggers,' I said and his face lit up. It would be neat to report that in his next over Jones was dismissed. He wasn't but my senior bowler was smiling again.

It was a consequence of Digby's considerable prodding that I might have been branded as a firebrand radical among the OUCC hierarchy – though somehow this never happened. By now Andrew was married and he thought it was iniquitous that his wife, Sue, was not allowed in the pavilion. And he was right. As at Lord's the pavilion in the Parks was deemed a male-only preserve. So at one committee meeting in 1976, despite initial opposition, we gently persuaded the powers that be to allow women to enter, beating Lord's by twenty-three years. This enabled everyone to sit inside and look up at the boards displaying Oxford teams including C. B. Fry, Douglas Jardine, Cowdrey, M. J. K. Smith and the Nawab of Pataudi.

There were some highlights on the field during that scorching summer and one of them took place in Barnsley. There the

Combined Universities were playing their last zonal B&H match of the summer and it was a bit of a struggle to get our best side out. Exams were rearing their ugly head and it was a long way from Oxford and Cambridge. So unusually we set off with the feeling of fulfilling our duty rather than relishing the challenge ahead.

Sadly Geoff Boycott was not playing for Yorkshire and he breezily wished us luck before the start of play. In our dressing room we had a Tyke, Steve Coverdale, the Cambridge wicketkeeper who was on Yorkshire's books – among other things he would become the chief executive at Northamptonshire in later life. Naturally we sought Coverdale's advice on the Yorkshire bowling attack he knew so well, a task he undertook most earnestly. 'Chris Old: he's quick and accurate; he can swing the ball away but the odd one comes in. Good bouncer.' Well, we knew Old was an international cricketer so there were no great surprises here; we moved on to Steve Oldham. 'He's quicker than he looks; he can swing the ball out – and in – and he gives you absolutely nothing.'

The pattern was set. No matter which bowler Coverdale was assessing it seemed that he was a world-beater. The others, by the way, were Howard Cooper, Arthur 'Rocker' Robinson and Alan Ramage, who may well have been a better footballer. Now we had to decide whether Coverdale should open the batting with Peter Roebuck or whether Gaj Pathmanathan from Oxford, a delightful man and a silky, though unpredictable, batsman from Sri Lanka, would be a better bet at the top of the order. After all those stern Coverdale endorsements it was hardly surprising that we opted for Pathmanathan. This proved to be a good decision.

Yorkshire, despite the presence of Bill Athey, John Hampshire and David Bairstow in their line-up, batted timidly. One could sense the eyebrows of the PA man heading northwards as

he announced the introduction of bowlers such as A. R. Wingfield Digby and R. le Q. Savage at the home ground of Dickie Bird
and Michael Parkinson. We started to enjoy the occasion. We all
bowled well; we were allowed to as Yorkshire crawled to 185–7.
Out went Roebuck and Pathmanathan and our Sri Lankan was
inspired. Immediately he took the attack to Old, who responded
with some inappropriate remarks about Pathmanathan's heritage.
For the first and only time in our experience Gaj, the mildest of
men, was enraged because of Old's outburst, which prompted him
to continue flaying his bowling all around the ground.

He hit 58 in no time and the rest of us finished off the simplest
of victories with seven wickets and eight overs to spare. Pathmanathan was man of the match. Boycott popped his head in the
dressing room to say, 'I wished you luck. But not that much luck.'
So we returned south in a more cheerful frame of mind and Yorkshire missed out on a quarter-final place.

Selection was trickier for the Varsity match. This was when I
deserted Trevor Glover's advice of 'picking your mates'. There were
three players for two places: Ken Siviter was a useful pace bowler,
apart from his tendency to bowl a proliferation of no-balls (batsmen sought that elusive 1000 runs by the end of May; we hoped
that Ken could avoid 100 no-balls in that time); Robin Topham, a
batsman, had come up on the rails late in the university season and
Rod Eddington, a Rhodes scholar, was an all-rounder from Western Australia (WA). I opted for Siviter and Topham. You are more
likely to be familiar with Eddington, who was the chief executive of
British Airways from 2000 to 2005, having previously run Cathay
Pacific.

Rod was in his second year at Oxford, having played a few games
under Trevor Glover the previous summer. He was a stalwart of

the cricket club, who would also become president of Vincent's. He played in that first match of 1975 against Sussex and early in his spell I dropped Greig at mid-wicket off his bowling, which was a pity – Greig ended up with 121. 'Nearly got the big fella early on,' he would explain to his mates that evening.

Rod, like Digby, was a mature student, having graduated from the University of Western Australia before heading for Oxford. He was more worldly-wise than most of us and he had a better grant; he also had an MGB and a moustache not so different from the one sported by Ian Chappell at the time. Back in Perth he had played for the university side in grade cricket alongside John Inverarity and Rod Marsh, two wonderful men, who, to my delight, keep popping up over the years.

In that first summer at Oxford in 1975 Inverarity was teaching at Tonbridge School and Eddington brought him along to the Parks, where we had an informal and stimulating training session with him. Inverarity might be regarded as Australia's answer to Mike Brearley, a cerebral cricketer who nonetheless had the capacity to get along with every type of player in his dressing room. Dennis Lillee thought the world of Inverarity, rather like Botham did of Brearley.

Rod bowled cagey left-arm spin with an arm that could have been a little higher, and he was a doughty batsman in the lower middle order. He was consumed by the game in between studying something incomprehensible to do with nuclear physics (I think). He was also a selfless clubman of boundless energy who could sort everything out, and in his first two years he flickered between the university side and the Authentics (the second XI). I recall quite a long partnership with him against Middlesex in 1976 – though he remembers it better.

Rod would happily talk cricket all night and he knew his stuff. Naturally he was fascinated by the art of left-arm spin and years later I invited him along to the *Observer*'s table at the Cricket Writers' Club annual dinner. There, more by accident than design, he found himself alongside Kevin Mitchell, an *Observer* sports writer for decades, who once bowled left-arm spin for Randwick CC in Sydney, and the great Indian spinner, Bishen Bedi. At their end of the table the talk was all left-arm spin but my impression was that Bedi, never the most reticent of men, barely got a word in.

To return to Lord's in 1976. Rod was in the twelve and after much agonizing I left him out and played Topham and Siviter, options that I think could be justified on purely cricketing grounds. Naturally Rod took this decision brilliantly. Throughout the three days of the Varsity match he was superb, upbeat and endlessly encouraging and helpful in the dressing room. I did not realize the extent of his disappointment until much later; he would not let it show. The blue, which the likes of Tavaré and myself had taken for granted, would have meant a great deal to him.

Many years later, when Rod was the chief executive at BA, I was working with *Test Match Special* (*TMS*) at Headingley and we had a minor crisis. The 'View from the Boundary' slot at lunchtime on Saturday had become one of the programme's highlights – it still is. For half an hour a prominent cricket enthusiast would be interviewed, usually by Jonathan Agnew, and over the years the guests have ranged from Mick Jagger to Daniel Radcliffe to Theresa May. But sometimes the celebrities cancel at short notice, which was the case in Leeds (most of them prefer Lord's).

There was an urgent conflab at the back of the commentary box since an emergency replacement was needed. This has rarely been an area where I could offer much help but I tossed out the name of

Rod Eddington, a suggestion greeted with much enthusiasm not just because time was running out fast. After one phone call Rod immediately agreed to be at Headingley in twenty-four hours' time – at least he would not have had a problem getting a flight.

In the meantime I gave Jonathan a few details about his new interviewee: WA, Oxford, left-arm spinner, distinguished career in aviation, head of Cathay Pacific before taking on the job at BA, knows his cricket. I also outlined how Rod at Oxford had come so close to getting a blue but then added that it'd be preferable not to dwell on that in the interview. There was plenty of other stuff to talk about. Agnew nodded gratefully.

Rod arrived promptly at Headingley an hour before his lunchtime slot and he was ushered up to the cramped old commentary box in the rugby stand. He sat quietly at the back while I was on air with Jonathan in the pit at the front of one of the smallest boxes on the circuit. It was a stiflingly hot day and as were commentating I took off my jacket and slung it on to the back of my chair. Soon it fell into the dust on the floor and Rod immediately bent over and picked it up before hanging it up on the nail in the wall, which served as a peg. Agnew, still on air, turned around and observed, 'Still doing those twelfth man duties then, Rod.' The interview was a great success.

So was that Varsity match for Oxford back at Lord's in 1976. The game seemed of huge importance to us. In that era the giants of the press corps would attend even if there were not many spectators beyond family and friends. John Woodcock of *The Times* was present, lamenting the fact that some of the Oxford players were wearing the wrong caps. The match was still – just – on the cricket correspondent's schedule.

Chris Tavaré, capping a season when he had batted at a level way beyond his peers, hit a superb 99 and we shared a partnership of 149. His century at Pagham against Sussex on a turning pitch a couple of weeks earlier had been a masterclass, which had the professionals gasping let alone his teammates. David Gurr and Richard Savage caused havoc among the Cambridge batsmen and, despite greater resistance in their second innings, Oxford won for the first time since 1966 by ten wickets. Perfect. As it happened we had not needed any runs from Topham or wickets from Siviter.

After the match I was given the unusual opportunity, readily accepted, of being elected as captain for a second year – the fact that Classics was a four-year course, rather than three, opened up that possibility. So life was looking up on several fronts. Earlier in the summer I had met Anna Stewart, a zoologist like Tavaré, who was among the first intake of women at Wadham College. In *Cherwell*, the students' magazine, she was described as 'Wadham's blonde' and that only added to the mystique. Even though her awareness of cricket was no more extensive than my knowledge of colour change in octopus we began to spend time together. To my delight we still do.

Oxford could not repeat the Lord's victory in 1977 but we had our moments throughout the season. Unusually we had the capacity to bowl county sides out, mostly because of the excellence of Gurr and Savage – and Digby had lost none of his pace – but we rarely scored enough runs; Tavaré was concentrating on his exams. In 1978 John Claughton took over the captaincy and I became a sporadic member of the team with my own finals looming. In fact Donald Russell, my tutor, politely informed me that if I wanted to get a degree it would be wise not to play any more cricket until after my exams. I knew he was right, followed his advice and scraped through. I was assisted by the guidance of Claughton and his meticulous notes – he was/is a proper classicist – even though he was a year behind me.

So I managed to leave Oxford with a degree, a few first-class runs and wickets, and, more surprisingly, a long-term partner. I had been offered the opportunity to go back to Blundell's to teach in the winter, which I accepted. Yet despite acquiring a flimsy knowledge of the works of Thucydides as well as discovering some of the intricacies of Greek vase painting of the fifth century BC and beyond, my career aspirations did not include much in the way of Classics and they would ultimately lie beyond the classroom.

FOUR

FULL-TIME PRO

THE SURVIVING SOMERSET CRICKETERS who played against Lancashire at Southport in 1977 neither need nor want any reminders of that game. But if they did one word would do: Croft. That is Colin Croft, the West Indian fast bowler, who was chosen as an overseas player by Lancashire ahead of Joel Garner.

That may have been a dubious choice by Lancashire and it meant that in the years to come Joel would always bowl very quickly against them when playing for Somerset. But on 1 August 1977 Croft scared the life out of most of us. There was a ridge at Southport. And there weren't any helmets. And we did not yet have Garner. And they had Croft.

The mind often plays tricks that are exposed by the scorecard, which is the bane of so many cricketers' favourite anecdotes. My memory has always been that we were not only terrified by Croft but also bowled out by him. In fact the scorecard tells me that he took just three wickets in the match. Peter Lee, meanwhile, a yeoman fast-medium bowler who had begun his career at Northamptonshire, took eleven. But none of us remembers much about that.

For decades I recalled being part of a Croft hat-trick (in fact I was merely out first ball to him in the second innings), and then I might recount how just before going out to bat I had to vacate the dressing room, which was square of the wicket, because Graham Burgess and Mervyn Kitchen, two men batting just above me, were unwittingly destroying any self-belief I might have possessed.

'See that ball, Budge? No, neither did I. We've got no chance out there.'

In my mind Burgess was there nodding vigorously in agreement with Kitchen as these two old Somerset pros were debating, with a bellyful of black humour, the wisdom of their chosen profession, the benefits of retirement and, more specifically, how the devil they were going to get out of Southport unscathed. I'm looking at the scorecard now. Burgess wasn't playing in that game. He couldn't have been in Southport talking to Merv. Neville Cardus, I now understand. You are forgiven the odd inaccuracy and even the occasional white lie that illustrated the truth so beautifully.

Thinking back to that match in Southport, however, I am confident of this much: the dressing room was square of the wicket just as it used to be at Old Trafford. Hence it was practically impossible to pick up the entire flight path of the ball especially when it was propelled by Croft. This was more than the human eye could cope with. Just occasionally there would be glimpses of the ball as it sped into the upturned gloves of the Lancashire wicketkeeper, John Lyon. Dressing rooms that are situated at square leg can easily fill waiting batsmen with dread when there are fast bowlers around. It was also like that at Hove in the seventies and eighties when Imran Khan and Garth le Roux seemed to be propelling an invisible ball.

In the first innings at Southport Somerset scored 308 runs. Viv Richards hit 189 of those, ferociously smashing Croft out of the attack in another scintillating innings. I note that I was the second highest scorer along with Brian Close, sharing a partnership of 69 with Viv, of which I contributed a surprising 31. Viv by his brilliance had masked the dangers of that ridge.

Somerset lacked anyone of Croft's pace in that match and Lancashire gained a small first innings lead. Then, with the exceptions of Richards and Close (of course) we were terrorized when we batted again. I remember Brian Rose inadvertently hitting Croft for six after the ball had flicked the top of his bat handle before flying over the wicketkeeper's head (as well as his own) and then over the rope. It was at this point that I was listening to Kitchen (but not Burgess) in the dressing room.

'I'll never see it. And I'll never be able to get out of the way. I'm done for,' he said (maybe to Derek Taylor, who was definitely there) as he removed his false teeth and put them delicately into his blazer pocket for safekeeping. I had to leave the dressing room as the conversation had become so doomladen.

Soon, after the dismissal of Close, it was my turn. Out I went and upon arrival at the crease there was an immediate problem since I didn't know where to stand as I took guard. Colin Dredge had bowled thirty-three overs in the Lancashire innings and, as ever, he had dug a deep pit on the popping crease with his left foot just where a right-handed batsman likes to stand. I could not put my right foot down there; I'd never get it out. But if I went backwards in my stance I would probably topple on to the stumps. And I had serious reservations about standing anywhere nearer the bowler, who was the snarling Croft. No happy compromise was forthcoming.

In any case this was a short-lived dilemma. Croft raced in. He briefly disappeared behind the umpire as he always did before darting out to the offside and then spearing the ball in my direction – very quickly. That delivery was a little short and on course for the ridge, which the Somerset players were all too aware of by now. I fended at the ball as it made a beeline for my head, which I was keen to jerk out of harm's way; the ball brushed my glove and then, as if in slow motion, it seemed to take an eternity to land in the safe hands of wicketkeeper Lyon about 35 yards behind the stumps. I suppose I was disappointed; I might have been relieved – it's a long time ago now.

Rest assured I will not be describing my every dismissal in first-class cricket (I've just checked; there are 409 others) but that one lingers in the memory. It is a chilling reminder of a bygone era when batsmen did not have helmets. We were bowled out for 83 in seventeen overs and lost the match by eight wickets; Peter Lee took 7–24 in that second innings, though he would acknowledge that the mere presence of Croft glowering at the other end had ensured him the majority of those. Croft somehow seemed more indifferent about hitting batsmen than any of his contemporaries. It was no fun facing him with just a cloth cap for protection.

So this is what I had chosen to do for a living once I had left university. Was that really a good idea? The only other option had been teaching. In fact I did teach for a short time back at Blundell's School in Tiverton after leaving university, which explains why I have always lived in Devon since then, but in my mind this was a convenient way to spend three winters and to earn some money while pursuing my true profession in the summer. It was a generous offer from the school since I would never be around during the summer term to share my cricketing expertise and, while I had a degree, I lacked any other teaching qualifications.

I taught Classics, which I was supposed to know something

about, a bit of Economics, when I really was bluffing, and some English. One of my pupils, Oliver Owen, would become the deputy sports editor at the *Observer* over two decades later and it remains my contention that I delivered my work to him far more promptly than he ever did to me. I can't find any lesson plans from that era. Most of the time I was busking.

I was always kept busy outside of the classroom when helping to run various rugby teams in the winter. So once I was that sad, solitary figure on the touchline in December somewhere near the top of Exmoor being pelted by driving rain late on a Saturday after-noon while my fourth XV lost 3–0 after a dubious penalty given by the home referee. Later I was promoted to run the senior colts with my old university colleague, David Fursdon, briefly a geography teacher who would eventually end up as the chairman of governors at Blundell's. Then I spent most of the time blaming his forwards for our latest defeat after he had already decided that my backs were the culpable ones.

On Thursday evenings from January onwards I would take one of the senior pupils, Hugh Morris, who would go on to cap-tain Glamorgan and play three Tests for England, with me up to the indoor nets at Taunton when the Somerset professionals would convene for some practice and some gossip. Hugh was a prolific runscorer at Blundell's as well as being a big-booted fly-half in the winter. When I first played against him in county cricket a few years later he would call me 'sir' but my razor-sharp antennae detected a certain irony.

I soon realized that I was a better cricketer than a teacher and that was where my longer-term future lay, even if there is a lot of evidence to suggest that in the late seventies and the eighties pro-fessional cricket was chaotically run. But at least playing the game for a living was becoming a significantly less dangerous proposition around this time. Despite all the recent innovations, the advent of the helmet, a piece of equipment so conspicuously absent from the dressing room back in Southport, remains the most significant change to cricket in the last half-century. It transformed the way cricketers bat.

Before 1978 it was a rare and traumatic event for a batsman to be hit on the head. In 1976 I witnessed Peter Roebuck being struck by Andy Roberts when playing at Fenner's for the Combined Universities against the West Indies. Off he went to hospital with his head swollen and he did not bat again in the match. It was a chilling moment even though he seemed to recover from the experience surprisingly quickly.

Eighteen months earlier we had all watched the 1974/5 Ashes highlights with Dennis Lillee and Jeff Thomson battering English batsmen on some unreliable surfaces in Brisbane and beyond. This was another world with Keith Fletcher being hit on the badge of his cap, David Lloyd in the box, as one or two diners may have heard him mention over the last few decades, and the reinforcement, Colin Cowdrey, a forty-two-year-old Michelin man, being pummelled repeatedly in the chest. This happened most frequently when Jeff Thomson was bowling at him in the Test match in Perth when, at the first drinks interval, you could see two eras collide. At the break Cowdrey, recognizing that he had never played against Thomson before and having just been battered repeatedly in the ribcage, instinctively held out his hand for a handshake with Thomson saying, 'Hello, Colin Cowdrey. I don't believe we've met.' Apparently Thommo was rendered speechless by Cowdrey's opening salvo and then he resumed the barrage after the drinks interval. On that tour the cricket was compelling; it was also X certificate.

Batting was a more frightening occupation back then. Some might conclude that tail-enders were more cowardly in those days but that would be a gross injustice. They just realised that they had to retreat to avoid serious injury. Priority number one was to make sure you were not hit on the head. Once the helmet became commonplace there was less excuse not to get in line. Increasingly being hit on the helmet became a routine event, an occupational hazard, and the notion that certain tail-enders should be exempt from a barrage of bouncers gradually disappeared. By the 2017/18 Ashes series it was commonplace for the England tail-enders to receive nothing but bouncers from Australia's (very) fast bowlers. And no one, including the umpires, complained. It would have seemed lily-livered to do so. In fact it was weak not to intervene.

The advent of the helmet meant that batsmen became more cavalier against the short ball since they trusted their headgear, but in 2014 we were reminded after the tragic death of Phil Hughes, the Australian Test batsman, that the helmet does not offer complete protection.

Back in 1977 intelligent opening batsmen were beginning to innovate. Mike Brearley sometimes wore a skull cap under his old-fashioned England one; Sunil Gavaskar of India had something similar under his white floppy hat. These were discreet additions unlike the headgear worn by Dennis Amiss in 1978. His protection resembled a white motorbike helmet and, preposterously, there were a few giggles when he first appeared underneath one in county cricket. Here was a superannuated Hell's Angel coming to the crease – though he was soon regarded as a very wise and pragmatic one.

In 1976 Amiss had been hit on the head when playing for the MCC against the West Indies at Lord's. As a consequence he overhauled his technique against fast bowling by opting to take a vast step back and across his stumps just before the bowler delivered. It was not pretty but in the final Test at the Oval he made 203 while Michael Holding was taking fourteen wickets in the match. Thereafter Amiss was eager to try any of the prototypes offering protection to the head. There was an irresistible logic to that and he has always acknowledged how the helmet prolonged his career.

By 1978 there were a few more helmets around but not enough. At Somerset there might be no more than two or three in the dressing room and, rather like village cricketers passing bats as the departing and arriving batsmen crossed on the outfield, there was a brief period playing against fast bowlers when we would snatch the helmet of an outgoing batsman as surreptitiously as possible before heading to the crease.

Initially the grille of the helmet often resembled an iron-barred gate rather than the slender wires of today and I rarely used it. In fact the presence of the grille on my helmet would sometimes betray my apprehensions. I would screw this cumbersome piece of equipment into place if the opposition included Courtney Walsh or Sylvester Clarke or Colin Croft (post 1977). However, my technique, for want of a better word, had been forged in the pre-helmet days. I think I was only hit on the head once – if we exclude a fierce straight drive by Brian Rose when I was the non-striker – and that was by a Gloucestershire bowler less familiar and less speedy than Walsh, named Richard Doughty. If I had been born twenty years later I guess I would have been hit too many times to remember.

Soon we all made sure we had a helmet in our cricket 'coffins'. Later in his career Peter Roebuck possessed one with just one ear flap on the left-hand side, which was something of a mystery to opponents. They all knew that Roebuck possessed a sharp, analytical mind and some spent time trying to figure out the theory behind his one-flap helmet; there had to be some logic there. I knew the truth: that my colleague was indeed blessed with the most fertile of minds, but that he could also be utterly impractical and slapdash. The simple explanation was that one ear flap on his helmet – on the right hand side – had broken and he could not be bothered to replace it; so he just carried on regardless.

However, Chris Balderstone, a fine cricketer for Leicestershire and footballer for Carlisle United, had been most impressed by Roebuck's batting and he had noticed the solitary ear flap. There must be something in Roebuck's innovation, he thought. So he meticulously removed one of the ear flaps from his own helmet. Sadly my researches do not extend to discovering whether this transformed Balderstone's game. Probably not, but here is another example of the lengths that the professional sportsman will go to in his search for that elusive, magic elixir.

The helmet was spurned by a few. Viv Richards famously never wore one because he felt that it might give the bowler some encouragement; initially Ian Botham seldom used one. Watch the video of him clouting Dennis Lillee and Terry Alderman at Old Trafford in 1981 and he is bare-headed (and note the helmeted figure of the more cautious Chris Tavaré at the other end). But it was the West Indies attack that prompted Ian to stick the helmet on. The one occasion I recall Botham beaten before he went out to bat (with a helmet) was at Old Trafford, earlier in 1981, when playing for Somerset. He had just returned from captaining England's winter tour to the West Indies and was still shell-shocked by the experience; the dressing room was at square leg again and there was Michael Holding bowling like the wind on a lively pitch. As he himself had predicted a couple of minutes earlier, Botham was dismissed without scoring – though he later combined with Garner to win the match with the ball.

Since then there have been odd occasions when the helmet has been mysteriously left in the dressing room. Once, but only once, at Southampton, Mark Nicholas came out to bat for Hampshire against Garner in a white floppy hat because he felt uncomfortable in a helmet at the start of his career. He soon opted to make the necessary adjustment. David Fulton of Kent in a Lord's final in 1995 batted against Wasim Akram of Lancashire in his floppy hat, a calculated act of defiance that seemed to work for a while – he made a brisk 25. But all the great players since Richards have worn a helmet when they deemed it necessary. Now an England player has to wear one whether he wants to or not to satisfy health and safety demands.

The helmet was most definitely necessary – for all except Viv Richards – during World Series Cricket, the project created by Kerry Packer in his fight to gain the television rights for cricket in Australia. In 1977 it did not take long for a stunned cricketing establishment to decide that World Series Cricket was a bad thing. And, to the vast majority of that establishment, so was Mr Packer. Even worse, it transpired that the England captain, Tony Greig, was a key lieutenant of Packer and one of his recruiting officers. Greig was prepared to forsake the England captaincy to launch the brave new world. As ever John Woodcock of *The Times*, who was among those who thought the end of civilization was nigh, found the most memorable phrases whether you agreed with him or not. He wrote of Greig: 'What has to be remembered, of course, is that he is an Englishman, not by birth or upbringing, but only by adoption. It is not the same thing as being an Englishman through and through.'

The feudal system of English cricket, where modest wages might, if you were lucky and accommodating, be augmented by the award of a benefit towards the end of a county career, was being challenged and those in charge were very unhappy about that. Alan Knott, Derek Underwood, John Snow, Dennis Amiss and Bob Woolmer, an eager latecomer, signed up alongside Greig for World Series Cricket. Meanwhile there was a wholesale exodus from the establishment game in Australia with Ian Chappell coming out of retirement to captain their side. The same applied among the West Indians, who were now on course to becoming the best team in the world under Clive Lloyd's leadership – their solitary absentee of note was Alvin Kallicharan. 'It was,' said Packer, 'the easiest sport in the world to take over since nobody bothered to pay the players what they were worth.'

In England the reaction to the Packer Circus, as it was first dubbed by John Arlott, bordered on the hysterical especially at Edgbaston, where Dennis Amiss was ostracized by some of his county colleagues. 'It was better to be on the pitch [scoring stacks of runs] than in the dressing room,' he recalled. 'It was a very sombre time so I tried to stay out there and produce as many runs as I could.' He produced a lot to ensure another contract with his beloved county. Amiss was the unlikeliest of rebels: he would end up as the chief executive at Warwickshire and vice chairman of the England and Wales Cricket Board (ECB) decades later, but back in 1977 nobody at Edgbaston was talking to him. Nor had anyone ever considered Underwood and Knott, who had always been so adored down in Canterbury, to be modern day Che Guevaras. Yet those Packer players attracted incredible hostility within the English game.

Around this time the PCA, which had been established in 1967, was still finding its feet and the issues of Packer and the rebel tour to South Africa in 1981/2 prompted several extraordinary meetings to which every county player was invited. John Arlott, a man who had a special affinity and affection for professional cricketers, was the PCA president at the time and had the daunting task of chairing two of those meetings at Edgbaston, during which there was much debate and considerable confusion. In the first of them I'm sure we passed two utterly contradictory motions within the space of half an hour on the Packer issue, upholding the rights of any cricketer to earn a living as a professional anywhere, yet deploring the advent of Packer and the exodus of England cricketers to World Series Cricket.

For some Greig, Amiss, Underwood and co. were cast as traitors. But those of us in the shires were more likely to be sympathetic, in part because we had overseas players in our county teams heading off to play for Packer. We were not going to brand Richards and Garner as traitors in Taunton. I have a clear memory of David Shepherd, who would become more familiar as a hugely respected international umpire, taking his place at the podium at Edgbaston and reading a statement in Churchillian tones (with a bit of North Devon) on behalf of his county's players. Shep was Gloucestershire's representative at the PCA and they were not inclined to condemn one of their colleagues, Mike Procter, either.

But there was rather more vitriol directed at the Packer players at Lord's, where they were used to the notion that they were the people running the game all around the world. The issue dominated the back pages for weeks and occasionally some of the front ones. Cricket made it on to *The Frost Progamme* where the heavyweights Kerry Packer, Jim Laker and Robin Marlar appeared with Packer winning on points, impressing everyone with his wit and articulacy as well as his determination to win. Soon there was a court case, in which the Test and County Cricket Board (TCCB) and the International Cricket Conference endured the equivalent of an innings defeat against the Packer organization.

Now there has been some revisionism. The Packer Circus was not such a bad thing after all. He introduced the idea of night cricket, which proved to be a spectacular success in Australia and thereafter in other parts of the southern hemisphere. In the twenty-first century the authorities seem to think that this might be the case in the UK as well, despite all the evidence to the contrary – it is either too cold or too light. Television coverage was also revolutionized by the advent of World Series Cricket. Before Packer no one really thought it was worthwhile having a set of cameras at both ends. He was also prepared to pay the players properly, although it took a long while for any increase in income to filter down to the professionals on the county circuit.

At the time it always amazed and perplexed me that the venom generated by the decision of players to sign for Packer was never replicated when so many England cricketers signed up for the rebel tours to South Africa in 1981/2 and 1989/90. By contrast there was almost a nod and a wink from the establishment towards the rebels when South Africa was the destination along the lines of 'Well, yes, we quite understand why you're going – had a wonderful tour there myself in '48/49 (or '56/7 or '64/5) – but I'm afraid we can't condone this in public.' Moreover there was certainly less condemnation of those embarking upon the rebel tours to South Africa from fellow professionals on the county circuit.

There were more PCA meetings on this issue, which were agony for Arlott. There he was up on the top table, ill at ease, not in good health and sweating profusely as well as being torn in several directions. On the one hand was his lifelong devotion to the professional cricketer, on the other his hatred of the apartheid system that he had witnessed first hand on the tour of 1948/9, hence his decision never to return to that country again. In 1970 Arlott, who had helped Basil D'Oliveira come to England, was out of step with the majority of his press colleagues and the cricketing establishment over whether fixtures with South Africa should be continued. So too were the Revd David Sheppard and the young Mike Brearley, who spoke out against the planned 1970 tour to England when the cricketing hierarchy was so desperate to maintain sporting links with South Africa.

At the meeting at Edgbaston, which was chaired by Arlott, there were explanations from some of the players involved on the rebel tour of 1981/2. The likes of John Lever and Peter Willey gave the pragmatic view, which was easily understood: playing cricket for a living was a brief career and they could not scorn the opportunity to secure the financial future of their families. Less convincing were the explanations of Woolmer and Knott, who spoke, not of their financial gain, but their missionary zeal to take the game to the townships of South Africa and beyond.

In all this the PCA should have felt uncomfortable that their senior officers were heavily involved in the rebel tours; there was rarely any evidence that they did. Jack Bannister was a founding member of the PCA and in time he became the secretary, treasurer, chairman and president of that organization. He was a stalwart in the evolution of the players' union, which does so much good work now. But he was also involved in the recruitment of English players for rebel tours to South Africa. The same applied to David Graveney, who was the manager of the 1989/90 tour. No one seemed to be too bothered about that.

By the time of that second rebel tour, which was thankfully terminated before completing its schedule, players in county cricket were queuing up to be invited for one last lucrative payday. For many it seemed the obvious thing to do. I recall a supper with Jimmy Cook, the South Africa opening batsman, and Chris Tavaré, who were both playing for Somerset in 1989, when Cook innocently said, 'You must come, Tav.' Then he was most surprised when Chris quietly explained that whatever the financial benefits he did not wish to play there. But he was in the minority among England players of a certain age. I was never asked to go though a few years earlier I had been briefly sounded out by Robin Jackman to see if I would be interested in playing for Western Province, an invitation politely declined.

Those that chose to go to South Africa were banned from international cricket but, in the long term, their careers did not suffer like the rebels from the West Indies, most of whom were ostracized for life. Nor did Cricket Australia rush to employ their rebels in later years. But Graham Gooch, Mike Gatting and David Graveney, for example, would all hold key posts at Lord's or with the England and Wales Cricket Board in later life.

That there should be a second rebel tour by English cricketers at the end of the eighties is an indicator of how blinkered those running the game could be during that period. They did not seem to sense that anything was wrong. For various reasons England players felt so insecure and resentful – a feeling that was just as strong, if not stronger, at the end of the decade than at the start – that they were eager to take the rand. Ian Botham and David Gower were the obvious exceptions, though Ian's solicitor took the precaution of flying out to visit him in India in 1981 when the first tour was being hatched to reinforce the negative aspects of becoming a 'rebel'. But the simple fact is that this pair did not go and that was the best choice. However damaging those tours were to the game in general they did my career no harm since the competition for places in the England side was diminished. The absence of Derek Underwood, John Emburey and Peter Willey certainly enhanced my chances of winning an England cap or two.

So here we have a picture of a fractured game, chaotically run. The best players were all too easily enticed by the offers from Kerry Packer in Australia or Dr Ali Bacher in South Africa. At county level there were still the remnants of the feudal system that had run the game for a century or more. The players felt undervalued and exploited.

In the real world one might have thought twice about entering an industry that was run so amateurishly – and indeed by amateurs. But I never stopped to consider whether it was a sensible idea to commit to life as a professional cricketer instead of trying for a proper job like teaching or farming (in fact I'd abandoned any notion of farming long before my teens – I never really understood how tractors or cows worked). Playing cricket for a living for Somerset was far too exciting a prospect for such measured calculation.

FIVE

GREAT LOSSES

ONE OF THE ODD things about Brian Close – and there were a few – is that most of the stories about him are true. This is not always the case in cricket. You probably know the dubious ones, the hardy perennials that are dug up especially when the topic of sledging arises.

I've always quite enjoyed the tale usually attributed to Viv Richards and Greg Thomas, the fast bowler from Glamorgan; indeed I may have spouted it a few times after some dinner somewhere: Richards plays and misses three times in a row; Thomas, with his Welsh twang, bellows down the pitch, 'It's round and it's red and it's got a seam on.' The next ball is hit into the river and Richards says, 'You know what it looks like. See if you can find it.' Boom, boom. I'm pretty sure it never happened.

It gets much worse and much uglier. Rod Marsh (supposedly) asks Ian Botham, 'How's your wife and my kids?' eliciting the response, 'The wife's fine but the kids are retarded.' Or there is the imagined exchange between Glenn McGrath and Eddo Brandes of Zimbabwe: 'Why are you so fat?' asks McGrath. 'Because every time I shag your wife she gives me a biscuit.'

I know Botham and Marsh well and can guarantee that they would not have sunk to such hackneyed, contrived, so-called 'banter'. It never happened. Nor did the McGrath/Brandes conversation, which sounds like the product of a third-rate writer of jokes for lurid Christmas crackers. It is hard to believe that anyone thinks these stories are true and as time goes by it's just as surprising that anyone thinks them funny.

It was different with Close, who arrived in Taunton in April 1971 after being sensationally sacked by Yorkshire the previous autumn, a decision, which its perpetrator, the autocratic Brian Sellers, would soon rank as 'the worst in my life'. Close himself did not possess a refined sense of humour but he generated mirth wherever he went. He also generated awe and admiration. There has never been a braver cricketer nor one with such a reservoir of self-belief. We may all have laughed at him but we marvelled at him as well. He was my first county captain and the most memorable. I think nearly all of my Somerset colleagues of that era would have the same view.

Ian Botham would most definitely say so even though he had a few ferocious rows with Close, all of which were over within a minute. They were generally about cricket and the way to play the game. The young Botham, who was a superb athlete in the seventies, once stopped the ball in the field brilliantly, surprising the batsmen who became stranded at the same end. Instead of trotting up to the stumps to remove the bails Botham hurled the ball in that direction with abandon. Close was furious that he should have taken such an unnecessary risk. Of course Botham's throw demolished the stumps, which meant that this was an even better time to deliver an almighty dressing down, an opportunity not to be shunned by the skipper. Yet those fleeting rows somehow seemed to enhance their relationship as did the fact that Ian's future wife, Kathryn Waller, was the daughter of a family friend of Close.

It may be that Close saw something of himself in the young Botham, the tearaway all-rounder of limitless ambition. Yet Close would only play twenty-two Tests for England spread over twenty-seven years. He was captain in seven of those, winning six and drawing one in 1966 and 1967. On his first tour, to Australia in 1950/1, he was probably a naive, headstrong, obnoxious upstart for much of the time but my guess is that he was given little or no support by the senior members of the party. He was only nineteen years old and left to flounder. He was probably not E. W. Swanton's cup of tea either, which was quite important in those days. Swanton, known as Jim, was the cricket correspondent of the *Daily Telegraph*, a broadcaster on *TMS* and a man of great influence in cricketing corridors. Johnny Warr, an amateur fast bowler from Middlesex, once described him as 'halfway between the Ten Commandments and Enid Blyton'.

In his own blunt way Close gave the young Botham the sort of advice that would have been of benefit to him at that age a quarter of a century earlier. And Ian, who often listened more than he let on, now happily confirms how much Close helped him in his early days. So does Viv Richards, who recognized bravery when he saw it.

Viv remembers how Close and his opening partner, John Edrich, were battered by the fast bowling of Wayne Daniel and Michael Holding on the third evening of the 1976 Old Trafford Test between England and the West Indies. 'When I was at short-leg Closey took another blow to the body and I whispered out of the corner of my mouth, 'Cappy, are you all right there, man? Are you OK?' (Richards did not want his colleagues to see him showing any sympathy to the batsman.) 'He just told me to fuck off.'

After that Test Close travelled straight to Edgbaston for a Gillette Cup match against Warwickshire on a lively pitch. His chest was already black and blue. A short ball from Bob Willis hit him there and he buckled at the knees. Up he got to finish as Somerset's top-scorer with 69 runs out of a paltry 140. No surprises there. But I was once a little startled when Ray Illingworth told me that Close was a bit of a hypochondriac in his youth – until they made him captain at Yorkshire. Yet by the time he appeared at Somerset, stories of his foolhardy bravery as a batsman or short-leg fielder ('catch the rebounds!') were legendary – and true.

Just remember he was forty-five years old when he was taking on the West Indies in 1976, the first season for over two decades that he had declined to put the Test fixtures in his diary. How he needed all that self-belief against that West Indian pace attack. He played in three matches and was dropped after the Test at Manchester. He was upset about that. He suspected that Tony Greig left him out because he was worried that he might be superseded as captain – by Close, of course. 'Players kept looking at me when I was at short-leg. So I put 'em in't right place,' he would tell us upon his return from the Tests.

Like most great players I have come across, he was never out. He was once the final victim of a hat-trick against Barry Stead at Nottingham, apparently playing an ugly swish. Upon his return to the pavilion he rounded upon the last batsman dismissed, a novice named Richard Cooper, who had, of course, been out first ball, saying, 'You told me it was swinging. But you didn't bloody tell me it was seaming as well!'

Close was not a natural coach like Tom Cartwright and he did not have any truck with the psychobabble that crept into the game after his retirement. Peter Roebuck would often recall an early game for Somerset when he was having trouble at the crease against a particular bowler. But there was one consolation: he had the vast experience of Close to call upon at the other end. So he went down the pitch to his captain in between overs in search of some guidance. 'I can play him all right, lad… but you might struggle' – not quite the response Roebuck was looking for.

As a captain Close was brilliant at driving home a victory, brimful of aggression, never letting the game drift. He did that regularly for Yorkshire and he demonstrated to the Somerset players how this could be done. Yet inevitably the mishaps remain longer in the memory. For example, when Jim Parks chipped a finger while keeping wicket Close naturally decided that he was the man to take over behind the stumps against Leicestershire in a Gillette Cup match, with Somerset's position well nigh impregnable. After a few fumbles Close concluded that the gloves did not fit well so he discarded them and opted to keep with his bare hands. As a consequence Allan Jones, a fast bowler who seldom saw eye to eye with his captain, was prompted to bowl faster; the odd ball drifted down the leg side and eluded the gloveless Close and the extras tally grew. Somehow Leicestershire reached their target.

But my favourite story has Garry Sobers coming out to bat for Nottinghamshire at Weston-Super-Mare. Close, inevitably, was fielding at forward short-leg and Cartwright was bowling. Between them in their contrasting ways they knew all there was to know about the game. But Closey being Closey would have a special plan for Sobers.

The crowd shuffled to the edge of their seats. The world's greatest all-rounder pitched against the ultimate English medium pacer and this inspirational, unconventional leader. Here was a moment to savour. So they watched Close move slowly towards the end of Cartwright's run-up as Sobers took guard. An important conversation was about to take place; a cunning plan was about to be hatched. Close, as planned, had memorably caught Sobers for a duck off a John Snow bouncer in the 1966 Oval Test; what would he come up with this time? He finally stood alongside Cartwright and passed on his vital piece of information. 'Right, Tom lad,' said Close, 'this lad's a left-hander.' Whereupon he walked all the way back to his post, perilously close to Sobers, at forward short-leg. Sobers duly went on to hit a century.

By 1977 it was time for him to go. He was disappointed that no trophies had been won in his seven years at the club. After his retirement Close wrote, 'I very badly wanted to win something for Somerset, to repay the county which had given me such a warm and sincere welcome when my cricket career seemed shattered. Unfortunately I failed in the end but we had fun – and a few near misses. I hope their memories of me are as warm as mine of Somerset and its cricket.' They are.

He came close to lifting a trophy. In 1976 Somerset only had to beat Glamorgan at Cardiff to win the John Player League. Somerset's supporters arrived so early that there was no one on the gate at Sophia Gardens, which prompted Welsh stewards being sent into the stands with buckets by Glamorgan's omnipotent secretary, Wilf Wooller, in the forlorn hope of a contribution. Somerset lost narrowly, in part because of Close's predilection for wearing tennis shoes on a damp surface, which caused him to slip at a crucial moment in the field and give Glamorgan's best batsman, Alan Jones, a reprieve.

The following year Somerset reached the semi-final of the Gillette Cup against Middlesex. The match was scheduled for 17

August but it rained for a week; a County Championship game between the two sides was rescheduled to Chelmsford and it was finally possible to play a fifteen-over game at Lord's on the 26th. Somerset were bowled out for 59 and lost by six wickets. I remember going to the crease at number nine and my prime goal was to try to bat out the overs. Close was distraught after that match. 'That's the story of my life – a complete farce,' he declared.

He was wrong. Close was one of the great figures of that era. He led England briefly with great success until his own obstinacy and the determination at Lord's to get Colin Cowdrey back saw him sacked before the 1967/8 tour to the West Indies. There had been some Yorkshire time-wasting at Edgbaston and he was not inclined to apologise. He led Yorkshire to the Championship four times, as well as winning the Gillette Cup twice before being sacked and reduced to bewildered tears in the autumn of 1970. Then he revived Somerset – and himself. Wherever he played he was always a mesmerizing presence both from afar and from within his dressing room. I wonder if he ever recognized what an inspiration he was – or a source of merriment.

Yet there was still the feeling of a career unfulfilled when he finally retired, though he seldom complained about that. Perhaps he really was unlucky. Such a thesis would be given credence by a recollection of Arthur Milton, who was on the books at Arsenal along with him. Needless to say, Close was a barnstorming centre-forward and Arthur always enjoyed recalling how his number nine went through a phase when his headers kept going over the bar. So the following week they practised little else. Close mastered the art of rising high and heading the ball downwards. Along came Saturday and Arthur twinkled down the right wing before sending over the perfect cross. Close soared like an eagle and a thunderous header sped downwards towards the goal. It hit the turf so hard it bounced over the bar.

Following Close as captain of Somerset would not be easy and it was not clear who should do it. With hindsight Brian Rose seemed the obvious choice but that was not the case at the time. Brian kept his own counsel in his corner of the dressing room, concentrating on scoring enough runs to guarantee his place in the team. No one really knew what he was thinking. Derek Taylor, the wicketkeeper and senior pro, was the safe, conservative option. Peter Denning, the other blond from Weston-Super-Mare, was another candidate. He growled a lot, hiding a far sharper cricketing brain than one imagined he possessed. He spent most of his time pretending to be a country bumpkin, despite attending Millfield School, St Luke's College at Exeter and having – it was rumoured – membership of the MCC.

'Dasher' Denning, who died from cancer in 2007, was a wonderful teammate. He was the most selfless of cricketers, who was great to have as a batting partner. He was a superb judge of a run and he was always prepared to scamper to the end where you had to face the big West Indian fast bowler. He had a bat so light that Ian Botham referred to it as 'Dasher's Swan Vesta' and he would use it to play the 'Chewton Chop' (his family were butchers in Chewton Mendip), a sort of cut shot that exasperated fast bowlers from Jeff Thomson downwards. Opposition captains needed at least two third men when Denning was on song. And he was always available for a nightcap at the bar and a chat when something was gnawing away.

But they were obviously right to appoint Rose as captain for the 1978 season. It transpired that he was tough; he would not shrink from difficult decisions and proved to be a fine strategist. There would not be so many flights of fancy on the field as when Close was in charge but the long-term goals were clearer. Rose knew he had gems in Richards and Botham and his plans meant putting his faith in the young players on the staff. He wanted his Somerset side to be meaner and more ruthless on the field. There was enough talent there to win something and we kept being reminded that Somerset had never won anything.

One offshoot of this appointment was that Rose would be trans-formed as a batsman. In the winter of 1977/8 he had toured with England alongside Botham, who was also on his first tour, and had gained his place as a diligent accumulator of runs mostly on the leg-side. But as captain Rose rediscovered the joy of playing his shots. He drove freely on both sides of the wicket and suddenly scored at a great rate alongside Denning at the top of the order. He knew he was never going to be dropped now.

This was not a bad time to be at Somerset. In 1978 I was still at university until the first week in July, after which I spent the rest of the season in the first team, more for my off-breaks than my runs. By now Peter Roebuck and Phil Slocombe were regulars in the side; Botham was established in the England team, bowling fast and swinging the ball prodigiously; Richards was already regarded as one of the best batsmen in the world.

Colin Dredge, dubbed 'The Demon of Frome' by Alan Gibson, who could spot a genuine character from a distant bar, was estab-lished in the side with his sling-shot, manual-defying action and his willingness to bowl up any hill and into any wind for as long as the captain wanted. Hallam Moseley would do the same but we were unable to play him and our latest recruit, Joel Garner, in the same team since there was a limit of two overseas players per side. In that season Joel's appearances were restricted to the Gillette

Cup matches and a few Championship games. Therefore Hallam played the rest.

So from July onwards I was on the road around the highways and byways that meandered to our county grounds, usually with Peter Roebuck as my passenger or driver and room-mate. These were happy, uncomplicated days. I have just been flicking through the pages of Pete's first two books, *Slices of Cricket* published in 1982, and *It Never Rains* (1984), in which he writes amusingly but not so flatteringly about my driving.

'Vic is a rural driver oblivious to others,' he avers, 'jogging along without a care in the world without indicators or mirrors. We are lucky if he notices anything more than twenty yards in front, apart maybe from a herd of cows. Vic's never quite sure whether to over-take or not, peering out of the side window to see if the coast is clear – and I use the word "coast" advisedly. If it's not clear as far as Dover we'll stay right where we are and Vic will start growling.'

This goes on and on for some time. I should point out that I am writing this the day after attending a speed awareness course (another one). Whether that is a good case for the defence, I'm not so sure. It is true, as Pete recalls elsewhere, that I once pulled up behind a line of parked cars, thinking them to be a queue wait-ing for the traffic lights to change. This exasperated Pete, who was far more patient at the crease than in a car. And we did once stop three times to ask the same policewoman in Derby the where-abouts of our hotel. We asked the right question but neither of us ever managed to listen to the answer. She threatened to book us if we stopped by her again.

We often got lost. On one occasion in deepest Yorkshire we were totally flummoxed. Dennis Waight was also in the car. He was the Australian physio, employed by Somerset in 1981, who also worked with the West Indies. At the advent of World Series Cricket Kerry Packer had allocated him to the West Indies squad whether they liked him or not. Clive Lloyd was so impressed by his work that he made sure that his team retained Waight after the settlement between Packer and the Australian Board. Thereafter the West Indies fast bowlers were seldom injured and they were grateful for Dennis's expertise. The cynics suggested that Somerset employed him to ensure that Botham, Richards and Garner got to the ground on time. In fact, he was brilliant at his job.

Dennis was a patient man but on this particular journey he was getting somewhat exasperated that we seemed to be going around in circles, and in the back of the car he was expressing his frustration in the broadest Australian accent imaginable. He spoke like a man who had just been plucked from the bush somewhere in North Queensland. We stopped the car – probably not that far from Barnsley – and Dennis marched into a pub in pursuit of guidance. After five minutes or so he returned still exasperated. In his inimitable tones he said, 'Aaargh, it's no good in there. Couldn't understand a bloody word they were saying.' No doubt the feeling was mutual.

We always travelled on Tuesdays and Fridays and the radio would be on. *Any Questions* on a Friday was our staple diet and this would inevitably rouse Roebuck's hackles as he dismissed some of the garbage being spouted, usually, but not always, by a Tory on the right of the party. Instead of *Any Questions* on the radio it would have been more soothing to stick on a Bob Dylan tape, or even Led Zeppelin.

Our hotels were modest and sometimes interesting. I have cause to remember The Diglis in Worcester, which I think is now a suave, boutique establishment. It is situated by the river and Brian

Close, well-fuelled, once made the return journey there by swimming across the Avon. Even in its refurbished state I doubt whether The Diglis would satisfy the modern player. It does not have a gym. But it suited us fine.

Here I had an unofficial stag night in September 1978. It coincided with the last game of the summer and the end-of-season party. It is possible that I had too much to drink. It is certain that my drinks were spiked and the prime suspect remains a current knight of the realm. I felt very poorly the following morning.

Remember how I mentioned the ruthlessness of Somerset's new captain. Well, here is confirmation: on that morning Rose made me bowl throughout the rest of Worcestershire's innings and I have the figures to prove it: 28–3–121–0. The following day things perked up. I was married to Anna in the Hertfordshire countryside. Pete Roebuck, who was obliged to wear a morning suit probably for the first time in his life, was the best man. 'If I'm the best man how come he's marrying Anna?' he asked.

We were back at The Diglis for the first game of the season the following May. I was rooming with Roebuck again on the night of the general election, but the elevation of Margaret Thatcher to prime minister was suddenly of minimal interest to me. I had received a phone call from Anna to inform me that she was pregnant. So once again my head was spinning in our creaking bedroom. I was unable to sleep but this was not because of the radio – there wasn't a TV in the room – informing me of the defeat of Shirley Williams in Hertford and Stevenage or Jeremy Thorpe in North Devon. It's a lovely hotel but I've always been a bit wary of going back. You never know what might happen there.

The summer of 1978 was a momentous one for Somerset but ultimately an unsuccessful one – even though it was probably the best season in the club's history at the time. We were in contention for everything and won nothing. It seemed that Brian Rose had only one observation to make at about 10.57 each morning. 'This is the most important day in the club's history,' he kept saying. At dawn on 2 September we had the chance to win two trophies, the first ever for the club. By the evening of the third the cupboard remained bare.

There were some epic games and brilliant innings along the way, usually from Richards. The first masterclass came against Warwickshire in the first round of the Gillette Cup. Somerset needed 293 to win, a mammoth target in those days, and Richards was 139 not out at the end. Better than any other cricketer of that generation, Richards could steel himself for the grand occasion – we always thought this was what separated him from Zaheer Abbas up at Gloucestershire. Richards might even rein himself in a fraction to ensure that he was there when it mattered. There was a relaxed intensity about his batting, if such a state is possible.

I was with him at the end of that game and, of course, he was a reassuring presence. He did not say much out in the middle but he always engaged with his partner. He did not bat in isolation. There was always the sense of 'we are in this together', which us lesser mortals obviously appreciated. But he did not like batsmen riding on his back, just hanging in there and relying upon him to do all the scoring. Provided you were alive, active and trying to contribute at the other end he was happy. He did not want any parasites. He did his best to make you feel good, a tricky task since he was usually batting sublimely at the other end. They seemed to bowl so much rubbish to him.

Richards could intimidate bowlers in a manner beyond any other player of my experience. Most batsmen are vulnerable on nought but Richards, by his delayed, swaggering entrance, could have the palms of bowlers sweating on a cold day before he had faced a ball. He oozed arrogance, a quality that deserted him when he was beyond the boundary, which made him unusual; most cricketers accurately reflect their character in the way they play. All the bowlers of that generation remember what happened when they were up against Richards – the same applies with Geoffrey Boycott. They knew, even then, that here was something to pass on to the grandchildren.

It was better not to provoke him. At Leicester in 1981 Viv was practising on the outfield on the first morning of the match when the tannoy opened up. It was Mike Turner, the no-nonsense chief executive of Leicestershire, on the microphone. 'Could the Somerset players please refrain from hitting the ball into the advertising boards around the boundary? And that includes you, Mr Richards.' A few of the Leicestershire players winced at this intervention and their worst fears were soon realized. After Garner had taken 7–41, Richards hit 196 out of Somerset's 356 in a match we won by ten wickets.

To return to the Gillette Cup match at Taunton in 1978: Warwickshire were beaten with time to spare with Viv smashing the last ball of the match from David Brown over the pavilion ('You know what it looks like, David…'). In the next round Pete Denning hit an unbeaten 145 at Cardiff; in the quarter-final Colin Dredge skittled Kent at Canterbury; for the semi-final, Essex, another county yet to win a trophy, came to Taunton. It was probably the best one-day match I played in; it was definitely the most agonizing.

On 18 August Taunton's little County Ground was packed and the gates were locked until the chairman of the club, Herbie Hoskins, decided to reopen them. Herbie was a local farmer from

Sparkford and worked on the time-honoured principle that one should make hay while the sun shines. Who cared if the ground was uncomfortably overflowing? You had to be there.

There was tension in abundance but once again Richards did not seem to feel it. He cracked 116 before falling victim to a brilliant catch by Mike Denness, but in stark contrast our captain Rose played five successive maidens from Stuart Turner. Roebuck was skittish; I scurried at the end and we had a highly respectable 287 from sixty overs. It was barely enough.

With the exception of Denness all the Essex batsmen scored freely, though none could produce the major innings. Even so they were always up with the rate. I bowled an appalling over just before tea and conceded 13 runs to Graham Gooch and Rose understandably looked elsewhere. Later I atoned with a rare intervention: a direct hit from mid-wicket accounted for Norbert Phillip, one of four Essex batsmen to be run out.

By the start of the sixtieth over Essex needed 12 to win with two wickets remaining – a tie suited Somerset. Colin Dredge bore the burden of bowling the final over. The first ball went for a single, the second for four, the third bowled Ray East. The fourth delivery was not so satisfactory as Colin contrived to bowl his first no-ball of the season, from which three runs accrued. Now Essex needed just four from three balls. Neil Smith, their wicketkeeper, swung and missed and from the next delivery there was just one run. So three were needed from the final ball of the match.

Everyone was on the boundary now, as was permitted in those days. I was at deep mid-wicket and came to the terrifying conclusion that this was the prime spot for the ball to come. Where else would J. K. Lever, a handy tail-end batsman, aim? I was desperate for the ball to go elsewhere. It did. Fittingly it sped to Rose at deep point. He lost it for a while amid the scurrying figures in the distance. Eventually he located it and sent it back to Taylor, the keeper, who dived at the stumps. Smith, in pursuit of that third run, was out but only by a couple of feet. Neither side deserved to lose that game. The Essex players nobly came into our dressing room to taste some bitter champagne. They would have to wait until the following year for some silverware.

Meanwhile nine consecutive wins in the John Player League had taken us to the top of the table. So everything hinged on the weekend of 2/3 September 1978. We were to play Sussex at Lord's in the Gillette Cup final and Essex back at Taunton on the Sunday. Well, we blew it. At Lord's we played with abysmal timidity against a good Sussex side. Only Botham with a belligerent 80 batted with his normal freedom; even Viv was subdued while scoring 44. Apart from Rose's 30 nobody else offered anything. It was as if we were intimidated by the occasion and the venue, and paralysed by all the hype that had preceded this weekend. Perhaps we tried to play safe to avoid too many mistakes, which is seldom a good idea.

The next day we were back at Taunton and, after contributing nothing at Lord's, I was omitted. Somerset liked to chase in these games and initially all went to plan. Essex were 92–4 after twenty-nine overs but they plundered another 98 from their last eleven. In those days 190 was not a bad score in a forty-over contest. Somerset were always struggling in their chase. The tension seemed unbearable towards the end. I left the viewing box on the side of the old pavilion, where the batting side would sit to follow the action, and opted to watch the last rites from the top of the indoor school, prowling up and down the roof, hoping for some mighty blow into the graveyard that would send 10,000 Somerset folk into ecstasy. In the middle Keith Jennings, more red-faced than ever, was swinging desperately and gallantly scampering singles but we needed boundaries. Four runs were needed from the last ball; Jennings heaved and ran and Somerset lost by two runs.

I returned to the dressing room. There was complete silence with bodies slumped dejectedly on chairs and benches. There was nothing to say; there were no post-mortems, no recriminations, no futile attempts to raise spirits. We were unaware that outside thousands of supporters had massed around the pavilion, cheering and calling for the players. Jock McCombe, an impish little Scotsman, who doubled as a dressing room attendant and Viv's cheery gopher, told us we had to go up into the viewing box. Nobody was keen on that. But Jock persisted and said we had to go up there; Roy Kerslake, our tireless cricket chairman and as much part of the team as the players, said the same.

So up we went. The reception we received was overwhelming. They cheered and cheered as if we had just won two trophies. I'm not sure if this made anyone feel any better but we never forgot those scenes; they were far more memorable than anything that followed our victories in later years. We felt that we had let them down; we had blown it on that last weekend. But they didn't seem to mind. They just stayed there chanting and cheering. We didn't deserve that. Tears flowed quietly down the cheeks of several players as we went back to the dressing room. Still no one spoke. Eventually the silence was broken as Viv withdrew to the bathroom with his treasured Stuart Surridge Jumbo bat and smashed it into little pieces.

SIX

GREAT WINS

AND SO TO THE 'glory years' of Somerset though they could not have started more ingloriously. On 23 May 1979 at Worcester, where we were scheduled to play our last zonal match in the B&H Cup, there was an incident.

Until then everything had been going swimmingly. We had even managed to cope with the late return of an injured Viv Richards from the Caribbean. Those images of the end of the 1978 season were still a constant spur. We trained hard under the guidance of Brian Rose, a PE graduate from Borough Road College as well as our captain, and we did not need much motivation.

This was my first full season on the staff since being a novice in 1974 before heading off to university. Naturally I was eager to nail down a regular place in the first team from May to September. I started well with bat and ball, which ensured I would be ever-present in the Championship side that summer while playing most, though not all, of the one-day games. By the time we arrived at Worcester – I guess we must have been staying at The Diglis again (much more of this and I must be entitled to a free weekend there) – we were unbeaten in all competitions.

On Wednesday, 23 May the match was scheduled to be on BBC TV (this must come as a bit of a shock to any younger readers) but it rained all day and no play was possible. Somerset had won all three of their previous B&H games and sat happily at the top of the table in their zone. Only a heavy defeat could prevent us from qualifying. On the next day it was possible – minus the cameras – to start at 1.30 p.m. There were about a hundred spectators in the ground.

On that Thursday morning there was time for us to consider all the permutations and the following, sadly, was one of them: in the event of a three-way tie at the top of the table the wicket-taking ratio of each side would determine who qualified. So we established that if we declared our innings on 0–0 and were therefore required to bowl just a few deliveries for the game to end, the mathematics dictated that we were guaranteed to qualify for the knock-out stages of the tournament.

There has always been the notion that Peter Roebuck and/or myself had dreamt up this scenario. But that's not my recollection. There were plenty of fertile minds in that dressing room. Rose, fiercely determined and quite capable of tunnel vision in pursuit of his goal, took the precaution of ringing up Donald Carr, the secretary of the TCCB, who may have come close to swallowing his pipe. He informed Rose that such a declaration was not in breach of the rules as they were written but he was not impressed by the idea.

Now everything happened all too quickly. There was a brief discussion among the team as Rose confirmed his intentions. Derek Taylor, a senior figure, was the one man to disagree with this course of action. The rest of us equivocated, still unsure whether Brian would go through with this cunning plan, which in the end would work no better than any of Baldrick's. I should have joined Derek in opposing the declaration.

By the time the game was due to start the Worcestershire players had a fair idea of what might happen. Out went our usual opening pair, Rose and Peter Denning; in the dressing room Viv was padded up, an indication that we still weren't sure whether Brian would carry out the plan. Rose played the first ball from Vanburn Holder and settled into his stance again; there was a no-ball; then once the over was completed Rose marched off towards the pavilion with Denning in his wake.

Worcestershire's captain, Norman Gifford, who was at backward point and well aware of what was going on, then displayed his shock/horror with as much melodrama as he could muster, his head in his hands in a picture of appalled bewilderment, Jacques Tati minus the subtlety. It took Worcestershire 1.4 overs to knock off the runs. So although we lost the match we remained top of the group. But there would be no quarter-final for Somerset.

Staring at the turf we scarpered back to the dressing room and within fifteen minutes most of us were in our cars heading for home, without showering. During the ten balls we were out on the field I felt about two feet tall. We should have known better. It might easily have wrecked our season. In the immediate aftermath we thought it might wreck our careers. Understandably there was an outcry, an inquiry and by a vote of 17–1 Somerset were chucked out of the competition – oddly the one vote came from Derbyshire, not Somerset, whose president and former captain, Colin Atkinson, was none too pleased with his players.

And then it rained and rained. So we found ourselves marooned in hotels on the road mulling over the events of 24 May and becoming ever more miserable. We were no longer the bright young things of English cricket but the most cynical of professionals, pariahs who would be tainted for life, or so it seemed. Rose was shattered by the whole affair and was contemplating resignation – even though we told him not to. A big factor for him was how our supporters back home were going to react and that was hard to tell from a claustrophobic, rain-drenched hotel in Birmingham.

We had to wait until 3 June and a John Player League match against Hampshire at Taunton to find out what they thought. 'Before the start of the game,' Rose recalls, 'the Somerset players, myself in particular, were apprehensive about the kind of reception we would be given in the wake of the Worcester controversy, even though we had received hundreds of good luck messages. I don't think any of us expected such a welcoming roar as the one that greeted us when we stepped out onto the pitch.'

As we chased 149 for victory Rose was run out for 25. From his reception as he returned to the pavilion one might have assumed that he had hit a century. Somerset won by three wickets and a corner had been turned. That declaration was a bad mistake, betraying a lack of judgement as well as our desperation to win at all costs. It also highlighted a defect in the rules, which were subsequently changed, but no one seemed keen to thank us for that. And yet, despite all the flak – maybe as a consequence of it – the team stuck together.

We lost just a single Championship match that summer, the last one when we played a weakened side at Hove prior to another momentous weekend in September. However, we drew too many matches partly because no captain was ever going to set us a target with Richards and, if there was no international cricket going on, Botham in our side. Essex, under the shrewd leadership of Keith Fletcher, romped to the Championship, having broken their duck earlier in the season by winning the B&H Cup, from which we had been banned.

Fletcher was a wonderfully adventurous county captain who wove his team of talented jokers into a superb side, yet when he ascended to the role of England captain and subsequently coach, he could not have been more cautious in outlook. Essex could ally sharp humour and hard cricket better than anyone else. Often when we played them Botham would be very funny in return but more easily distracted by the by-play. John Lever, David Acfield and Ray East, especially East, could be hilarious and yet keenly competitive at the same time.

Fletcher would look on wryly shaking his head at all the madmen around him but he was too shrewd to stifle them. Somehow it was uplifting that he could smile at Keith Pont, who was fielding at third man at both ends, grabbing a stray bicycle on the boundary and cycling across the square to his position on the other side of the ground.

I have a happy picture in my head of East at Taunton on a wet and windy day, which caused piles of sawdust to be placed at the end of the bowlers' run-up. During a stoppage in play East surreptitiously picked up some sawdust in his left-hand. Soon any spectators who happened to be looking in his direction saw East bend his neck and place his left hand by his lower ear; with his other hand he banged the side of his head and then they 'witnessed' sawdust trickling from his head, through his hand and down to the ground. This time Jacques Tati would have been happier with the performance.

So by the time we reached September Essex had long since won the B&H Cup and tied up the Championship with thirteen victories in twenty-one matches. Now it was our turn. We were in the Gillette Cup final again and we had the chance of winning the John

Player League on the Sunday, a remarkable mirror image of the previous season.

Along the way there had been a few scrapes, most notably in the quarter-final at Taunton against Kent. At one point Somerset, batting first, were 126–8 but Graham Burgess, now thirty-six years old, delivered a calm, measured innings of 50, which spanned thirty-five overs and, with the help of the tail, extended our total to an unexpected 190. Then Garner and Botham let rip against Kent's batsmen, who looked increasingly pallid as they made their way to the middle. With the crowd erupting at the prospect of an unlikely victory Taunton was suddenly an intimidating venue.

Garner took five wickets; Botham snatched three as well as pulling off two stunning catches at second slip. Asif Iqbal (10) and Chris Cowdrey (12) were the only men to reach double figures and Kent were all out for 60. But it would have been very different if Burgess had not raised spirits by eking out those extra runs.

Burgess loved the game, which is not always a characteristic of the professional cricketer; he was the sole survivor of Somerset's first appearance in the Gillette Cup final in 1967, which I watched as a twelve-year-old. He would often rhapsodize about the quality of other players on the circuit. In particular he would watch the two Richards at Somerset and Hampshire intently and end up shaking his head with awe. He himself was very gifted, one of those big men who could time the ball delicately and a bowler who was capable of swinging the ball in both directions with a minimal change of action. He was a selfless cricketer, cheerful but not the most industrious and his powers of concentration were not limitless. In the summer of 1979, as a one-day specialist, there were other vital contributions from Burgess, but none more important than this half-century.

This time as we prepared for the final we declined to be intimidated by the pomp and grandeur of Lord's. We turned up in our jeans and T-shirts, raising a few eyebrows as we made our way to the dressing room. Those notices requiring – not requesting – everyone practising at the Nursery End to wear whites prompted everyone to pack their blue tracksuit bottoms.

Even more important than the colour of our practice gear was the determination of our West Indians that we should not blow it again. Northamptonshire put us into bat and after a bright but brief opening partnership Viv Richards prevailed once again. 'I willed myself until it physically hurt,' he explained afterwards. 'There must be nothing irresponsible. It wasn't a day for daring, carefree sixes.' Richards hit 117 out of our 269–8. And then Garner took over, grabbing two early wickets. There was a 113-run partnership between Geoff Cook and Allan Lamb. Then Cook was run out by a fine throw by Roebuck, a relatively rare event; Lamb was superbly stumped by Taylor, whereupon Garner took charge again, finishing with 6–29. Even so Richards was man of the match as Somerset won by 45 runs. So after 104 years we had a trophy.

Throughout the day John Cleese had been a guest in our dressing room. He hailed from Weston-Super-Mare and was a genuine fan of Somerset cricket. Earlier in the summer he had entertained us all to dinner in London, an occasion we all enjoyed immensely; the only problem, I suspect, was that we wanted to talk of nothing other than *Monty Python* and *Fawlty Towers*, while he was rather more interested in having a cricketing chat. On the day of the final he sat quietly in a corner of the dressing room, anxious not to be a distraction. A year or two later Jeffrey Archer would not be quite so reticent.

I have just been thumbing through Somerset's 1980 handbook,

a publication, incidentally, that was initially overseen by a players' company, which had been the brainchild of Brian Rose. Our captain's faith in Somerset's marketing department at the time was limited – actually I'm pretty sure there was no marketing department. I have rediscovered a brief piece by John Cleese on that final. The first two paragraphs, in a curious way, reflected our approach to the match.

Although I have supported Somerset for 104 years – since 1948 – I'm afraid I did not enjoy the Gillette Cup final very much. I'm sorry if this sounds ungrateful, but please remember Nelson probably didn't 'enjoy' Trafalgar; nor, I suspect, did Henry V giggle his way all through Agincourt.

At decisive moments of world history like these, lounging around 'having a good time' and 'thoroughly enjoying oneself' are not appropriate; what matters is winning. At all costs. Losing is NOT a viable alternative. Even a moral victory is right out – of about as much interest as a blow on the temple with a wrecker's ball. 'The game's the thing,' you cry. Ha, ha, ha! Can you imagine Napoleon addressing his troops just before Waterloo? 'Remember, chaps, it's only a battle. Fight hard but fight fair. And the important thing is I want everyone to really enjoy himself. May the best team win.' I think not on the whole. So the 1979 final never looked like being a barrel of laughs. Especially after 1978.

It seems that Cleese easily understood how the players were feeling. We were just desperate to win something.

There was no time for great celebrations since we were off to Nottingham for the final match in the John Player League. If

Middlesex could beat Kent at Canterbury we would be champions provided we won as well. On the way north Rose and Denning, captain and vice-captain, stopped off at Watford Gap service station for eggs, bacon and sausages – and, in Denning's case, his usual bucketful of tomato sauce. There they were greeted by coachloads of Somerset supporters making the same journey who were mildly surprised to meet their heroes in such mundane surroundings.

Understandably we were more relaxed that Sunday. Somehow we knew it was all going to work out. Pete Roebuck top-scored with 50 out of our total of 185, which was usually sufficient in those days – although it becomes increasingly hard to understand how – and Nottinghamshire never threatened to overhaul their target; they were beaten by 56 runs. Down at Canterbury Kent did no better since they lost by 55 runs when chasing Middlesex's 182. We had won another trophy.

Graham Burgess lit a fag and drank some bubbly. Then he levered himself off his bench and wandered out to the balcony of the away dressing room at Trent Bridge, where there were some pretty hanging baskets. He carefully tied his boots together and then he hung them around one of the baskets, declaring to anyone listening, 'That'll do I.'

Over the next four years we would finish runners-up in the John Player League three times and win three more Lord's finals (two in the B&H Cup in 1981 and 1982 and the NatWest trophy in 1983). In the Championship we only really threatened in 1981 when we finished third with ten wins behind Nottinghamshire and Sussex. In that season Joel took 87 wickets at 15.08 apiece in the Championship, stunning figures, yet he tended to be even more devastating in limited-overs cricket when he knew that he would only be required for a maximum of twelve overs per day.

How he was never the man-of-the-match in one of the finals beggars belief and reinforces the notion that it's a batsman's game, not that this would have worried him greatly. He took 6–29 against Northamptonshire in the 1979 NatWest final when Richards scored 117. Against Surrey in the 1981 B&H final he took 5–14 but Richards then cracked 132 not out and was given the award; in 1982 against Nottinghamshire Joel finished with 3–13 but the perceptive judge of the award, Tom Graveney, gave it to me for my 2–24 (mind you, the two were Derek Randall and Clive Rice); in 1983 against Kent Joel had figures of 2–15 but Bob Willis's verdict was final. I got the award for a brisk 29 and 3–30.

The simple fact is that in these big games Joel was just as critical to our success as Viv. As a bowler Joel was mean, fast and accurate, almost an elongated Tom Cartwright. He hated giving anything away, which was in stark contrast to his character off the field. He was – and still is – the most generous of men, seldom without a wide grin on his face. When playing at Taunton he would frequently do a lap of the ground when Somerset were batting and he was like a pied piper. A long queue would form around him and Joel would sign autographs for hours and chatter away with the fans.

One of our gripes was that he was too genial. We had played against Colin Croft at Southport and beyond, and there was always Sylvester Clarke at Surrey. Both hinted at menace before the game as well as during it (though I remember a genial chat with Clarke in the physio's room at the Oval when he was aching from bowling so many overs and I was badly bruised as a consequence of facing some of them). Joel took no pleasure in hitting a batsman and he quite liked a gentle life but it was foolish to take advantage of his good nature.

In a match at Bath against Northamptonshire he was bowling

at Stuart Waterton, their wicketkeeper. Joel may have been bowling at Cartwright pace, not extending himself hugely but still bang
on target. Then Waterton innocently pulled a ball away for four to
the square-leg boundary. Suddenly Joel took offence and was ener-
gized. He bellowed down to Waterton gruffly, 'You want something
to hook; I'll give you something to hook' and he suddenly found
another 10–15 mph. A third slip was summoned, then a fourth; up
came a forward short-leg. Waterton and his partners could only
contemplate the folly of hitting Joel for four.

He was devastating in those one-day games. Because of his
height Joel's yorker was even more potent and he could hit the
splice of the bat from a remarkably full length – so I'm told. I never
faced him apart from the odd little loosener in the nets. None of us
were inclined to go into the nets if he was going to bowl properly.

I enjoyed fielding when he was bowling at the end of the innings
in one-day games because I, too, liked a quiet life. Garner was brilliant at the death, mixing yorkers and rib-ticklers. Often I would
be at mid-off or mid-on and in his last couple of overs Joel would
send me to the boundary. 'Are you sure you want me out there?'
I'd ask, 'I don't think he's going to hit you that far.' He was sure so I
dutifully disappeared to the boundary but I have no recollection of
any nasty, swirling skiers heading my way.

Before those Lord's finals we would have a team dinner, which
was a very rare occurrence; the club were paying so we all turned
up eagerly. Having assembled, enjoyed the food, shared the wine
and, possibly, passed the port it seemed appropriate that we should
have a discussion about the game the following day. These meetings became a ritual rather than a source of any tactical wizardry.

For example, if we were playing Nottinghamshire we would
diligently go through their batting line-up. 'Tim Robinson, good

player, might struggle against Joel though. Randall? We'll bowl Joel at him. Rice? Well, Joel always bowls well against him. Hadlee? Dangerous player but might struggle against Joel.'

In fact they always seemed to struggle against Joel. As a consequence, whenever Somerset played at Trent Bridge in the early eighties with Joel anticipated to play, the pitches were always brown and slow – against everyone else they were usually emerald green in the middle so that Hadlee could hold sway. Joel nearly always bowled fast against Clive Rice and if this was not the case Viv would trot down to the end of Joel's run-up and say, 'Hey Joel, you know where he's from?'

There was one little flaw in our pre-final planning. After a couple of drinks we may not have taken into account the fact that Joel was only allowed to bowl eleven overs in the B&H Cup. At these dinners Botham might intervene at any moment and he would be brimful of confidence. I'm sure I remember him saying, 'Whatever you do, don't bowl short at Hadlee' and the next day Ian inevitably greeted his rival with a stream of bouncers. Soon it would start to get out of hand and Rose would spread his hands in exasperation and leave the table. But by then we were all fairly relaxed and there was the possibility of a good night's sleep ahead.

Goodness knows where Joel went once those dinners broke up. But he often declared that before a big game he would prefer to sleep soundly for five hours rather than toss and turn for nine. This was a formula that seemed to work rather well for him.

Joel, the batsman, could also be captivating. He used a plank that I could barely pick up. He had a technique that was sound and he could hit the ball an awfully long way if everything clicked. He would be elevated up the order in one-day games for a last-minute thrash, occasionally with spectacular results. He quite fancied himself in the longer form of the game as well but he lacked patience. He would bat properly for a while, blunting the bowlers easily enough and avoiding any major mishaps when running between the wickets – he was always unreliable in this department – and then he would have a horrible heave and be dismissed. He once returned to the dressing room in a grizzly mood having attempted to hit the ball to the Quantocks and being clean bowled. He threw his railway sleeper of a bat into his bag in pained exasperation before bellowing to all and sundry, 'I done swipin'.' But he hadn't.

So Joel was a gem, far more easy-going than Viv and more approachable for the fans. Everyone warmed to him. And that's still the way. I once bumped into him during an England tour to the West Indies when Barbados were playing against Jamaica in a rural ground in the north of the island. He knew everyone there and was, of course, incredibly hospitable, summoning up spicy chicken and rice from nowhere and plenty to drink. Before I left I was determined to reciprocate somehow. 'At least, let me get you a drink,' I pleaded. 'OK, a bottle of vodka and a big bottle of coke will do it,' he replied with a grin.

In 1980 the West Indies were touring England so we needed some reinforcements. Viv recommended a fellow Antiguan named Hugh Gore, who did not prove to be a great success as an overseas player. He was a delightful, laid-back character but he must have been the slowest West Indian 'fast' bowler to be enlisted by an English county during that period. He bowled left-arm over the wicket and the ball was in the air for so long that he did at least give it every opportunity to swing, which it did occasionally. He never played again in first-class cricket after his brief excursion onto the county circuit.

Our other signing was more interesting and better known. Out of the blue Sunil Gavaskar turned up. We all met him for the first time on 9 May at Canterbury on the eve of a B&H Cup match. The following day Somerset required 243 for victory. Rose and Gavaskar, opening the batting, put on 241 together in forty-two overs.

Both played brilliantly and most startling was how superbly they ran together, given that they had never met until the previous evening. It might have been Rose and Denning out there, a long-standing pairing that seldom bothered to call at all.

Sunil was a fine acquisition. He did not score a stack of runs but he played half a dozen brilliant innings in both Championship and limited-overs cricket, which left us gasping just as Richards had done upon his arrival. Sunil was also a puzzle. This was the hard-nosed, bloody-minded cricketer who had blocked for sixty overs in a World Cup match against England at the Oval in 1975; who, when given lbw to Dennis Lillee at the Melbourne Cricket Ground (MCG) instructed his partner, Chetan Chauhan, to leave the pitch with him. And he often seemed to be in dispute with his own cricket board, something that happened less frequently in his broadcasting career. Yet throughout that summer all we saw was a mischievous, eager-to-please visitor to our dressing room with a delightful sense of humour. 'How is it that our bowlers are so much more friendly than theirs?' he would ask innocently. Botham took the mickey out of him constantly, homing in on his fear of dogs and his total inability to dive in the field; Sunil happily responded in kind.

We much enjoyed his company and that of his wife, Marshniel, and son, Rohan, who thought Viv Richards was the best player in the world. And we marvelled at his batting. I think he had a good time as well. He was able to walk down the high street in Taunton and do some shopping with his wife without being swamped by fans. For him that was a priceless luxury.

This became even clearer to me many years later when covering cricket in India. Sunil was working with *TMS*, among several other outlets, and he was travelling with us to the ground in Chandigarh. On our way it became apparent that he was getting restless. 'You don't have the right pass,' he said. We tried to reassure him that we would be able to get the car right up to the gates of the stadium. 'That's no good,' he said. 'We have to be able to drive inside the ground.' In our innocence we thought Sunil was being a bit of a prima donna. Upon arrival at the ground we got out of the car just outside the gates. Within half a second Sunil was swamped by well-wishers. It was a terrible struggle for him to inch towards the gates amid the crush. Now we understood why he had been so uncomfortable on the journey.

Back in 1980, with Botham and Rose in the Test team against the West Indies, I captained the side quite frequently; it might have been tricky for a twenty-four-year-old to do this with a player of Gavaskar's stature in the side. But he made it easy. I enjoyed the experience, though it would have been easier if I'd had Garner rather than Gore taking the new ball. There was a sort of tacit understanding that I was the heir apparent at Somerset.

In our different ways we were all eager to learn and improve as cricketers though that process was dependent mostly on trial and error. There was not much coaching going on. Tom Cartwright, the coach when I joined the club, had moved on to Wales, the home of his delightful, sparky wife, Joan, and there he had begun working with Glamorgan. So Peter Robinson, the archetypal old pro, who would do anything for the club – and indeed he fulfilled most roles over four decades – was now the coach. But his role had little in common with the position of coach in the twenty-first century.

Robinson seldom travelled with the first team and we were left to our own devices. Instead he spent most of the time looking after the second team, which was hardly surprising since there was no one else on the coaching staff. So we might consult among ourselves but there was little or no formal coaching once in the first XI. This may have suited me.

Pete Roebuck and I were very different in approach, a topic we would discuss at length on some of our car journeys or meals in deserted Greek restaurants. Pete was much more technically minded. He would take to the indoor school and the new bowling machine and groove his shots for hours on end. He would analyse his dismissals and seek solutions, and he would consult with Viv or Brian, or indeed Peter Robinson in between matches. By contrast I was reluctant to analyse too much on the basis that I did not want my mind cluttered by too many technical concerns when I went out to bat. Admittedly this was an easier course to take now that I had all-rounder status, which allowed a certain freedom in my batting. So every innings would be an adventure; for me it was more about touch than technique and I could never be sure whether the touch would be there.

It would have been easier to tinker with my bowling since that is a more mechanical process. But even here I was essentially self-taught, working it out as I went along. I bowled too much off the back-foot, which meant that I was less likely to find the zip and pace that the best spinners generate. I tended to pivot more on my left heel than my toes, which is not what the manual requires. I was a little slower than the average spinner but at least there might be a deceptive loop to my deliveries. I would have enjoyed the presence of the speed gun so that I could check my pace and the extent of any variations. I would have a few checklists with the wicketkeeper: how high was my arm? How close to the stumps was I at the non-striker's end when I released the ball and, most importantly, was I following through with sufficient energy after delivery?

Looking back I would have liked the option of bowling more quickly. When that ball is turning, quicker is usually better. But by the eighties I had a natural pace and it was usually counter-productive for me to try to bowl much faster like John Emburey or Phil Edmonds were able to do. I began to become more effective in limited-overs cricket mainly because I was capable of bowling a consistent line, which to the right-hander meant that the ball would (nearly) always be hitting his middle and leg stumps. In those days it was possible in England to bowl with six men on the leg-side in one-day cricket and it now seems incredible that most batsmen would obediently hit those leg-stump deliveries to the leg-side, where the majority of the fielders were stationed. More-over posting a long-on was generally a reliable deterrent; most batsmen would respect his presence and not try to clear him.

I also discovered that the bigger the occasion the more effective I might be partly due to that lack of pace. It is one thing to launch an assault against an accurate spinner in a routine Sunday match somewhere in the shires; it is another to do that in a Lord's final with the cameras rolling and a trophy up for grabs. On the grand occasion it was a source of anguish for some batsmen whether to risk a headlong attack against my gentle off-breaks, which increasingly had a good chance of landing in the right place, or to wait for the bad ball. I think that helps explain my relative success with the ball in Somerset's three finals in 1981, '82 and '83 (the tally is

32–9–78–6, since you ask). Oddly enough, despite all the exotic shots of today it is still easier for a spinner to prosper in the shorter game than in Test cricket (Moeen Ali and Adil Rashid have often found that to be the case).

BY 1983 A few cracks were appearing at Somerset and changes were in the air. Derek Taylor, our trusty wicketkeeper, had retired. He was the solid senior citizen in the side and a superb gloveman, especially adept at standing up to seam bowlers. He giggled a lot, especially for a man brought up at the Oval; he loved a bit of gossip when reuniting with his old Surrey colleagues or his twin brother down at Hampshire. He batted more like an old pro than the rest of us and was oblivious to the cries of 'C'mon, Taylor' that were often heard as he was carefully laying the foundations of his innings. His running between the wickets was more conservative than my driving (in a car) was alleged to be. He always seemed like the most sensible man in the dressing room so it was a source of great merriment when he contrived to be out 'obstructing the field' in a Sunday League game at Edgbaston in 1980. Brian Close always said he was 'the most responsible player in the side', which wasn't that difficult. He departed at the time of his own choosing, and that's not always the case with professional cricketers.

Taylor was replaced behind the stumps by Trevor Gard, who came from South Petherton in south Somerset. He was no more than five feet five inches tall and he had wonderful hands though his lack of inches could sometimes make keeping to a rampant Garner a trial. He scored his runs no more quickly than Taylor and in smaller quantities. He was – and still is – a delightful West Countryman, who does not like to get too excited about anything. Which is not really what is required from the modern wicketkeeper.

Sometimes his sense of fair play could be infuriating. I once delivered one of my most vociferous lbw appeals, which was rejected. It did not help my cause that Trevor behind the stumps had not joined in the appeal. So at the end of the over I asked him why, 'Missing by a quarter of an inch,' he said.

Now and then Trevor would do his best to be the fulcrum of the fielding side, issuing encouragement to one and all from behind the stumps as the modern keeper should. But this did not come naturally to him. On one occasion a weary Botham had just returned from a Test match. The toss was lost, Somerset were in the field at Taunton and the new ball was naturally entrusted to him. He bowled three slow, exploratory, lacklustre deliveries after which Trevor decided it was time for his first intervention of the day. 'Keep going, Both,' he chimed at 11.01 a.m.

Ian thought the world of Trevor and delighted in his successes in 1983. At Hove in the quarter-final of the NatWest Trophy Sussex were bowled out for 65 in 40.4 overs. Joel Garner took 4–8, Ian 4–20. Arthur Milton was doing the man of the match award and was left with a tricky choice. As ever he found a neat solution. 'I can't separate the performances of Joel and Ian,' he announced at the end of game presentation ceremony, 'so I'm giving the award to Trevor Gard.' Trevor had taken five catches, a couple of which were superb. In the 1983 NatWest final against Kent he produced two brilliant leg-side stumpings off Richards and me that swung the course of the match.

One other stumping by Gard lives in my memory though it was not a match-winner. But his victim at Weston-Super-Mare in 1983 still recalls the occasion with considerable anguish. One of my off-breaks turned more than anticipated and as it passed the leg-stump the batsman toppled forward out of his crease. Gard whipped off the bails and up went the umpire's finger at square leg: Boycott st Gard b Marks 83. Geoffrey is still bewildered how that could have happened. Thank you, thank you, thank you, Trevor. But he did not last that long in the side. In 1987 he was replaced mainly because his contributions with the bat were so limited, even though his keeping was generally beyond criticism.

Captaincy issues were now surfacing. Rose had been in charge for six momentous years but now his body was starting to rebel. He could only play in seven Championship matches in 1983 and was injured throughout our entire NatWest campaign. During the World Cup, when I joined Ian Botham in the England team, Peter Roebuck had captained the side and had been surprised how stimulated he was by the challenge. Otherwise Botham led the team in Rose's absence.

In 1982 I had a received a surprising invitation from Tom Cartwright, who asked whether I would be interested in captaining Glamorgan. I was flattered and the prospect of captaincy intrigued me. So along with Anna I made a highly confidential trip to Cardiff to discuss this possibility with Tom and Ossie Wheatley, Glamorgan's chairman, a secret expedition somewhat undermined by the fact that my sponsored car, parked at the Angel Hotel next to Cardiff Arms Park, had my name scrawled all over it. Anyway I concluded that I was too much of a Somerset man to leave and, in any case, Glamorgan only really prosper when there is a Welshman in charge.

However, the chances of my captaining Somerset in the short term were receding fast since Ian Botham wanted the job. No doubt this was linked to his experiences as England captain. He was appointed – with Mike Brearley's blessing – in 1980. The major handicap he encountered was that nine of his twelve Tests in charge were against the mighty West Indies – the other three were against Australia. Nobody beat the West Indies at this point in history.

It had not worked out but naturally Ian thought this to be a coincidence. In reality, at the age of twenty-four or twenty-five he was compromised as a Test player when captaining the side. Ian was at his most dangerous as a cricketer when had leeway to be a bit irresponsible, when he had the freedom to go for it. While in the ranks he did that with spectacular success. But how could he do that as captain when he was duty-bound to be responsible? Suddenly he was shackled. The irony and the agony for him was that his incredible performances in 1981 against Australia, immediately after his tenure as captain had ended, only served to strengthen the argument that he should never have been made captain of England in the first place.

So Ian, unsurprisingly, was eager to disprove that theory and captaining Somerset successfully might help to demonstrate that. He had his eyes on the captaincy in 1983 and the absence of Rose gave him an opportunity. The swiftest way for him to show his suitability for the job was to lead us to victory in the NatWest Trophy. Five consecutive wins would do it and five wins were delivered.

During those games Ian confirmed that he was an excellent captain on the field, alert, astute and full of ideas. He read the game well and backed his judgement. He almost won the semi-final against Middlesex off his own bat. In front of 20,000 spectators at Lord's he made 96 not out and relished blocking the last balls of the game with the scores level, since he knew that a tie would send Somerset into the final.

Then in that 1983 final on a grey, seamer-friendly day at Lord's in September, during which Derek Underwood was not required to bowl a ball, he decided at tea time, when Kent had nine wickets in hand, 'sod the conditions. We'll try taking the pace off the ball.' Viv and I bowled in tandem for a while and the plan worked. Here was another example of fine, intuitive captaincy.

With another trophy won the case for Ian to take over from Rose seemed irresistible. Moreover Ian would have been furious if any another option had been pursued. At the end of the season I was asked whether I would be his vice-captain. Of course I would. So the inevitable decision was taken. Was it the right one? Probably not. Ian knew the game as well as anyone but the role of a county captain required more than that. Essentially the captain ran the show in those days with minimal support, and Ian did not really have the time or energy to do that alongside his international commitments.

Of course there is no guarantee that I would have been able to do the job well. This was rather more complicated than captaining Oxford University. The perception may have been that, even if the case for Botham had not been so compelling, I was not tough enough for the post, especially in a dressing room that contained Ian (for some of the time) and Richards and Garner (when the West Indies were not touring); I would be too easily manipulated by the superstars, who would do as they pleased. We'll never know since they had long since disappeared when I was eventually made the official club captain at Somerset.

SEVEN

CAPS NO. 55 AND 499

THE ENGLAND HIERARCHY HAS recently created the tradition that a debutant in any of the three formats is presented with his first cap by an old England player. It is a good idea that links the past with the present, and echoes the All Black notion that each generation is somehow looking after the shirt before passing it on.

I have been delighted to give a cap to a debutant on three occasions and when doing so have felt almost as nervous as the recipient. The last time was at Lord's in 2018 when I was thrilled to give a cap to an Old Blundellian off-spinner, Dom Bess, who played for Somerset and who had been taught by my daughter, Amy. The first occasion was in Mumbai when I was asked to give Joe Root his T20 cap in 2012. There was a reason why I was invited to do this. Everyone else had left the country. It was 22 December, the last game of a long and successful tour of India, and most of the obvious candidates to welcome a new player into the fold were already popping the angel on top of the family Christmas tree.

Even the head coach, Andy Flower, had gone home so the invitation to present the cap had come from Richard Halsall, his deputy. It is only a two-minute ceremony on the outfield about fifty minutes before the start of the game and it requires a quick, encouraging word from the old player, which is followed by much clapping of hands and patting of backs in the huddle. Nonetheless I was apprehensive mainly because I reckoned that there might be a fair number of players in that huddle who had little idea of the identity of this old bloke clutching a new cap in his hand.

In Mumbai I was grateful for Halsall's clever turn of phrase. He introduced me to the huddle by saying that I had played forty games for England. He was not lying. I played six Tests and thirty-four ODIs but somehow, by conflating the two formats, Halsall managed to make this seem like a more substantial international career. It sounded rather more impressive like that. Anyway, I duly delivered the cap to Root who neither batted nor bowled in the game. But England won in the last over in front of a full house at the Wankhede Stadium and I've always assumed that this was a consequence of my stirring words before the match.

Back in the eighties as a sporadic England cricketer I was more effective, especially as a bowler, in one-day cricket than in Test matches. In the limited-overs format my control and gentle loop could work well since the need for the batsmen to hurry up would often create chances. In Test cricket more was required from a spin bowler, more zip through the air and spin off the pitch that might actually dismiss batsmen when they were defending.

Moreover I soon came to realize that Test cricket was, psychologically, far more challenging. It was the waiting that could be such a torment for a new player. I might fail with the bat or bowl poorly early in the match and it could be three interminable days before the chance to atone came along, by which time the brain could be addled, conjuring up all kinds of imminent disasters. At least in ODI cricket there was not too much hanging around, not too much time for the mind to go down those dark alleyways.

My first appearance for England in 1980 came as a bit of a shock. Ian Botham was the new captain and his first undertaking was to the lead the side in two ODIs against the West Indies. He certainly had not given me any indication that I might be selected for these matches. I doubt whether this had been part of any long-term plan.

On 22 May Somerset were due to play Hampshire at Bournemouth in our last zonal fixture in the B&H Cup. This time the mathematics were not as complicated as they had been at Worcester in 1979. Neither side could qualify for the quarter-finals whatever the result. Botham had arranged to meet with the chairman of selectors, Alec Bedser, at Bournemouth to discuss the make-up of England's one-day squad.

At our hotel I met up with Brian Rose and Peter Denning on the eve of the match and everything was quite relaxed. After the pressures of 1979 when every day mattered so much we found ourselves with the prospect of a relatively inconsequential game. There would be no curfew; in fact there never was a curfew – winning sides seldom have one.

At the bar we discovered there was a Pernod night (there may have been some tennis tournament to promote). So there were endless supplies of free Pernod, a drink that had never before passed my lips. Well, the captain and vice-captain were showing no inhibitions so I merrily joined in, supping Pernod with them with some abandon into the early hours.

The following morning we were all a bit fuzzy. Somerset batted first and were soon 23–3 but then things obviously looked up. I can report that I was 81 not out at the end of our innings when we had reached a respectable total of 204; then I took 1–26 from my eleven overs. We won by 55 runs and I received the Gold Award, maybe from Alec Bedser – as with most of the details of this match that do not appear on the scorecard I cannot be entirely sure. Two days later it was announced that I was in the thirteen-man squad for the two one-day games against the West Indies. I wonder whether this would have happened without the soothing qualities of all that Pernod, though curiously I don't think I've ever drunk a drop of it since. In my relaxed state a surprisingly good and pleasingly 'alliterative' performance in front of Bedser and Botham at Bournemouth had catapulted me into the England squad.

The other notable inclusions were Lancashire's David Lloyd, who was recalled at the age of thirty-three after an absence of two years, and a first summons for Chris Tavaré, my old teammate from university. The conditions and notes for acceptance from the TCCB soon arrived in a brown envelope and I read them eagerly. They required me to ring Lord's immediately to confirm whether I was 'completely fit' (well, more or less), available and requiring a cap and sweaters ('yes, please'). The fee was £280 per match (£140 if twelfth man or one of the reserves); the evening meal allowance was £7. The sponsors, Prudential Assurance, were giving £2500 in prize money to the winning side in each match.

The first game was at Headingley. I was immediately struck by the levity within the dressing room. It may have been forced but the likes of John Lever and David Lloyd did their best to relieve the tension that comes with a new regime. They were all intrigued to see how Ian was going to react to the captaincy. At the end of a brief practice session Geoff Boycott asked me to stay behind to bowl some more at him in the nets, an invitation I was very happy to accept. When he had finished batting he asked me if I'd like him to bowl at me, an invitation I declined. But I was impressed that he had asked. No doubt my old Latin teacher would have explained that this was a '*Num*' rather than a '*Nonne*' question, namely one expecting the answer 'No'.

It was grim and grey at Headingley; I was unsurprisingly omitted from the eleven and the match ran into the second day. West Indies were bowled out for 198 in dodgy conditions; in the continuing gloom England mustered 174 with Tavaré unbeaten on 82 when the last wicket fell.

Straight after the game we drove down to Lord's for the second match on the following day in front of another full house. The sun appeared and I was selected instead of Lloyd. I remember snippets of the match, in which England bowled first again. Ian brought me on early in part because no wickets had fallen, so Gordon Greenidge and Desmond Haynes were still at the crease. Peter Willey was at mid-off, a cricketer of few words, but beyond the grimaces a very warm-hearted one. He uttered a gruff 'good luck' before I set off to deliver my first ball in international cricket. Behind the stumps was David Bairstow, bright red and beaming every time I landed a ball anywhere near a good length. 'Well bowled, well bowled,' he bellowed, far more convincingly than Trevor Gard could ever do. It was typically over the top from Bairstow but on this particular day hugely appreciated.

It did not go too badly. I dismissed Greenidge and Haynes, who both mishit catches to the leg-side. Out came Viv and he was in responsible mode. So he did not attempt any extravagances; he just milked me in risk-free manner. I bowled my quota of overs without interruption and figures of 11–1–44–2 were respectable enough. That Viv had played so sedately against me may not have been a compliment. In later life I worked out that, as a point of principle, Viv attacked the bowlers who were meant to be the dangermen. They had to be annihilated rather than blunted. So he would aim to assault Bob Willis or Derek Underwood since they were reckoned to be the best but he might be more passive against the lesser lights. I once tried to cheer John Emburey up with this thought after he had been mauled by Richards in the Antigua Test of England's 1985/6 tour to the Caribbean. But it didn't work.

West Indies made 235. Thanks to Boycott and Willey England responded with a 135-run opening partnership but we had slumped to 178–5 when I joined Ian in the middle. I had never seen him so animated. At county level a guffaw and a quip were never far away when batting with him. But here he was really pumped up – understandably since he was seeking his first win as an England captain. 'We've got to do it,' he said. 'I don't care who you want to do it for but we've got to do it.'

I was impressed and responded by making a very useful 9 (well, we did manage to put on 34 together before I was bowled through the gate by Michael Holding). There were still 24 runs needed when I departed but Ian, 42 not out at the end, willed England to a three-wicket victory. It has not occurred to me before but this might have been his high point as England captain. It was certainly his solitary victory over the West Indies when in charge.

The man of the match was Boycott for his 70 and the ceremony was mildly reminiscent of the scene in *The Sound of Music* at the end of the Salzburg Festival. 'There were some fine performances here today but the winner is… Geoffrey Boycott… [cough, splutter, anxious look left and right as nobody appears on the balcony to receive the award]… And the winner is…' There was no Boycott anywhere to be seen. It transpired that he was already on a train heading north (though probably not singing, 'The hills are alive…'). This was a surprise to most of us but it was also understandable.

Yorkshire were playing Sussex at Middlesbrough the following day and Geoffrey wanted to be in the best possible frame of mind to open the batting against Imran Khan and Garth Le Roux. *Wisden* records that on that first day at Middlesbrough, 'Boycott was painfully cautious'. But he did score 85.

Thus ended a satisfactory debut marred only by the schoolboy error of mistaking Eric Bedser for Alec just as we were leaving Lord's. Inevitably they were dressed identically – they say it was not until after Eric's death that Alec felt able to wear his England tie (Eric never won a cap).

For Ian the next fifteen months were a struggle. Throughout 1980 and 1981 he played nineteen Championship matches for Somerset as well as most of the key limited-overs games. In an age of central contracts this now seems a ridiculous workload for the England captain. But that was how it was, which explains Boycott's Friday night dash to Middlesbrough after the Lord's ODI. Bob Willis, when he was made England captain a couple of years later, was also in charge at Warwickshire but he was able to leave himself out of county games so that he could ensure that he was as fit as possible for Test matches. At Edgbaston they sometimes felt short-changed by this, and one of the locals would always bellow out 'Bowler's name?' when Willis came on to bowl during one of his rare county appearances.

Ian was denied that luxury at Somerset. Back at Taunton we did our best to support him when he returned but it soon became obvious that he was shackled when captaining England. There were other impediments. At the start of that season he played in the Parks against Oxford University – for some reason – and injured his back, which became an underlying, long-term problem. He was never as flexible again.

It is a remarkable fact that Botham the bowler was never better than in 1978 and '79 and yet he still had thirteen years as a Test cricketer ahead of him. In those two seasons his body was still supple.

He could bowl at pace, terrorizing the lower order and one or two at the top as well, and he could swing the ball prodigiously. He was hostile, skilful, a tremendous physical presence and bursting with confidence. From the eighties onwards it was more a case of him imposing his personality on the opposition for his wickets. Even in 1981 when he won the match against Australia at Edgbaston with his spell of 5 for 1 in 28 deliveries, the ball was not moving much. He just willed them out – once he had been persuaded by Mike Brearley that he was the right man to be bowling.

Another problem was the brilliance of the West Indies. Against them Ian hit a ceiling; he prevailed against all the other Test nations but never the West Indies. Their bowlers were in a different parish; he could never bully them at the crease. His highest score in twenty Tests against them was 81 and he averaged 21 with the bat in those matches. Deep down Ian knew and tacitly acknowledged that Viv was the king. Ian might have been able to overwhelm international cricketers around the globe by the sheer force of his character. But that would never be the case with Viv.

So for Ian the timing of the offer of the England captaincy, which he could never turn down, was dreadful. In hindsight his team did not play so badly in that summer of 1980. The Test series was lost 1–0 thanks to West Indies' narrow victory by two wickets in the first game at Trent Bridge. Four Tests were drawn, sometimes with the home side hanging on grimly, but that was comfortably England's best effort against the West Indies throughout the decade.

At the end of the summer Ian went off again to Alec Bedser to pick the touring side for the Caribbean and we were all intrigued to know who was going. 'Well, I didn't get everyone I wanted,' he told us on his return, 'but at least that bastard from Surrey is not going.' The bastard to whom he referred was Robin Jackman, the thirty-five-year-old seamer who had taken 121 wickets in 1980 at an average of 15.40. Jackman could be a nauseating opponent because he never shut up when he was bowling. It is always the way that the bowlers who lack extreme pace have the most to say; Malcolm Marshall, Michael Holding and Curtly Ambrose barely opened their mouths on the field (Dennis Lillee may be the exception that proves the rule here). They did not need to say anything. But the likes of Jackman and Paul Allott, while staying the right side of the line, just had to have a word.

Ian does not change his mind about anything readily, which is highlighted and reciprocated in his ridiculous four-decade-long feud with Ian Chappell, but he soon had to welcome Jackman into his tour party. In the Caribbean Bob Willis was injured and replaced by Jackman, seemingly a comparatively minor event in a traumatic tour. In fact Jackman's arrival sparked a major incident. Before the second Test he was refused a visa to enter Guyana because of his South African connections. A. C. Smith, the tour manager, took the precaution of contacting nearby gunboats belonging to the Royal Navy and the Test in Georgetown was cancelled. Later in the tour Ken Barrington, the much-loved assistant manager, especially by Botham and Jackman, died suddenly of a heart attack in Barbados. This was no ordinary tour for a new captain.

Upon his return to Taunton Ian was still somewhat shell-shocked by the experience, but he was happy to confide that he had changed his mind on Jackman, 'I got him completely wrong; he's a great bloke.' By the same token Jackman, a sensitive man behind the bluster, who would have felt the early negative waves from Botham, had revised his opinion too. However, I can predict no détente in the Botham–Chappell relationship even though they now share approximately 139 years between them. It's a shame. You would have thought they had a lot in common.

That series in the Caribbean was lost 2–0. Ian bowled lots and batted very little. His rejoinder to his best batsman, Graham Gooch, that he should save his energy by cutting down on his early morning runs, did not augur well. Ian was soon under the pump the following summer when the first Test against Australia was narrowly lost. Then in the second Test there was the pair at Lord's where the silence in the Long Room, when he returned to the pavilion after his second failure, was deafening. The magic was fast disappearing.

Just before that Lord's Test Ian played for Somerset against Glamorgan. He was already at a low ebb as the arguments raged over whether he should continue as England captain. He had agreed to attend a grand sportsman's dinner in Cardiff. He would not pull out of this engagement but it was the last thing he wanted to do. He grabbed Peter Denning and me and said, 'You're coming with me.' He needed some company and, perhaps, some insurance that he would not get marooned with some well-oiled armchair experts.

Gareth Edwards, rugby legend, and Mike England, the former Wales football captain, both spoke superbly and I was beginning to fret for Ian who had to follow them. I can't remember what he said but I was mightily impressed. He managed to joke about his situation in a self-deprecating way and soon won them all over. I see that he scored an unbeaten century in the game against Glamorgan as well but he obviously could not carry over that form into the Test match, after which he resigned. Bedser, who was never much of a political spinner, confirmed that he would have been sacked anyway. We all know what happened after that.

By the time I reappeared as an England player, much had changed. Not only Botham but also Keith Fletcher had been ditched as England captains, while Mike Brearley, the saviour in 1981, had withdrawn gracefully. Meanwhile the likes of Geoffrey Boycott, Graham Gooch, John Emburey, Derek Underwood and Peter Willey had ruled themselves out of England contention by going on the rebel tour of South Africa in March 1982. Not many of the rebels were at their peak, but it was still quite a star-studded side. So Bob Willis was now the England captain with Botham and David Gower as his lieutenants.

In the summer of 1982 England defeated India 1–0 in a three-match series and then won the first Test against Pakistan at Edgbaston. I was called up to Lord's for the second Test – Geoff Miller was ill – but I did not get a game and ended up as twelfth man. After two days, scurrying around in the dressing room as helpfully as possible, I went off to play for Somerset. By the fifth day England, with Gower deputizing as captain for the injured Willis, had been thrashed by ten wickets.

Another invitation arrived from Lord's. Alongside those conditions of acceptance came a white invitation card, the sort you might stick on the living room mantelpiece if tempted to impress guests with your important connections: 'The Test and County Cricket Board Selection Committee invite V. J. Marks Esq. to be available to play, if selected, for England v Pakistan at Headingley. RSVP The Secretary of the TCCB'. This time the notes told me that the fee was £1400 (£409 if not selected) and the meal money had mushroomed to £10. We were expected to report to the England captain at Headingley 'not later than 3 p.m. on Wednesday, 25 August" – the match started the following day. I was also informed that on the eve of the game 'the cricketers and selectors will dine together at the Dragonara Hotel in Leeds'. As a potential debutant I must have sat next to Peter May, who had now taken over from Alec Bedser as chairman of selectors, but I cannot remember anything about the meal.

This time I was in the final XI. By now my old friend Tavaré was established in the side and about to play his seventeenth Test match and there was one other debutant whom I did not know so well, Graeme Fowler. I had met him a week earlier when captaining an England B side against Pakistan at Leicester, and I had been struck by how fearlessly and funnily he had taken the mickey out of Peter Roebuck, who was also playing in that game. Not many did that on first acquaintance with Pete.

As Graeme has explained in his recent book *Absolutely Foxed*, he, Tavaré and I would spend a lot of time together on England tours over the next couple of years, usually eating together early in the evening before we all went our separate ways – we are still waiting for Tavaré's memoirs for absolute confirmation that we all enjoyed each other's company. Initially Graeme played the fool, the irrepressible imp from Accrington, daft yet devilishly quick-witted. No doubt this was an early defence mechanism for he was less experienced than me, the other debutant – at least in terms of cricket played and years lived – when we both turned up at Headingley and he was less familiar with the other players in the team. Soon Chris and I came to appreciate that there was a deep-thinking, sensitive soul somewhere beyond the mischief. Mind you, the mischief never disappeared for long.

But at Headingley we were still getting to know one another although I was already grateful to him. My car had broken down and I'm pretty sure that Foxy's dad managed to fix it while Graeme and I were doing our best to survive our first Test match for England. Neither of us had brilliant starts. My first five overs were, at best, ordinary. Javed Miandad couldn't believe his luck. Thereafter, with the pitch seaming slowly, the seamers did all the work with Jackman bowling tirelessly.

In his first innings Fowler was bowled for nine by Ehteshamuddin who had been plucked out of league cricket in Bolton after an injury crisis had struck the tourists. I was bowled by a more familiar figure on the international circuit, the wrist-spinner Abdul Qadir. Without playing a shot. Oh dear.

It was just before tea and I had played well – for seven. I just wanted to get to the break. I saw this ball, wide of off-stump and for a millisecond there was a feeling of relief as I came to the conclusion that this delivery was too wide to be of concern. My wicket would be intact at the interval and a significant landmark reached, still not out at the break in play. That would have been true if Qadir had propelled his leg-break. I think the ball, Qadir's googly I now realize, struck the middle and off stumps. Aaaaargggh.

Pakistan had a lead of 19 in what was obviously going to be a tight match. In the second innings our three pacemen patiently worked through their line-up, which included Zaheer Abbas, an ageing Majid Khan as well as Miandad. Predictably Imran Khan proved an obstacle and, with our pacemen needing a break before the second new ball, Willis, with some reluctance, I guess, turned to me.

Imran opened his shoulders hitting a couple of fours. But then I was bowling to Sikander Bakht, the number ten, who had defended

My first team photo and already I'm on the front row. STANDING L TO R: Lionel (tractor driver), Arthur (cowman), Joe (carter), John (my brother). Sitting l to r: Charlie (shepherd), Joan and Harold (my mother and father), Fred (handyman).

My mother was always a hands-on farmer's wife.

Bring it on.

Blundell's School XI 1972. Jerry Lloyds on my right.
Master-in-charge John Patrick back right.

A meeting of non-quiche eaters. Ian Botham receives his
county cap from Brian Close in 1976.

With Anna
having finished
some exams
at Oxford.

Still with Anna,
in 1978.

Oxford University 1977. STANDING L TO R Arthur Milton (coach), G. Pathmanathan, M. L'Estrange, D. Brettell, D. Gurr, P. Fisher, R. le Q Savage, D. Kayum, K. Siviter. SITTING L TO R C. Tavare, J. Claughton, me, A. Wingfield Digby.

What a man! No backward step from Brian Close, 45, on a dodgy pitch at Old Trafford in 1976 against Michael Holding and co, who were eager to make him and Tony Greig do the grovelling.

A cover drive pre helmets, velcro, hair loss and jumbo bats. It must be c. 1976.

Relief after a quarter-final victory in the Gillette Cup at Canterbury with Dennis Breakwell and Phil Slocombe, 1978.

Jubilation at 10.15pm in the dressing room at Taunton after an epic semi-final against Essex, 1978. Pete Roebuck seems to be getting on OK with Viv and Ian.

The mood is frostier now. It's 1987 at Taunton. Ian, now playing for Worcestershire, and Pete are not talking. And I'm stuck in the middle.

At Lord's on my England debut in a one-day game in 1980 with Tavare prowling at cover and captain Botham at mid-wicket. Gordon Greenidge is not backing up much; he must have been wary of going to the other end.

Even I don't look utterly convinced that Sikander Bakht, my first Test victim in 1982, has made contact with the ball. There would be repercussions.

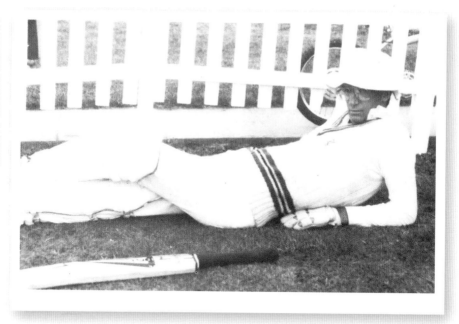

Roebuck reclines circa 1982.

At Lord's in 1983 and it's tense which is why we're watching
on TV rather than parading on the little balcony.

stoutly for an hour alongside his captain. Sikander propped forward and the ball ballooned to Mike Gatting at short-leg. We all appealed and umpire David Constant raised his finger. With nine wickets down and a limping no-hoper as a partner, Imran was out swinging in the next over.

Who can be 100 per cent certain? But I'm pretty damn sure Sikander did not hit the ball. The Pakistan players were absolutely convinced. My first Test wicket – and there would not be many more – was a bogus one. It was also an important one since England's target was now no more than 219. It was also a dismissal of some long-term significance – though I would like to stress that I was an unwitting provocateur here – since relations between the cricketing nations of England and Pakistan would be strained, to put it mildly, for a decade or more.

Imran was furious at the decision and this galvanized him to herculean efforts in the fourth innings of the match. Now Fowler, with Tavaré a more passive accomplice, produced a terrific, gutsy innings of 86, which should have made victory a formality. England reached 103 without loss.

Then Imran dismissed Tavaré and Mudassar Nazar, bowling his low-slung in-swingers, dispatched the middle order. Meanwhile Imran was tirelessly steaming in at the other end; he had Derek Randall lbw second ball and I was in just before the close. At least Ian was still there when play ended with England needing 29 more runs with four wickets remaining.

The following morning Botham became another Mudassar victim with 20 runs still required. So it was left to Bob Taylor and me. It was slow going; there were byes and leg-byes as Imran tried bowling around the wicket partly because of dodgy footholds when he was over the wicket; it was ugly; it was unconvincing. But we got there. Taylor hit the winning runs and England were victors by three wickets. The series was won.

But there would be repercussions. The issue of umpiring bedevilled England–Pakistan Tests for years. When England, with Mike Gatting as captain, next visited Pakistan in the winter of 1987/8 there was the Shakoor Rana affair in Faisalabad to compound the animosity on either side. The two men clashed on the field just before the close of play, a day's play was subsequently lost, which suited Javed Miandad and his team well, and cricket made the front pages for the wrong reasons. I remember being rung up by the sports editor of the *Daily Telegraph* to write about this, preferably in a critical way, an invitation I declined. I was not ready to start slagging off my fellow pros. At about this time Tom Graveney, who had played in Pakistan in the fifties and sixties, was not at his most conciliatory. 'They have been cheating us for 37 years and it is getting worse. It was bad enough when I toured in 1951,' he said.

Amid the furore in Faisalabad the England management in their wisdom – apparently after a suggestion from that great lateral thinker, Robin Marlar, to the chairman of the TCCB, Raman Subba Row – decided to give all the players a £1000 hardship bonus, confirmation, perhaps, that the management of English cricket in this period was not entirely flawless. The players took the money but not many of them thought this was a very good idea.

The animosity between the two cricketing nations kept bubbling over; there were two tense, often ill-tempered series in England in the nineties, both won by Pakistan. After the incident in Faisalabad England did not tour Pakistan again until 2000/1 when Nasser Hussain, the captain, became an unlikely yet most effective diplomat. By then the wisdom of Imran Khan's oft-stated argument had been recognized. Imran had been the first to advocate the use of neutral umpires in international cricket and that dismissal of Sikander Bakht back in 1982 can only have confirmed his view. Just about everyone agrees now that Imran was right all those years ago. It was just a pity that we didn't listen to him earlier.

So I had been there at the climax of a tight England victory and they were about to name the party for the tour of Australia and New Zealand. And they picked me, albeit as one of three off-spinners along with Geoff Miller and Eddie Hemmings. Even at this distance there were one or two strange decisions in the selection of that touring party. Mike Gatting was omitted. This was a surprise but his Test record up until then had been modest despite his obvious ability to dominate for Middlesex. Phil Edmonds was also ignored, which had less to do with form than the fact that Willis saw him as a potentially disruptive influence. Well, it would indeed be a congenial tour, but not an entirely successful one.

EIGHT

ONE-DAY CRICKETER

IN THOSE DAYS WE did not have to do much before boarding the back of the plane to Australia. I sent off my waist, chest and inside-leg measurements for the uniform and those wonderful touring sweaters. At some point we would all assemble at Edgbaston for a quick chat and a few health checks. Bernard Thomas was the physio, one of just four non-players in the touring party – manager Doug Insole, assistant manager Norman Gifford and scorer Geoffrey Saulez were the others – and he gave us a piece of paper as we left, which bore the instructions 'Get fit' and 'See your dentist', so I dutifully arranged to play squash with mine.

It would not be possible now but a couple of weeks before we left for Australia Ian Botham invited/volunteered me to join him in a charity football match against his beloved Scunthorpe United at the Old Showground. In our celebrity side were a couple of my boyhood heroes, Mike Summerbee and Colin Bell, once of Manchester City, as well as Billy Bremner (Leeds United), so I was unusually wide-eyed in the dressing room. I remember Billy was almost sent off by the time we were 3–0 down. An exasperated referee kept trying to explain to him that this was only an exhibition match. Against the odds I opened our scoring from all of two yards.

We convened at Lord's just before the flight to Australia. I had no idea what to take, which meant I took too much. Immediately I was impressed by Geoff Miller who arrived with no more than a half-empty hold-all. As an experienced tourist he had worked out that this was all that was needed once we had been given our track-suits and uniforms. The dinner jacket was no longer compulsory for an England tourist. Chris Tavaré was probably the only one to pack his pyjamas, though on a later tour Richard Ellison, also of Kent, would do the same. Chris would also take the shrewd pre-caution of bringing his own pillow on overseas tours.

The rooming list was organized by Bernard Thomas and it was always a source of keen interest. In fact Bernard organized a lot of things; if we wanted leather jackets or carpets in India he knew where to go. However, his day job was to keep us fit and healthy, which he attempted to do in a most predictable manner. We did the same stretching exercises in the same order on every day of the tour. He knew little about cricket but since he was no more than five feet four inches tall his shoulders were the perfect receptacles for Willis's feet when the captain wanted to stretch his hamstrings early in the day.

Bernard needed to be sensitive to which pairings might work when concocting the rooming list. The pattern was that we would have the same room-mate for two or three weeks and then a new list would be announced. At the start he'd try to pair new tourists with old. My first partner was Robin Jackman. Like Botham before me, I did not necessarily regard close proximity with him as great news. Until then most conversations between Jackman and me had centred upon the shortcomings of my batting and they had been conducted – exclusively by him – out in the middle. Within twenty-four hours, I, like Botham, realized that I had been totally wrong about him.

Jackman was great company, knew the ropes – explaining vital minutiae like how best to organise the laundry – and was quick to brew the early morning tea. Later I would learn from Pat Pocock that he had roomed with Jackers for years when playing for Surrey and it was a happy union even though their routines were rather different.

Pocock was usually an early-to-bed man, whereas Jackman was not. He liked a few drinks, often into the early hours. So Pocock would take precautions before he went to bed. He would remove all furniture that might be in Jackman's slipway after he merrily returned from the bar; he would leave the bathroom light on and there, by the basin, the Jackman toothbrush would be lovingly coated with the Jackman toothpaste to speed up the journey to bed. And they lived happily ever after. I did not spoil him that much upon our arrival in Brisbane but I quickly came to realize that it would be much more fun to play in the same side as Jackman than against him.

The players hardly ever have room-mates now. That changed after the tour to Zimbabwe in 1996 when, according to David Lloyd, the coach, England 'flippin' murdered 'em', 0–0. That was a dire expedition from England's perspective and Lord MacLaurin, as the chairman of the newly formed England and Wales Cricket Board, flew out to do some trouble-shooting. One of the issues to emerge was the players' accommodation. Malcolm Ashton, who was in the party as the scorer/admin man, has told me how they carefully selected Jack Russell's room to demonstrate to Lord MacLaurin the unsatisfactory, cramped conditions they had to endure. Jack would have two cricket 'coffins' full of paraphernalia, a few easels as well, no doubt, since he's a talented artist, alongside countless pairs of sweaty inner gloves spread around the room – and there was still the clobber of his room-mate to take into account. It looked awful. Lord MacLaurin inspected Russell's room and then decreed that the players should have single rooms thereafter.

As we get older the prospect of sharing a bedroom becomes less appealing and outdated. But there were benefits in the system. Usually you got to know your room-mate well and this became a valuable safety valve especially when someone was feeling low. It was expected that you would try to look after one another.

Despite Bernard's attempts to seek out compatible pairings there would be the odd aberration, whereupon a wee bit of diplomacy was necessary. The Botham–Eddie Hemmings union was obviously not one made in heaven so it was quickly claimed that Eddie's snoring was keeping Ian awake and a swift change was made. Eddie and Ian were never going to be bosom pals and later in the tour at Brisbane it was interesting to note their reactions to the emergence of a piglet, which had been smuggled into the Gabba in an esky (a portable ice box) on the outfield.

On one side of this unfortunate piglet was scrawled 'Botham', on the other 'Eddie'. There was this perception among quite a few Australians – and one or two Englishmen as well – that both of these players were a little overweight. The crowd and the viewers on TV thought the sight of this piglet on the field of play was hilarious. Ian managed to laugh it off; Eddie showed no signs of being amused but at least by then they were spared the necessity of discussing this incident together just before lights out.

I found myself having to make the odd adjustment in my rooming arrangements on tour. I may not be spilling too many beans when I tell you that the lifestyle of Tavaré, for example, had lit-tle in common with that of Botham (although this pair got along famously), but I was required to adapt to the routines of both. On a later tour – to India – when I was chairman of the social committee I had to fine Allan Lamb for being inconsiderate to his room-mate, Phil Edmonds, since for some strange reason Lamb wanted to sleep with the curtains closed. Mind you, whenever Lamb stirred in the morning he immediately had the radio and the TV blaring simulta-neously at full volume. With a room-mate it was harder for a mem-ber of the party to become reclusive – oddly that might be the case with Derek Randall despite his being such an extrovert on the pitch.

The Ashes tour of 1982/3 did not start well for me and I was reminded of that recently. Just before England's last trip to Australia in 2017/18 Matthew Engel, the *Guardian*'s cricket correspondent in 1982, and later the editor of *Wisden*, suggested doing a conver-sational piece for the paper on that tour. The notion was that this tour was our first with England, for me as a player, for him as a cricket correspondent. This was an excellent idea since he volun-teered to write it all up.

'Am I allowed to mention Harry Frei?' asked Engel. I had just about forgotten about him. A lot of sportsmen have the capacity to sweep away memories of former humiliations; in fact this can be a very handy attribute. But proper journalists remember everything.

Harry Frei was a bustling left-arm pace bowler as well as a fine Australian Rules footballer. He made his debut for Queensland in the first match of England's tour. On the first day I had just taken a tumbling catch off Geoff Miller and then was summoned by the captain, Bob Willis, to bowl. In my first over I had the left-handed Trevor Hohns caught at slip in the classical manner. Things were looking up.

Out came Frei, who hit my next two overs for 38 runs. I did not bowl too badly, just stupidly. Frei kept swinging at good-length deliveries and the ball kept disappearing over mid-wicket. After a couple of swipes I looked to captain Bob at mid-off. 'Keep tossing it up. He'll get out,' he insisted. This piece of advice proved unhelpful. Frei kept clearing the boundary. A wiser man would have fizzed the ball through to him after his first two heaves had been successful. So, before I could blink, 1–0–1–1 had become 3–0–39–1. And I felt like a novice again. In the second innings I bowled a lot of overs with little reward and already I could sense that any chances of making the Test team were receding fast. Frei's 57 remained the highest score of his career.

So I was a bystander throughout the Test series and when I did play in the odd state game I did nothing of consequence. It did not help that early on I fell into the trap of thinking, 'I bet they [the rest of the squad] are all wondering, "What the bloody hell is he doing here?"' I eventually came to realize – but not until my second tour – that the other players do not generally think like that.

It was a wretched time. I can understand how cricketers are more likely to become depressed on tour. Sometimes there seems to be no escape from a vicious circle. Too many failures and you are out of contention; then there is too much time on your hands; your sole purpose is to ferry drinks and to support the others as cheerfully as possible during the big matches. The temptation is to conclude that if you keep playing badly, doing your job so ineffectively, then you must be a bad person. Guilt creeps in since there is a wife and young child back at home battling away in your absence, while you are wasting time in the sun. All too easily the bar becomes a haven – in fact on that tour it became quite a haven for those who weren't in the least bit depressed – and the determination to keep working incessantly in the nets diminishes. After a while the prospect of actually playing becomes a bit alarming.

So being a bystander on tour is not much fun though I did have the minor distraction of filing a few pieces for *The Cricketer* magazine. Christopher Martin-Jenkins was then the editor and he had asked for some dispatches from the dressing room, which was the first time that I was ever paid for writing something. I was obliged to have my pieces vetted by the manager, Doug Insole, before sending them off but he did not interfere too often. All I can recall is one little snippet from a team meeting that Insole allowed through: 'The team was also urged to improve its appealing, an area in which the Australians are undoubtedly superior. When appealing the Australians make a statement; we ask a question.' A nice attempt at antithesis for the Greek scholars (I think).

I was also in a privileged position to witness the tour. There in the corner of the dressing room was Ian, no longer the raw tearaway of 1974. Now he was England's most recognizable sportsman – beyond all the footballers. In 1981 he was the BBC's Sports Personality of the Year – not that this is necessarily an accurate barometer of achievement – and one of only four cricketers to win the award. (The others are Jim Laker, David Steele and Andrew Flintoff; nowadays, even though Joe Root is one of our greatest ever batsmen, cricketers seldom make the shortlist.) Ian was box office all right after his deeds in the 1981 Ashes series. The Aussies desperately wanted to see him in action and the vast majority of them wanted to see him fail. Actually everybody wanted to see him, whether it was Mick Jagger, Elton John, both of whom kept popping up on tours in the eighties, as well as less convincing celebrities like 'Lord' Tim Hudson who, to the mild horror of Ian's wife and solicitor, wanted to become his agent, a goal he achieved all too easily.

Ian felt the pressure on this tour and he may not have helped himself greatly. He was a little over his optimum fighting weight but he kept assuring us that he would be able to turn it on when it mattered. But by his own standards he could not deliver in that series. As Engel observed in that 2017 *Guardian* piece we did together, 'It was the first tour when you could sense Beefy starting to live on his memories, believing in his own infallibility. The curse of Headingley '81.'

Once the Test matches came around Ian was not so blasé. In fact he was unusually tense. All eyes were upon him especially when he made his entrance with the bat. And he knew it. Throughout that series whenever England were batting he would sit down at the back of the dressing room with Geoff Miller and play cribbage. He was in no way disdainful of what was going on outside; he just wanted an escape for an hour or two. So he kept playing cribbage to take his mind elsewhere. By Melbourne he would be saying, 'You now owe me $977, Dusty.'

Ian was also in huge demand away from the cricket as well. One evening he grabbed Geoff Cook and me with his time-honoured 'you're coming with me'. He had agreed to go to a hospital where a young man was recovering from an accident, which had destroyed any chance of him continuing his passion for playing sport. On the way Ian was uptight and nervous, chain-smoking cigarettes – and he wasn't smoking them at the time. We were ushered into the ward and, like a light switch, Ian was ablaze, flirting with the nurses – in a manner that would be acceptable even in 2019 – cracking jokes and chatting away to the patient. It was a brilliant, warm-hearted tour de force. We left and back in the car he was exhausted, chain-smoking again.

England were unable to retain the Ashes although the series was still alive at the start of the final Test in Sydney, which does not happen very often. The nadir was in Adelaide and it began with the toss. Bob Willis wanted to bat; his chief advisors, Gower and Botham, wanted to bowl. Willis won the toss and bowled. The players' dressing room is square of the wicket there and I watched the first over intently. Willis marked out his run and steamed in and the ball kept plopping into the gloves of Bob Taylor at ankle height. After that first over it was obvious that we had made a ghastly mistake. Willis, especially, knew and he began to punish himself for not following his own gut instincts. It almost destroyed him as a captain.

Nonetheless on that tour Willis was quite an inspiration. By then he was thirty-three, old for an opening bowler; he had sparrows' legs, wonky knees and a spindly upper body that any teenager would do his utmost to hide from his peers, yet somehow he willed himself to keep bowling faster and more accurately than the rest. He was our best bowler in the series and he could not have driven himself harder. He still has that wonderfully dry, sardonic sense of humour and made every effort to incorporate the newcomers, which would involve adorning them with nicknames. Some of them, sadly, stuck for a while: Foxy [Fowler], Rowdy [Tavaré], Flash [Cowans], Sugsy [Pringle] and Skid [me].

In his early England days I think Willis was a back-of-the-bus man, at the hub of any social activity. As a captain he felt obliged to distance himself a little. He built up a close relationship with the manager, Doug Insole, who would have strong views about the cricket. Otherwise Willis would run the show, with Gifford on hand to organize the nets and Botham and Gower as his chief lieutenants. The captain could never rest. But occasionally and engagingly Bob would sometimes revert to his old self.

Naturally he was our main spokesman but his relationship with the press was spiky, having taken a nosedive in 1981 when he delivered that famously glum, otherworldly interview on TV to a startled Peter West after he had taken 8–43 to win that match at Headingley. Upon arrival in Australia Willis stressed that we should not waste any of our time consorting with the press in the hotel bar, a message he delivered forcefully. A few days later Peter Smith of the *Daily Mail*, who was the unofficial leader of the press party, pointed out that some of the players were now completely ignoring the press. Apparently Graeme Fowler had taken the advice too literally and shunned even a 'Good Morning' in the lift on the way to breakfast. So there was another meeting suggesting that we should, at least, be civil to the correspondents following the tour. Note how in those days press and players tended to be in the same hotels. Today that is seldom financially viable for the newspapermen.

It all settled down in the end on that tour, but there would be a few issues the following winter. Willis remained suspicious of the press for the rest of his playing career. On the 1985/6 tour of the Caribbean he was the assistant manager, combining not very successfully with the manager, Tony Brown, and he was apparently asked by a BA steward if there was anything that could be taken home for him. 'Yes,' he said, 'thirty-four journalists and two camera crews.' And when he was still captain Willis declared, 'I don't know what I'm going to do when I give up but I can tell you this: I'm not going to go on TV slagging the players off.' Which is what he does now rather brilliantly on Sky TV's *The Verdict*.

We lost badly in Adelaide to go 2–0 down in the series and Ian decided that morale was bound to be raised by a whisky and ice cream evening at the hotel. That didn't seem to do any lasting damage because England had an epic three-run victory in the Boxing Day Test in Melbourne a couple of weeks later. On the eve of the match we had celebrated Christmas, always a difficult time on tour, and from my perspective it had not gone frightfully well. Anna had trekked from England to discover that the lunch was an all-male affair, which did not please her greatly. Needless to say, two years later when I was chairman of the social committee in India, the tour party's Christmas lunch in Calcutta welcomed women and families.

On Boxing Day Chris Tavaré superbly carried out the plan to take the attack to Australia's off-spinner, Bruce Yardley, while scoring 89 – we had been becalmed by him earlier in the series thereby allowing the Australian pacemen time to rest. Norman Cowans had his best match as an England cricketer, taking eight wickets in the game. Needing 292 to win Australia were 218–9 on the fourth afternoon. Willis set the field deep for Allan Border so that his bowlers could bowl at Jeff Thomson, who was seldom in trouble. On the fifth morning Australia needed another 37 runs and 18,000 locals came in for free. Australia inched towards their target without too many alarms. Then Thomson, just as we had all started to give up in the dressing room, edged a catch off Botham to Tavaré at second slip, the sort he usually snaffled. This time he only managed to parry it but Miller, at first slip, was alert enough to complete the catch behind Tavaré's back.

Great game, great result, but the comeback could not be consolidated in Sydney, where the final Test was drawn. It was a match remembered – by English followers, at least – for the poor decision in the first over of the match by umpire Mel Johnson not to give John Dyson run out (he was at least two feet adrift and would go on to make an adhesive 79) and the gutsy 95 scored by Eddie Hemmings as a nightwatchman.

Now the focus turned to the one-day series with England in their pastel blue outfits, which I kept but somehow never used for golf and gardening as originally planned. We had just one practice match in this format, which was no use to anybody and which does not qualify even as a footnote in cricket history. But I have never forgotten the game. It took place in Launceston in Tasmania on a poor pitch; the home side were bowled out for 112 (Marks 3–13).

In the Tasmania side was Michael Holding – the West Indies must have had some windows in their schedule because Joel Garner was playing for South Australia that winter. Our reply started poorly and then took a turn for the worse. Derek Randall was hit in the mouth by a rising delivery from Holding and there was blood everywhere on the popping crease as he was led from the middle. From that moment on Holding reduced his pace and bowled fuller. 'I realized that I could have hurt some more batsmen on that surface,' he said afterwards, 'but why would I want to do that in a match like this?' I just have this sneaking feeling that Colin Croft would have taken an alternative view. Since I was yet to bat I have never forgotten Holding's generosity.

The ODIs, which comprised a triangular tournament against Australia and New Zealand, led to a best-of-three final, most definitely a post-Packer format, and provided fiercer competition and better pitches. Day/night cricket was new to most of us and at Sydney under lights the atmosphere was unforgettable. There was an invisible wall of sound coming from the stands. Running between the wickets had to be organized via sign language rather than word of mouth. Very often Rodney Hogg's eyes seemed to be popping out of their sockets. In darkness the Sydney Cricket Ground provided a unique sporting stage and a brilliant spectacle.

Let me briefly call upon Engel's report from thirty-six years ago of the first game in Sydney. 'Marks's very appearance was a surprise after his months in obscurity. But he not only appeared, he had the courage to try, as he might on English wickets, to beat the batsmen in the air with loop and guile. And to a large extent he succeeded.' I took 2–27 from ten overs. But we failed by 31 runs to chase down the target of 181.

By the end of that 139-day tour – we went to New Zealand for three more games – I had played in twelve of the thirteen ODIs, having been omitted from one shortened game in Melbourne. Despite some superb innings by David Gower, who had been our best batsman for the entire five months, we lost more than we won, but I seldom got collared, picked up a few wickets and Willis's confidence in me as a one-day bowler had grown. I did not contribute many runs though I do recall, in my own mind at least, hooking Jeff Thomson for four at Sydney. In fact it was more of a shovel but I felt pretty pleased with myself once the ball had crossed the ropes until I heard Rod Marsh bellowing from behind the stumps, 'Jeez, Thommo, you're bowling at half-rat power.'

In the 1983 World Cup back in England the following summer we won a lot more than we lost. There were just eight teams divided into two groups. Perversely we played each side in our group twice. Why there weren't just seven matches with everyone playing each other and the top four becoming the semi-finalists I don't know, but since the early days no one has constructed a satisfactory format for the 50 over World Cup. Recently the tournament, which has such enormous potential, has become a marathon as the TV companies and the International Cricket Council (ICC) seek to exact every last dollar. Hence the shrewd cricket fan tends to ignore everything for a month, after which the competition reaches the knock-out stages when it can become truly exciting. Unfortunately by then a good proportion of the players who have been zig-zagging around the host country – or continent – are exhausted.

In 1983 England won five of their six group games as they cruised to their semi-final. I was now England's leading wicket-taker in the competition with 13 and, apart from losing a tight game against New Zealand at Edgbaston, we had seldom been troubled. Five of those wickets came at Taunton, where we beat Sri Lanka in a run-drenched contest. England's first appearance at Somerset's home ground was a thrill for my parents, who were among the capacity crowd no doubt trying to remain anonymous – at least until I had taken a few wickets. Sadly Ian was run out for a duck so the locals had to make do with a Gower century.

At Old Trafford on a horribly sluggish pitch – mind you we batted pretty tepidly on it – we were defeated by India in the semi-final. It does not read like a thrilling game for the neutral. England were bowled out for 213 in sixty overs. India knocked them off with five overs to spare. Graeme Fowler was our top-scorer with 33 and, though favourites to reach the final, we were outplayed when it mattered.

So the assumption was that the West Indies would prevail in the final, just as they had done in the first two World Cups. No one challenged that notion when India were bowled out for 183 at Lord's. However, from the moment Viv Richards was caught by Kapil Dev to make the score 50–2, India believed while the West Indies, to general consternation, shrivelled away. This was supposed to be a Caribbean coronation. Maybe that is why Clive Lloyd promoted himself up the order to number four. Throughout most of the tournament he had batted at five, but on this day he decided to go in before Larry Gomes. It is hard to work out why he should change the batting order. Perhaps towards the end of a brilliant career he wanted to decorate the world's finest cricketing stage one more time, a dangerous thought.

The Indian team, under their quixotic captain, Kapil Dev, was inspired and won by 43 runs. The impact of this victory was enormous. Until then the Indians had not taken much notice of one-day cricket. Their focus had remained on Test cricket; the fans worshipped their Test cricketers. But at a stroke this victory changed all that. It became apparent that the Indian fans were now desperate to see their heroes playing ODI cricket on their own turf. Touring schedules were changed and so were the TV schedules. A passion for fifty-over cricket swept through the sub-continent.

There was a similar volte-face with even greater consequences when India won the inaugural T20 World Cup in 2007 in Johannesburg. Until then they had been sniffy about T20 cricket. But when M. S. Dhoni's side prevailed in a thrilling final against Pakistan this format was then embraced in India. In 2008 the Indian Premier League (IPL) was formed and the ultimate success of that tournament has transformed how cricket at the highest level is conducted, a more dramatic change than the one we witnessed after the advent of World Series Cricket in the late seventies.

The IPL looks as if it is here to stay; the best players can become millionaires in the space of five weeks. Hence they are no longer dependent upon the generosity or otherwise of their national boards. This provides challenges for the administrators in the cricket-playing nations and a terrific bonus for the players, especially those capable of clearing the boundaries at will. Most old players doggedly stick to the line 'I'm glad I played in my era'. However, I fancy this is now the time to be a top-class professional cricketer (although it's a pity about all those cameras on the mobile phones). Today's best players can now fashion their careers in a variety of ways – rather than be told what to do by their boards. Hence the structure of cricket at both international and domestic level has never been more volatile while players can skip around the world's T20 tournaments, a situation that stems from India winning the 1983 World Cup and the 2007 World T20 tournament.

With my stock relatively high after the World Cup I played in the first Test of the summer against New Zealand at the Oval, which may have been quite a good advert for the one-day game. My 100 per cent winning record in Test cricket was sustained but the match was a turgid affair. I failed to score runs and took 3–78 from forty-three very cunning overs in the second innings. As far as I can recall the most entertaining passage of play was in the first innings when Phil Edmonds, off two paces, bowled several bouncers at Richard Hadlee, which were brilliantly taken by Bob Taylor standing up behind the stumps. This only seemed to confirm Bob Willis's suspicions about Edmonds being disruptive, and he was ignored after the second Test match though the fact that he ricked his back getting out of his car hastened his absence.

Unfortunately I was omitted after the first Test match. But they picked me for the winter tour to New Zealand and Pakistan, an expedition that for some reason prompts the exclamation, 'Ah, you mean the sex, drugs and rock 'n' roll tour.'

NINE

ON TOUR

WE ARRIVED IN FIJI just in time to celebrate the advent of 1984, which we did with gusto. It was a novel way to start a tour. Austerity was not so prevalent in the eighties. Late in Andy Flower's time in charge of the England team the prevailing wisdom seemed to be that boot camps and boxing in windswept parts of the northern hemisphere would bind a touring team together nicely ahead of the next cricketing challenge. At the start of 1984 we preferred to go to Fiji in preparation for England's tour of New Zealand and Pakistan.

We were in Suva for five days and there, in between the showers, we played two matches on a matting pitch, the second of which we only won narrowly. Sadly cricket in Fiji does not appear to have been inspired by our visit since their standing in world cricket has diminished since then. But the visiting England team greatly enjoyed the hospitality on offer, which would become a regular occurrence during the first half of this tour.

The New Zealand leg was lively. There were parties often attended by the players of both sides; there was alcohol and there was a bit of dope smoked along the way. There was also Ian Botham.

And this cocktail aroused the newshounds. If only I had written a book about this expedition rather than the next one the following winter I could furnish you with all the salacious details. In fact I'm relieved that *Marks Out of XI*, still available for the odd penny (leaving aside the delivery costs), dealt with England's 1984/5 tour of India, the assassinations of Mrs Gandhi and the UK's deputy high commissioner, Percy Norris, the Bhopal disaster and an epic England victory rather than a grubby defeat and a bit of pot smoking in the odd corner of New Zealand.

There was definitely no pot smoking in the Christchurch dressing room during the Second Test, which England lost by an innings and 132 runs even though New Zealand scored only 307 in one knock. This was the one allegation seized upon by the England tourists since it was the one that could be denied specifically and with conviction. Let me quote our captain, Bob Willis, who may have found writing a tour diary (with the consummate help of Alan Lee) a bit of a trial. 'Some of the innuendoes I found absolutely absurd, including one unsubstantiated allegation that certain players were smoking pot in the dressing room at Christchurch. How anyone can honestly believe such a thing could have happened is completely beyond me, but I didn't feel like laughing about it.'

We were not all ascetics on that tour, as evidenced by the odd team meeting when Bob Taylor and Chris Tavaré were mysteriously absent until it became apparent that the agenda did not relate to them. And there may have been a bit of dope in the birthday cake we gave to our manager, A. C. Smith, who would stick by us nobly when the *Mail On Sunday* and *Daily Express* came out with their various allegations. But there were no late-night brawls on the pavements. No one was hurt. No one ended up in court.

The allegations of pot smoking excited the journalists the most.

I have just come across the relevant issue of *The Cricketer* magazine, which reminds me that I was still sending dispatches 'From the Dressing Room'. In Christopher Martin-Jenkins' editorial he consulted 'purely hypothetically' a medical expert, who was also 'a well-known cricketer', about the effects of smoking pot.

The expert's conclusions suggest to me that some dope should almost become compulsory after an England ODI victory, especially in Bristol: 'It is similar to drinking alcohol without producing the associated aggressive tendencies. In fact the individual becomes less gregarious and is inclined to become slightly withdrawn, experiencing inner tranquillity... It seems likely that smoking pot the night before an important cricket match would have little effect on playing ability but might affect any decisions taken on that evening.'

On this tour, as in many others, so much hinged on Botham. He was still gold dust for the newspapers and this obviously had a major impact on the relationship between press and players. At the start of Ian's career the general rule was reckoned to be 'what happens on tour, stays on tour'. The correspondents would stick to the cricket rather than pursuing the detail of any off-field activities (though this was not a universal rule since there was, for example, much debate about the constant presence of Peter May's fiancée on the 1958/9 tour of Australia).

Unwittingly Ian changed all that. Yet the situation was complicated by the fact that Ian had become friends with some of the leading lights in the press box. He welcomed into his company the likes of Peter Smith of the *Mail*, Pat Gibson of the *Express* and Chris Lander of the *Mirror* and no doubt some good nights ensued. Lander, famously, turned up at John O'Groats to cover the first day of Ian's first walk in aid of Leukaemia research in 1985 and ended up doing the entire trip, which meant – among many other things (like blisters) – he had to trek back to the northern tip of Scotland to collect his car when it was all over. Years later Ian climbed up to the pulpit of Wells cathedral to give an address at Lander's funeral in May 2000, a sight that I could not have envisaged in 1974.

Ian brought these journalists into his circle. As a consequence they became loyal to him; they would not be prepared to shop him for any off-field excesses. But inevitably there was increasing pressure from the newspaper offices back home to investigate the latest Botham saga. This left some of the cricket correspondents in a tricky position and on the 1983/4 tour of New Zealand and Pakistan the situation was exacerbated by all the allegations flying around.

The *Mail On Sunday* sent out their own news reporters to get the story. The cricket writers would insist to us that they gave them little or no assistance, and as a consequence of his loyalty to Botham Peter Smith had to leave his job at the *Mail* prematurely – for a short time he would work as a media liaison officer for the TCCB. Smith was determined to stick by the old rules.

So while this was never his intention, Botham's very presence on tour widened the gap between the press corps and the players. On the 1954/5 tour of Australia the *Times* correspondent, John Woodcock, was ill during the Adelaide Test so the captain, Len Hutton, invited him to spend the entire match in the England dressing room, where he could lie down on the physio's couch if he was feeling queasy. That would not have happened to any member of the press corps towards the end of the 1983/4 tour when tensions were rising. And today even Mike Atherton would have to find somewhere else to lay his aching head.

So there was the sense of the media landscape changing in the early eighties. Did the demand to deliver something sensational coincide with the publication of more untrustworthy scoops? Well, let me quote one of the great cricket correspondents.

> The pendulum has swung full distance. Dullness is feared and avoided. So unfortunately is fact. The newsroom has invaded sport and on the occasion of Test matches the cricket correspondent is often reinforced by a columnist or newshound, who, with furrowed brow, scours hotels and pavilions on his dark and dubious assignments. The technique of the game now ranks below the 'story' and you will often hear reporters at the end of a full day's cricket lamenting that 'nothing has happened'. No one has fallen dead while taking guard or been arrested while placing the field.

Whose observations are these? Woodcock? Selvey? Berry? Atherton? No, this was R. C. Robertson Glasgow, once of the *Morning Post*, the *Telegraph* and the *Observer*, writing in 1949. Has everything really changed so much since then?

Maybe the newshounds eager to monitor Botham's every movement on the 1983/4 tour were not such a new phenomenon, after all. In a different way Botham provided an equally tricky challenge for his captain. Bob Willis and Ian were great friends and they had played many Tests together by the time Willis took over the captaincy. But he was not in the fortunate position of Mike Brearley – or even Keith Fletcher – of having a young Botham in his team still reaching for the stars.

Botham was the potential match-winner and a very powerful presence in the dressing room. It would not have been easy for Willis to read the riot act to him. Therefore it must have been a difficult balancing act for Willis to manage him. In fact in his later years Botham was only really effective overseas on the 1986/7 tour of Australia when Mike Gatting was captain and, for a briefer period of time, during the World Cup of 1992 in Australasia when Graham Gooch was in charge.

On this tour Ian started excellently with a century in the Wellington Test alongside Derek Randall (164), which gave England a first innings lead of 244, but New Zealand comfortably batted themselves to safety with centuries from Martin Crowe and Jeremy Coney. Next came the debacle in Christchurch on a seamer's paradise, which meant that the emergency reinforcement, Tony Pigott of Sussex, had to postpone his wedding in order to win his solitary Test cap (ahead of the unfortunate off-spinner). New Zealand were 87–4 at lunch on the first day and during the interval Willis quite rightly pointed out that we had bowled total garbage in the morning session. We were worse in the afternoon. The batting also left something to be desired against Richard Hadlee, who exploited helpful conditions brilliantly: England 82 all out was followed by 93 all out.

This defeat condemned England to lose a Test series in New Zealand for the first time. There was one Test to go but it was played in Auckland on a very flat, slow pitch, which duly produced the bore draw that suited New Zealand nicely. I was selected for this game and added three wickets and six runs to my Test tally.

Once again I had more success in the ODI series, which we won 2–1. At the Basin Reserve in Wellington, perhaps the only Test venue that doubles as a roundabout, I took 5–20, which remained England's best figures in ODI cricket until Mark Ealham dismissed five Zimbabweans for 15 runs in Kimberley in 2000 – and all of his victims were lbw. I cannot confirm the validity of those umpiring decisions since I was not there but my press colleagues in Kimberley telephoned so that I could give my reaction to this record-breaking event. No doubt I tried to be suitably gracious – even though every single Zimbabwean batsman was deemed to be lbw (have I mentioned that already?).

Let's return briefly to Wellington and a brown, slow pitch, which made fluent strokeplay tricky. I was summoned to bowl when the score was 18–0. When I had finished my ten overs it was 63–5. John Wright, Bruce Edgar, Geoff Howarth and a brace of Crowes all succumbed thanks to the sluggishness of the surface and their yearning to accelerate, plus the fact that the off-breaks were landing in the right place.

We must have looked like a slick unit out there for a while. At the team meeting we had worked out precisely where every fielder would be stationed for my bowling for left- and right-handed batsmen. I had the envelope in my pocket with all the details. Such a plan made sense because it is important to have the best fielders in the key positions. So, for example, David Gower, one of the best, would be at mid-wicket while we would hope to hide Willis and his wonky knees at backward point. It all went perfectly until a single was taken and a right-hander came on strike. Eight fielders moved seamlessly into their new position but dear old Derek Randall wandered around like a headless chicken until the envelope had been extracted from my pocket.

Without doubt Randall would have been in a key position since he was a superb fieldsman. In the ring he would gallop in for fifteen yards before the ball was bowled; Gower would take two paces. Yet both were brilliant. Randall also had an acute cricket brain though there were times when he managed to disguise this fact quite convincingly.

So we won that game and I was the man of the match. Had this happened in 2019 I would be grabbed by the ECB's media manager straight afterwards and escorted along with a security officer to the press conference room, where there would be TV cameras and microphones waiting as well as a reasonable quorum of scribes anxious to hang on my every word. Then I would grant a gracious interview to *TMS*. I think I would have quite enjoyed this experience: 'Let us now turn to the dismissal of Martin Crowe...' Sadly this did not seem to be the case in 1984; just a hurried chat for a second or two outside the dressing room, probably with Peter Smith, was all that was required.

That evening, I discover by dipping into the Willis tour diary, I joined the captain, Botham and Fowler at an Elton John concert. Elton had carefully planned his concerts in New Zealand to coincide with England's one-day schedule so some of us attended all three. In Wellington we were at the side of the stage about ten yards from him and the band. At the time Elton was chairman of Watford FC and it was clear that his interest in sport was genuine. I did not spend anywhere near as much time with him as Ian or Graeme (have a look at *Absolutely Foxed*), but I do have a recollection of Elton saying that Ian would not be able to get away with quite so much if he were on Watford's books, though this should not suggest that Elton's tour of New Zealand was an entirely puritanical expedition. Even so, Elton John's longevity suggests that he must have looked after himself pretty well.

Elton's friendship with Ian endured. In 2006 he and his band appeared at the County Ground at Taunton. Ian was there and a happy man, surrounded by his family. 'This is not so bad,' he said. 'There's my mate out there hammering out the songs and here I am in my box in my own stand.' Ian's mother, Marie, was there too and it was her birthday; in the middle of the show Elton followed 'I'm

Still Standing' and 'Bennie and The Jets' with a special rendition of 'Happy Birthday'. Ian bundled Marie out on to the balcony of the Botham Stand and she waved to the assembled throng rather like the Queen Mother.

BACK IN 1984 it was time to set off for Pakistan, where we would play three Tests and two ODIs. The schedule was ridiculously tight with no warm-up games so a substantial delay because of engine failure was unhelpful. We had taken the precaution of packing some alcohol. There were no problems at customs but some of the vital cardboard boxes were leaking ominously as they were creaking around the baggage carousel at Karachi airport and our manager, A. C. Smith, dutifully leapt on board in an attempt to rescue the situation – and the boxes – while still retaining his dignity. He did this as well as any man could.

It was only in Pakistan that all the allegations surfaced in the English newspapers. I was the chairman of the social committee, a role that had been undertaken on my first tour by Geoff Miller, a hard act to follow (in fact, he still is). No doubt you might conclude that on the New Zealand leg of the tour this was a redundant position – and there may be a grain of truth in that. There was not much need for additional entertainment there. That all changed in Pakistan. By the time the 'disgraceful' behaviour of England's cricketers overseas was dominating the back and front pages at home, we were probably in the team room doing charades and other nonsense at the behest of a social committee that comprised me, Fowler and Neil Foster, a trio unjustly referred to as 'The Mafia' in Willis's diary.

My dressing-room dispatch for *The Cricketer* reminds me of

evenings watching repeats of *Minder* in that team room; of the wailing of sirens and horns as our armed police escort ferried us to and from the grounds; of enjoying the Watermill Theatre company's production of *The Merchant of Venice* in Lahore (I'm sure Celia Imrie was one of the cast); and 'consuming countless crates of Fanta'. There is no mention of drugs or sex or even rock 'n' roll for that matter.

On the field we were cunningly ambushed in Karachi. In the first Test there was some assistance for the bowlers and the home side won it, albeit in a panicky way – they lost seven wickets, five of which were taken by Nick Cook, before they knocked off the 66 runs required for victory. It was the first time that England had lost a Test in Pakistan. Once more my batting was hopeless and my bowling no more than adequate.

In the first innings I was caught off bat and pad from the bowling of Sarfraz Nawaz, surprised by late in-swing when the ball was old. At the time this was mysterious. Now we all know that Sarfraz, with Imran Khan a willing pupil, was one of the first to recognize and develop the possibilities of reverse swing. In Australia they would refer to this phenomenon as the ball 'going Irish' but such a description is woefully politically incorrect in the twenty-first century. Sarfraz would skilfully manipulate the ball into the right condition ensuring that one side was bone dry, the other shiny and then he would work his magic. At the time we thought it was just freak in-swing.

Sarfraz was Pakistan's busiest pace bowler and never delivered a poor spell in that series. In the second innings at Karachi he had Mike Gatting lbw, padding up; the raised finger that sent him on his way belonged to Shakoor Rana. A decade later when Waqar Younis and Wasim Akram were in their pomp we were all familiar with reverse swing. It had become a wondrous art form – and another source of much controversy between England and Pakistan.

In that second innings in Karachi Gatting may have been grumpy about his lbw decision but there were no doubts about my dismissal: I was bowled – again – by Abdul Qadir, who took eight wickets in the match. Unsurprisingly I thought Qadir was a genius. He had tormented me every time. But others could also recognize his threat – and his artistry. With a wonderfully fluid, vibrant action he fizzed the ball down and it might be the leg-break, or the googly, or the top-spinner. I could not tell one from the other. Batting is hard enough when you are unsure which way the ball is going to go upon landing. It is even trickier when you don't know where the damn thing is going to land in the first place.

The best spinners make the ball dip viciously at the end of its flightpath. Qadir, Shane Warne, Bishen Bedi and Muttiah Muralitharan could do that to order. The lesser mortals would find that bit of magic sporadically. So when confronted by Qadir one could be so easily lulled – or at least I could. When the ball was in the air it might look innocuous and the mind was bewitched. 'This looks like a full-toss. Runs to be gleaned here… Hang on, it's dipping a little… It's a half-volley… Not to worry… Let's just lean into it… Oh no… it's still bloody dipping.' By this time I'm groping forward as the ball lands on a perfect length; and I'm lunging out of control yet again.

I was humiliated by Qadir in that second innings. It was almost a relief to be bowled by him. I had seldom felt so low as a cricketer. I knew I could bat a bit even though this faith was fading fast. Qadir was making me look like a complete no-hoper. I was contributing nothing with the bat, way out of my depth and this incontrovertible fact was increasingly hard to disguise.

Even our press corps spotted it. In those days we would await the arrival of the English newspapers with eagerness even though they were three or four days old. It was often our only contact with home since the phone lines were so unreliable. So we would scour them, absorbing every detail, including, of course, the cricket reports. Pat Gibson, a man who would become a great guide and mentor when I started as the cricket correspondent of the *Observer* in 1990, could not resist this observation in his paper: 'I don't know what Marks read at Oxford. But it certainly wasn't wrist-spin.'

By now the tour party was starting to disintegrate. Ian's knee was causing him extreme pain. After sixty-five consecutive Tests for England he would miss the match in Faisalabad and fly home for treatment. Moreover Willis was laid low with stomach cramps and fever. He would also miss that game and head home early. David Gower took over the captaincy and when it came to selecting the side for the Test match it was just a case of leaving out the only fit man remaining; this was Chris Tavaré, who had long since struggled to score any runs. Once the Test at Faisalabad was underway several more players were soon struggling with stomach upsets.

Throughout all this our hosts had sought to be as accommodating as possible. Our Lahore hotel had agreed to ship out our evening meals all the way to Faisalabad, a distance of about 140 kilometres, a luxury enjoyed by the majority of the press as well as the players though the atmosphere in the dining room was, by now, often a little frosty. My recollection is that the food was much better than the conversation.

Moreover it did not help the situation greatly when Ian Botham, in his hospitable bed back in England, confided to Pat Murphy of the BBC, 'Pakistan is the sort of place every man should send his mother-in-law to, for a month, all expenses paid.' No doubt it was a joke. But it was not a very good one; nor was it a very timely intervention. A. C. Smith had to use all his powers of diplomacy, which were considerable, to ensure that our excellent evening meals from Lahore kept coming.

I had never encountered a pitch like the one in Faisalabad. There was not a single blade of grass to be seen. It was 22 yards of hard, rolled mud and it was very good for batting. The ball bounced truly and slowly throughout. Pakistan declared at 449–8. Despite some groaning and clutching of stomachs in the dressing room we had reached 361–6 when I went out to join captain Gower – I had been demoted below Bob Taylor because I had played Qadir so dreadfully in Karachi. My innings began frenetically. I had decided that there was no point in blocking badly so that if the ball was full I opted for some rather extravagant, and, no doubt, ugly drives. Gower came down, not to urge caution, but to say, 'This seems to be working; you may as well carry on like this.'

In fact I settled down. Having somehow survived for half an hour I realized that the pitch was so slow that Qadir could be played off the wicket. I could wait for the ball rather than lunge, which is what you are supposed to do anyway. The cut and the sweep were less risky shots, and I could defend on the back foot even if this sometimes looked like an adult version of French cricket. At last I had a method – and it worked. Meanwhile Gower was batting superbly; this was not champagne Gower, but pragmatic Gower, who still possessed a certain grace. The captaincy combined with England's plight on tour had combined to galvanize him. We added 167 together, of which I contributed 83.

We declared with a lead of 97 but the match was inevitably drawn. At the end of it I bowled a fairly respectable left-handed delivery – just for fun – and Zaheer Abbas, who saw this act as a source of runs rather than merriment, leapt out of his crease to drive the ball imperiously through the covers for four. Given the background to the match it was quite a good England performance but the scorecard shows only the dullest of draws.

I played a better innings in the final Test in Lahore, where I top-scored with 74 in England's modest first innings total of 241, adding 120 with Fowler, who was, unusually, batting at number six. The method, hatched in Faisalabad, was still working. So, at last, I was making a contribution. England conceded a first innings lead of 102 but Gower was majestic again in the second innings (173 not out) and I scored 55 alongside him in a partnership of 119.

The captaincy seemed to be spurring Gower on, which often happens at the start of a new regime. In the Lahore dressing room he had been given a most unusual task by the tour management. Bob Taylor, the most fair-minded gentleman of cricket, had briefly lost his temper at one of the umpire's decisions and had remonstrated unacceptably. So it fell upon the new England captain to reprimand a man actually sixteen years his senior. It was the mildest dressing down I have ever witnessed but it ticked the box. Gower, by the way, was capable, occasionally, of delivering a serious bollocking, which would be all the more effective because of its rarity value.

With England one down in the series Gower declared on the final afternoon, leaving Pakistan a target of 243 in what would become fifty-nine overs. At one point Pakistan were coasting at 173–0 and *Wisden* reminds me in disapproving tones that '[Nick] Cook and Marks, the spinners, shared seven overs in more than half an hour. Had England won, as it briefly seemed they might, the victory would have been more than they deserved.' It was not so much the slow over rate that undermined Pakistan but an inspired

Norman Cowans, who conjured five wickets from nowhere. And there was some panic from Pakistan, who finished on 217–6.

Thus ended my Test career in distant Lahore after hitting three consecutive half-centuries for England: 83, 74 and 55. Since then Alastair Cook is the only Englishman to finish his Test career with two half-centuries in his final match. A surprised Andy Zaltzman, now *TMS*'s one-day scorer in between his serious job as a comedian, furnished me with this statistic in 2018 during the Oval Test. I must ask him about three consecutive half-centuries. However my prime role in the side was to bowl off-breaks; they may have been steady but they were not very potent. At least now I did not feel out of place in a Test match dressing room; I was no longer agonizing over whether I should be there. And scoring those runs in Pakistan would boost my confidence as a cricketer. The summer of 1984 would be my best for Somerset. Somehow I ended up ninth in the national batting averages, scoring 1,262 runs at an average of 52.58 and taking 86 wickets at 25.96. And I would be selected to tour again the following winter, though, as it transpired, I reverted to being a one-day specialist – and an author. Of course, I would have liked to have played more Tests but – despite the statistical quirk – I can understand why they did not pick me again. So, I suspect, can everyone else.

FOR THOSE CRAVING a detailed account of England's 1984/5 tour of India – and Australia – join the chase for the remaining copies of *Marks Out of XI*, which may have been my most significant achievement on that tour. I did play in all the ODIs, a series England won 4–1 and, in between chronicling the Test series, I carried out the drinks to our brave boys, barely spilling a drop along the way. But the cricketing significance of that trip lay with the Test series.

In fact it was a brilliant tour in many ways, a throwback to the old days, which is remembered fondly by all its (England) participants. A lot of stuff happened. A few hours after our arrival in Delhi the prime minister, Mrs Indira Gandhi, was assassinated and we all thought we would be going home. Thirty-six hours before the first Test in Bombay, Percy Norris, the UK's deputy high commissioner, was also assassinated on the morning after he had entertained us so generously at his apartment. We were then certain we would be going home. There was the terrible Bhopal disaster stemming from a gas leak at the Union Carbide pesticide plant, a story that some of the cricket correspondents were obliged to cover – indeed, one or two of them actually got quite close to the affected area. There was also the small matter of a general election. Somehow against this chaotic backdrop we stayed on and, having lost the first Test in Bombay, came back to win the series. There was the making of a good book there somewhere.

Only four of the tour party had been to India before. We had been given an idea of what to expect but any first visit there is likely to be a shock to the system. Initially we were imprisoned in our hotel in Delhi with smoke rising ominously from the centre of the city, a consequence of the unrest after Mrs Gandhi's assassination. We took refuge in Sri Lanka for ten days before returning to Bombay and only then could we venture out of our hotel. I joined Graeme Fowler and his camera for a short walk around the streets near the Gateway of India. Soon Foxy spotted a cherubic eight-year-old girl and he took a photograph. Within seconds we were surrounded by her entire family, all gently clutching our arms, persistently, passively begging for rupees. They followed us all the way back to the hotel. No pre-tour talk prepares you for that.

In Jaipur we stayed in a palace, where you could have had an indoor net in the bedroom before going out to the gardens to watch the snake-charmers in action. By way of contrast in our Rajkot hotel the washing facilities comprised one big plastic bucket and one small plastic bucket and the pillow was like a lump of granite – suddenly I understood why Chris Tavaré always took his own pillow to the sub-continent. Because this was such an inexperienced tour party we were able to take some enjoyment from the Spartan conditions – provided we were feeling healthy. In Rajkot we had an epic snooker and table tennis competition against the press with both sides claiming victory, which begins to makes this expedition sound like one penned by Arthur Ransome. Needless to say, this would not happen today either.

Moreover it was quite a curious tour party. Bruce French was desperately keen to visit the Himalayas and he was allowed to do so; David Gower and Tim Robinson had a little holiday in Rajasthan looking for tigers; Allan Lamb disappeared with his wife to Fisherman's Cove, south of Madras, for a few days by the beach. There was more time to explore and the tour management was enlightened enough to allow players to recharge away from the cricket. As a consequence and with the prompting of Anna, I visited backstreet temples in Calcutta, the Hooghly River, Mahatma Gandhi's shrine as well as the luxurious Tollygunge Club, where Geoff Boycott spent the last few hours of his England career, and the Royal Calcutta Turf Club. Today the England tourists do not have so much time to explore and they are likely to be more familiar with the country anyway; the hotels are usually luxurious wherever you go. A trip to India is not quite such an adventure now.

Fortunately we had Pat Pocock on our tour to tell us what it was really like in the sub-continent in the good old days. I enjoyed his story of welcoming Colin Milburn to Pakistan in March 1969. Milburn had been spending the winter in Perth, playing for Western Australia when the summons came to be a replacement on the Pakistan tour, which had been hastily arranged after the D'Oliveira affair had led to the cancellation of the scheduled trip to South Africa.

England's hotel in Karachi was not that salubrious, but Pocock came to an arrangement with another establishment nearby, which offered accommodation several grades below that being enjoyed by the tourists. Pocock persuaded the owner of this ramshackle building to let it masquerade as the England team hotel for the afternoon. Pocock met Milburn, who had been living in West Aussie luxury in Perth, at the airport; he reassured him that team hotel was not that brilliant but it was home. He escorted him to the seedy establishment that was pretending to be England's base and then he watched Milburn's jaw drop to the floor. Two days later Milburn, playing what would be his last Test match, hit a brilliant 139 in Karachi before the match was abandoned because of rioting at the ground.

One reason why England's trip to India in 1984/5 has often been regarded as a throwback tour was the absence of Botham. He had decided to take a winter off and this meant that the newshounds lost interest in how England's cricketers were behaving on tour. Moreover the serious turn of events beyond the cricket bound together the players and the press corps, which numbered little more than a dozen. We were all in the same boat, wondering at various stages whether the tour would continue. In fact we were often in the same bus as well.

Every day the press would accompany us on the way to the ground, which would never happen now. The security measures were not especially sophisticated. In Bangladesh in 2016 there was a monumental convoy each day to ensure the England players' safety, with all the neighbouring streets cleared and snipers stationed on rooftops around the entrance to the grounds in Dhaka and Chittagong. The precautions were not quite so extensive in India in 1984 but there were soldiers with machine guns – as well as the press (with their pens) – on the team bus and we seemed to take a different route to the ground each day. We stayed in the same hotels as the press, frequented the same bars and generally enjoyed one another's company. With so much uncertainty around we all felt that we were in this together.

This was reflected in the Christmas celebrations in Calcutta. The tradition of the press hosting a drinks party for the players on Christmas morning prevailed – it would not do so for much longer on tour. Goodness knows what was in the cocktails concocted by Chris Lander and the ubiquitous photographer, Graham Morris, but they were merrily swallowed. There were entertainments, some of which were musical. Even now I can recall snippets of 'I'm dreaming of Sivaramakrishnan' composed by Peter Baxter of the BBC and Michael Carey of the *Telegraph*. Even better, their 'Old Man Robbo' was a memorable tribute to Tim Robinson, who had such a prolific tour as an opening batsman – 'He's not like Gower, he's not like Gatting. For some strange reason he keeps on batting...'

There was also a sketch, which we thought was hilarious at the time, depicting the selection committee before the tour. Sadly the script no longer survives but Chris Cowdrey played Peter May, the chairman of selectors (and his godfather), I did my best in the role of A. C. Smith while Richard Ellison was a surprisingly convincing Alec Bedser. It ended with the May character on the phone to Colin Cowdrey, saying, 'Don't worry, I've got the lad in.'

Gower was impressive on that tour, and was England's best batsman in the winters of 1982/3 and 1983/4. It is a myth that he did not stretch himself as a batsman at Test level, though the same could not be said of him on the county circuit, where he must have been an exasperating colleague at Leicestershire as he seemed so easily bored. He had more time than anybody at the crease. I sought his advice once about how to deal with short-pitched fast bowling. 'I try to get into the right position to hook the ball as that makes me watch it more closely,' he said. 'But if I don't like the idea of playing the hook shot I get out of the way.' Well, that was only moderately helpful. For most of us there was never enough time for all that decision-making. But for Gower, at his best, there was.

However his reputation as a captain is not a source of wonder; it does not help that he won five and lost eighteen of his thirty-two Tests in charge of England. His record suggests that he struggled to arrest a decline. After a while he could only shrug his shoulders. Like Botham he encountered the West Indies in their pomp, and in 1989 the bulk of his team was planning to go on the second rebel tour to South Africa when they were supposed to be busting a gut to retain the Ashes. Oddly on the two tours when I witnessed him in charge he did the job very well. In Pakistan the elevation to the captaincy inspired his batting; in India he had a modest series with the bat yet led the side most effectively. It was a united, if not supremely gifted, tour party, which kept plugging away throughout and did not complain much. The Indian side was older and more divided.

Critical to England's success were the contributions of Gatting and Phil Edmonds. Gower had argued that Gatting should be his vice-captain and this responsibility enhanced Gatting as a crick-eter. He was never the type of character who functioned well as a bit-part player; he yearned to be centre stage. Early in his career he had been overshadowed by Botham as a player and as a presence in the dressing room. That all changed in India, where Gatting rel-ished being Gower's sergeant-major and he liked the idea of batting in the key position of number three. And he was an exceptional player of spin bowling. His century in the first match in Bom-bay was his first for England in his thirty-first Test, six years after his debut.

Edmonds was the most gifted finger spinner available but he could be difficult and always had the capacity to wind up Bob Willis as well as Mike Brearley. But he did not bother Gower, who never felt threatened by Edmonds' haughty, independent streak. In fact Edmonds recognized, without publicly acknowledging this, that he had reason to be grateful that Gower was prepared to give him another chance.

We enjoyed Edmonds' quirky presence on tour and he bowled more overs than anyone in that Test series, though he did not travel very far while doing so since he lost his run-up completely. It was all he could do to shuffle one step, like a nervous duckling on a riverbank, up to the popping crease, but he possessed such a classical action and a strong body that he could still deliver the ball with some venom. At the other end Pocock, at thirty-nine years of age, was still experimenting but his presence provided Gower with a canny pair of spinners who seldom relinquished control on surfaces that turned far more reluctantly than many Indian Test pitches of recent years.

Given the turmoil at the start of the tour it was hardly surpris-ing that England lost the first Test though Gower was at pains not to use this as an excuse for defeat. Early on in the tour passions had indeed run high. At one meeting soon after Mrs Gandhi's assassination and before we took refuge in Sri Lanka, there was manager Tony Brown in the team room, brandishing Allan Lamb's passport, challenging him to take it if he really wanted to go home. On the eve of the Test in Bombay we heard of Percy Norris's assassination just after posing for the team photograph in the grounds of the Taj Mahal hotel; we were told to go back to our rooms; we thought about packing our bags. Soon Gower and Gatting toured the corridors to announce that we were going down to the Wankhede Stadium for practice ahead of the Test match. 'What, target practice?' asked Graeme Fowler.

On the first morning of the match Graham Morris, who had taken that team photo, arrived at the stadium in his flak jacket, which was crammed with hardware, and in his best Irish accent he said, 'Excuse me, I'm from the IRA. Could you direct me towards the England dressing room, please?' The official politely obliged. Despite Gatting's second innings hundred, England lost and we all feared that now India had taken a lead in the series the rest of the tour would be played out on flat pitches. After all, this was what happened on the 1981/2 tour when Keith Fletcher was captain.

Gower kept stressing that there should be no excuses; no moaning about umpiring decisions or the peculiar challenges of touring India. We should avoid the siege mentality and embrace the country as best we could (which meant that we were all happy to set off at 5 a.m. for a trip to the Taj Mahal except for Gatting – 'I've seen it before').

In the second Test in Delhi the team competed well but were frustrated at lunch on the final day, when the match appeared to be drifting towards a draw. India were 95 runs ahead with five wickets remaining and a bat-pad catch against Sandeep Patil had just been rejected to the fury of the normally philosophical Pocock. The mood in the dressing room was angry rather than optimistic and this was when Gower surprised us. Essentially he was a gentle cajoler as a captain but now he was suddenly very animated. This was no time to start moaning; there was still a chance, so let's go out and grab it.

It may not have been Churchillian but it seemed to do the trick. Kapil Dev holed out against Pocock after lunch – he would be dropped for the next Test in Calcutta as a consequence, which caused quite a furore – and there was panic in the lower order as the prospect of defeat loomed large. Against the odds England needed 127 for victory and those runs were knocked off in the final session for the loss of two wickets.

After a draw in Calcutta England won in spectacular style in Madras with Gatting and Fowler (in what would be his penultimate Test – the rebels were coming back) scoring double centuries. Perhaps Fowler has more cause to be aggrieved about the sudden termination of his Test career than I have since his last three scores for England were 201, 2 and 69. Neil Foster in his first Test of the tour took eleven wickets in the match on a bouncy pitch. After a draw in Kanpur on a surprisingly flat surface – they said that the groundsman had a cousin who was a useful batsman, supposedly snubbed by Sunil Gavaskar years before – England had won the series 2–1, despite everything.

For good measure we won the one-day series comfortably when I played – reasonably well – instead of the venerable Pocock. In Chandigarh in the final match it rained heavily overnight and since 25,000 spectators had been waiting for five hours in the stands we played a fifteen-over match in soaking conditions and I promise you that Gower came up to me before the game to say, 'You're play-ing today – as a specialist batsman.'

So that Indian tour was something of a triumph. Sadly after three and a half months in the subcontinent, which earnt me £9500, we were required to go to Australia for a one-day tournament cob-bled together to coincide with the installation of floodlights at the MCG. We did not play very well there.

So there you have it. The England career would never be resumed except for a surprise call-up in 1988 for an ODI against Sri Lanka at the Oval. The game clashed with the NatWest final – as well as one of my benefit matches, as it happens – and they did not want to deny the two counties involved the presence of any of their England players at Lord's. So that may explain my selection. By then the England set-up was not in a great place after a trau-matic season of four captains and a catalogue of defeats. I believe I was the thirty-fourth player in that summer to put on an England shirt, not a record I boast about frequently.

TEN

PERTH

IT TOOK ME AN awfully long time to bowl my first ball on Australian soil. In September 1981 I was playing grade cricket in Perth in front of half a dozen onlookers and in the opposition for Melville CC were the Australian Test opener, Graeme Wood, and Dennis Lillee. I could not work out where all the spectators were hiding since Lillee was by now one of the greatest fast bowlers ever to have played the game.

My captain summoned me to bowl and I set my field meticulously like the good old English pro I was supposed to be, and I was about to propel my first delivery in the Antipodes when there was a yell from the man at deep square leg. I stopped in my tracks and was impressed. Clearly my new teammate on that distant boundary was desperate to check that he was standing in precisely the right spot. I applauded such attention to detail. I gave him an encouraging thumbs-up and set off again but stalled once more amid more shouts from that distant corner of the ground. Then I realised that these frantic yells had nothing to do with field placements. 'C'mon. Knock the bastard over. Let's have him. Take him out,' he was yelling in splendid isolation from a distance of 75 yards. And

I was only going to bowl a gentle off-break. Grade cricket in Perth, which I enjoyed hugely when playing for a warm, welcoming club called Bayswater Morley, where Bob Massie, Bruce Reid, Wayne Clark and Marcus North learnt their cricket, could be quite a noisy experience despite the lack of spectators.

In the late seventies and eighties grade cricket in Australia was a common destination for English county cricketers eager to improve their games while enjoying some winter sunshine during the six months when they were no longer employed by their clubs. During that period David Gower, Robin Smith, Derek Randall, Dermot Reeve, Brian Rose, Tim Lamb, Derek Aslett, Paul Terry and, a little later, Alec Stewart were among those who played in Perth.

You may not be so surprised to learn that Bayswater Morley CC was not one of the swanky clubs by the sea or the great Swan River – like Claremont Cottesloe or Nedlands, which were nestled alongside million-dollar residences. The club was situated in a nondescript suburb about fifteen minutes from the city centre. The pavilion was a functional one-storey building; outside there were two cricket pitches and some turf nets, which would be occupied every Tuesday and Thursday night. If you did not turn up for those training sessions there was little chance of playing at the weekend.

In those days the English envied the Australian grade system. Perhaps they still do. It provided such a beautifully simple pyramid, which has been almost impossible to emulate in this country. The major clubs in Perth would have four grade sides plus their junior teams and anyone playing in the first-grade competition would be noticed if he kept performing well. This was the straightforward route into the state squad, the state team and from there you could graduate to the Test side.

As a first-grade cricketer you would encounter state players throughout the season and occasionally, as was the case with Lillee and Wood on my debut, Test players. The matches would generally be played over two Saturdays. This helped to concentrate the mind – especially of batsmen. It might be that you only had two or three knocks in a month, which was a major contrast with county cricket where there was always another chance around the corner. To augment their pool of players, many of the clubs in the major Australian cities were prepared to bring over an English professional.

In the eighties the standard in Perth was high – I reckoned it was somewhere between first and second XI county cricket – and it was very competitive as well as noisy. One example of that has stayed with me. Early in the season we were playing South Perth. A particularly mean seamer, who played one game for Western Australia, Kim Hagdorn, was bowling against us and his long-sleeved shirt was not properly buttoned up. Hence it was flapping wildly in the breeze as he delivered the ball and was therefore causing quite a distraction to the batsman, who, quite reasonably, asked him to do up the offending button. The bowler snarled and rather than accede to the batsman's request, he removed his shirt before growling, 'Can you see all right now?' It was never like that in the Parks, especially in April.

I had ended up at Bayswater partly because Peter Denning, my Somerset colleague, had played there and had put me in touch with Ray Robinson, one of those irreplaceable club stalwarts who fixed everything. Ray found Anna, me and our two-year-old daughter, Amy, somewhere to live, a car and a sort of job (I think I was supposed to be indexing the loans manual at the Perth Building Society). Ray and his wife, Marg, could not have done more to welcome a wide-eyed young family to Perth.

Initially the cricket was a struggle. I had been warned that it would not be possible to swan in and dominate simply because I happened to be a professional in England. We lost our first four games and the mood was bleak. The club's coach, one of the old school, was, I think, the most lugubrious man I've encountered in cricket (he only lasted a season since they managed to entice Wayne Clark, who would guide Yorkshire to the County Championship in 2001, back to the club the following year). With plenty of prompting from the coach our players were descending into a pit of gloom. I tried to explain that they were not professionals; they were supposed to be playing for fun; it was time to lighten up. This was not the effete Pom speaking; I was being pragmatic. By then I knew enough to recognise that you don't play well when utterly miserable.

Then in November something extraordinary happened – and I have the framed scorecard in front of me to prove it. Via the impeccable hand of Betty Lawrence, our scorer who would effortlessly consume a packet of Winfield cigarettes in an afternoon while keeping the tally, I can relive a game at Hillcrest Reserve, our home ground, against Claremont Cottesloe. Bruce Reid opened the bowling; runs were hard to come by but so were wickets. Just before the first break after ninety minutes' play Claremont were 50–0 from twenty-four overs, when I dismissed their opening batsman, Cook.

OK, we'll cut the long story short. We bowled another sixty-two overs after the interval, during which time Claremont were dismissed for 118 and the scorecard reveals that my figures were 34.1–21–28–9. Well, it must have turned a bit, I suppose, and I did not bowl much rubbish. Even so, at this distance it's hard to imagine how this ever came about.

One factor, which helps to explain the desultory run rate, was the nature of the outfields at most club grounds in Perth at the time. They consisted of thick-leafed couch grass. This type of grass acted as a brake so it was hard for batsmen to deflect the ball into the gaps in the field. Hence there were no easy singles. The nurdle, the refuge of so many old English pros, was taken out of the equation.

Even so taking nine wickets so cheaply was extraordinary. This was the first nine-wicket haul in the club's history – not even Tony Lock, once of Surrey and England and Jim Laker's old partner, managed that when he played a few games at Hillcrest in the sixties – and it cheered everyone up since we finally won a game. The season improved after that. We won four of our last eight matches so that a potentially disastrous season became one of positive rebuilding – yes, I'm sure they were 'taking the positives' even back then. And in the following years Bayswater became quite a force.

My memories of those six months are almost entirely positive. There was an easy generosity and hospitality about everyone in Perth. Bayswater Morley had some good cricketers as well as Reid, who would go on to play for Australia. An off-spinner, Brett Mulder, would play twenty-five games for Western Australia; Gary Ireland, a pocket battleship from the mining town of Collie, was our best batsman and should have played more for the state side. He had a fine sense of humour, which was drier than the Gibson Desert though not as dry as that of Jimmy, his older brother, who, as an opening batsman, had designed his own skull cap (the second and final thing he had in common with Sunil Gavaskar – he was also the same height). They were all good company in an era when those tough Tuesday and Thursday training sessions would be followed by several cans of Swan lager in the clubhouse (well, one has to show a willingness to integrate in a foreign country).

The clubhouse was quite a social hub. Very early on there was a club function, where it was announced that the food was now on the table. As one, everybody stopped talking even if in mid-sentence and zoomed in like locusts; with almost the same alacrity all the men convened at one end of the clubhouse, the women at the other. The English pro would not be pampered but once they realised that you were prepared to muck in they welcomed you warmly into the fold. For the first time in ages I was obliged to bring something for tea on match days and I was made aware of the 'No Swiss rolls' rule. Swiss rolls are tasty, cheap, convenient and readily available but apparently at Bayswater there had been instances of the tea comprising eleven Swiss rolls and nothing else.

We enjoyed a little glimpse of WA; the Swan River and King's Park in Perth, which provides a wonderful view of the water and the city, offering a spectacular welcome to new visitors. Later we made a couple of trips down south. One was to Esperance on the south coast of the state, where some friends from Devon were farming. It does not look far on the map but it was about 500 miles. To break up the journey we would look forward to reaching destinations like Dumbleyung and Newdegate. A cream tea with scones and Lapsang Souchong may not have been available but there would be a garage there and just possibly a pub. Upon arrival we were shown around part of Jeremy's farm and were taken aback to see so many sheep skeletons on the land. Adopting the laconic turn of phrase of most West Aussies out in the country, he just said, 'Well, we've been a bit short of rain down here over the last year or two.'

We made friends with some of the younger players. As well as sharing the odd beer they showed us the delights of the Swan River and taught us how to play euchre; three or four of them would appear on our doorstep in Devon the following summer.

They stayed with us for a while and managed to find somewhere to play cricket in the West Country. Once they decided to come and watch Somerset at Taunton. They dutifully followed the signs saying 'Cricket' but neglected to take any notice of the next bit, which was 'St Thomas'. Cricket St Thomas is a country mansion near Chard, which was then a popular wildlife park, and that is where they ended up. It is about twenty miles from the County Ground at Taunton.

I found it considerably easier to find the WACA stadium when I was in Perth and naturally I went down there a few times. The most memorable game I witnessed was a fifty-over match between Australia and the West Indies. Along with a few thirsty Bayswater colleagues I watched from square leg; Michael Holding was at full throttle and I have never seen a wicketkeeper standing so far behind the stumps – and still Jeffrey Dujon was taking the ball at head height. I now had first-hand knowledge that cricket at the WACA could be an awesome spectacle. It had the fastest pitch in the world. I had no idea that this would one day become my home ground for a season.

That winter was fun; I'm sure it helped my cricket and, being in a foreign country, I took the opportunity to grow a beard – to no obvious benefit. I kept it for about a year. We saw kangaroos bouncing around at dusk, learnt about reticulation and redbacks, and enjoyed the luxury of being able to slip on a pair of shorts and not much else just about every day we were there. When it finally rained we went out into the garden to get merrily drenched. At the beginning of April we somehow squeezed Amy into the bassinet again and headed for home, somewhat alarmed that the United Kingdom was now at war with Argentina after the invasion of the Falkland Islands.

My Bayswater teammates would have been mildly astonished to see me again the following winter as a member of England's tour party to Australia. They would also have been surprised that I would end up playing a few more games for them five years later. In mid-September 1986 I was tucking into some breakfast in Tiverton when the phone rang. The conversation does not really need to be précised. It went: 'Rod Marsh here. Do you want to come and play for WA?'

I only knew Rod as a formidable opponent, who had shared a few beers on the 1982/3 Ashes tour and I was surprised by the invitation. However, the idea fitted since there were no concrete plans for the winter. I explained the offer to Anna, pointing out that the cricket would be demanding and that there were no guarantees that I would succeed – though I may not have dwelt too long on the intricacies of how tricky it might be to gain significant purchase with my off-breaks on the rock-hard surface at the WACA. She encouraged me to say yes. Leaving aside the cricketing challenges the idea of another winter in Perth was attractive. She was keen to go and she was right to be so. When Marsh rang back as arranged twenty-four hours later I said, 'OK'.

Marsh had retired from cricket by now but was one of the selectors of the state team. I learnt afterwards that he had checked out my credentials with Bayswater Morley and also my old university friend, Rod Eddington. Marsh had played grade cricket for the University of WA alongside Eddington and they had kept in touch ever since.

He called barely three weeks before WA's first Shield game. They don't muck around in WA. They had decided after some early season trial games that they needed a spinner from somewhere, especially for the trips to the Eastern states, where the ball might turn. I don't think I was their first choice. Apparently their enquiries to the Indian leg-spinner Laxman Sivaramakrishnan and Surrey's Pat Pocock had come to nothing. At least they knew I was prepared to drink the local beer. Not that the coach, Daryl Foster, was keen on too much beer-drinking, a stance which had provided him with some headaches especially when Marsh was in the team. Foster's mantra has stuck in my head: 'If you drink, you run.'

So I set off for Perth with Anna and Amy due to follow a fortnight later, and before I could blink I was making my debut for WA against South Australia at the WACA. It was a young side, denuded by the exodus of the likes of Kim Hughes and Terry Alderman, who, eighteen months previously had chosen to go on a rebel tour to South Africa. At thirty-one I was their oldest player and their slowest. When we went for training runs, which seemed to happen all too frequently whether we had been drinking or not, Bruce Laird, now retired but on the coaching staff after a distinguished career as the gutsiest of opening batsmen, was detailed to run with me so that I did not get lost – or dispirited.

Graeme Wood was the captain and before the first game he asked me where I usually fielded. 'Well, I'm not too reliable in the slips… and I don't have a very good arm,' I replied candidly. 'Go to square leg,' he said. Chris Matthews, a burly left-armer, who would soon make his debut for Australia against England in Brisbane, bowled the first over. For South Australia Andrew Hilditch, the former Test opener, who was always described as 'studious' since he had already qualified as a solicitor, was on strike.

Hilditch clipped the ball towards square leg and set off for his first run of a new season only to be sent back by his partner. In the meantime I had gathered the ball cleanly before dutifully throwing it back to the keeper, Tim Zoehrer. The batsmen were still in confusion; Hilditch was stranded out of his crease and joined a very small, melancholy list of cricketers who have been run out by Marks. Now to my mild alarm I was engulfed by the rest of the team, all of whom seemed to be about six feet six inches tall (some of them were) as they descended upon me for a merry celebration. This was an excellent way to endear myself to my new colleagues, who seemed to be as surprised as I was by this turn of events.

The rest of the day went pretty well too. I finished with 3–37 from eighteen overs, including the wicket of David Hookes. *Wisden* records that 'Hookes promised much but fell to Marks in both innings, aiming to hit him out of the ground.' Why did they always try to do that to me? I finished with six victims in a match WA won by eight wickets and in my solitary innings I hit a skittish 24, which included a few offside carves. 'Do you always bat like that?' asked coach Foster as politely as possible. 'I'm afraid so.'

So that game eased the passage into a new team. I was taken aback by the youthful zest of our side. Back at Taunton in a tired old professional way most of us would lounge in the back of the dressing room most of the time when Somerset were batting – unless Viv or Both were playing one of those innings – taking only a passing interest in proceedings out in the middle. Here the non-participants were constantly on the edge of their seats, watching every ball and bellowing 'Save yer legs' every time one of our batsmen hit a boundary.

They were zestful *and* talented, which is a handy combination. Geoff Marsh, provided he was not playing for Australia, opened with Mike Veletta. Tom Moody, a beanpole and a strikingly mature twenty-one-year-old, was at three with captain Wood at number four. Wayne Andrews, with a bat no heavier than Peter Denning's and an equally idiosyncratic technique, was at five.

Wood was a fine captain, even though he did not appear an obvious one from a distance. He had always been regarded as a self-contained, verging on self-obsessed, cricketer, who seemed too wound up with his own game to lead the team, rather like Brian Rose back at Somerset in 1977. But once given the captaincy his perspective changed. He opened out a bit and was stimulated by the challenge, plus he had an instinctive cricket brain. He was no great orator. Often he left the pre-match talks to Daryl Foster, who was more familiar with this territory as a lecturer at the University of WA. Sometimes after the game was over for the day Wood would switch from Graeme to 'Basil', who was a different character altogether, wilder and more unpredictable. My new colleagues knew Basil better than I ever did. But by 11.00 a.m. the next morning he would be Graeme again – and back in charge.

Geoff Marsh, the vice-captain, was always a terrific man to have in any team. Allan Border thought so much of him that he threatened to resign the captaincy when Marsh was dropped from the Australian side after the Adelaide Test in 1992. In the end Border was cannily persuaded to continue as captain by chairman of selectors Laurie Sawle (another West Aussie), who could see the wider perspective. 'If I were you I'd have a think about that resignation offer overnight, AB.'

Marsh was still forging his Test career in 1986 but this did not prompt any airs or graces on his part. When we played Tasmania in Devonport the team was staying in a basic but comfortable motel in substantial grounds. 'Right, I'll be doing breakfast on the barbie,' said Australia's opening batsman. Sure enough, he was up with the lark, grilling the bacon and frying the eggs before play and I tried to imagine recent England opening batsmen undertaking that task. John Edrich? Unlikely. Geoffrey Boycott? Probably not.

Marsh would end up as Australia's coach; I imagine he was in the Trevor Bayliss mode. He was with the side from 1996 to 2001, a bountiful period for Australian cricket, and was a good fit for that team. Marsh would not have been over-technical and he would never seek the limelight himself. 'I've got some of the best coaches in the world around me,' he would say. 'They're all in the team.' He also had two fine captains, Mark Taylor and Steve Waugh. Any sane coach would give those captains freedom to lead, which is what Marsh did. Recently we have glimpsed him in the stands at Australian Test matches, every inch the nervous dad, as both his sons have been in the Australian team, most notably the one that defeated England in the 2017/18 Ashes series.

Later Tom Moody would also become an international cricketer and a much-respected coach, as well as an occasional columnist for the *Observer*. He was in charge of the Sri Lankan team that lost in the World Cup final of 2007 in Barbados, after which he probably should have been appointed England coach after Duncan Fletcher; instead they opted in haste for Peter Moores, which did not work out so well. Even then it seemed that the ECB was concerned to look dynamic and in control to such an extent that they decided to appoint their chosen man with unnecessary haste before that World Cup was over. So there was no inclination or time to talk to Moody. In 2014 Moody, after one polite inquiry, did not bother to pursue the England job after the departure of Andy Flower since he realised that they wanted an Englishman (Moores again).

Instead Moody's coaching career has followed the modern pattern. For many the plum jobs are in the IPL, where in six or seven weeks it is possible to earn as much as any international coach who treks around the globe for twelve months of the year. He has been in charge of the Sunrisers Hyderabad, who won the IPL in

2016, and he has been involved in just about every T20 league that has been created around the globe. In addition he commentates on the game impressively and still he might have time to see his family now and again.

So much for WA's batsmen. Our strongest side contained three left-arm pacemen: Bruce Reid, whom I knew from Bayswater Morley, Chris Matthews and Peter Capes. In theory they should have created some gorgeous rough for the off-spinner but the surface at the WACA was so hard it never crumbled. Meanwhile Ken MacLeay, who would end up rearing prize-winning cattle in Margaret River, bowled clever away-swingers. It was a strong attack and I soon realised that my main job, especially in Perth, was to sustain the pressure already created. Before every match there was the clarion call. 'Bowl dry. Hit the top of off-stump.' It was not a bad shout.

Soon England were in town to play their final warm-up match before the first Test. I was perfectly happy to be omitted from this game, which allowed the young off-spinner Brett Mulder, another Bayswater man, a game – we sometimes played together for the state team later in the season. I went to watch for a while and met up with some of the team and the press and I could understand how Martin Johnson, then of the *Independent*, came up with his famous assessment of Mike Gatting's side ahead of the Brisbane match. 'There's only three things wrong with this England side,' he would muse in his column. 'They can't bat. They can't bowl and they can't field.' That line has survived thirty years; maybe that's the nearest to immortality that a cricket hack can hope for.

I also saw Matthew Engel, who was on his first tour as the *Guardian*'s cricket correspondent, but not at the WACA. He got in touch on the day we had arranged to go to Waterworld with Amy and Anna's sister, Charlotte, who was staying with us. So we persuaded Matthew to come along with us. The sun was out again and five of us bumped down the rapids inside our rubber rings or sped down the waterslides at great pace and we had a great time. Matthew hid his exhilaration rather better than the rest of us but nobly claimed to be enjoying himself.

The England players also seemed to be enjoying themselves but they were not at their best at the WACA against my new colleagues. Ian was still in party mode; Gower bagged a pair and the tourists just hung on for a draw. In Brisbane a week later Botham hit 138, Gower, dropped early on by my new teammate, Matthews, who seldom fielded in the slips for WA, made 51 and England beat Australia by seven wickets. I was once obliged to ask Ian to choose his 'greatest game'. To my surprise he chose this one. Perhaps he had forgotten the Jubilee Test in Bombay in 1980 when he ran amok with bat and ball, but I could understand why he might steer clear of the bittersweet triumphs of 1981.

I think he just enjoyed that tour in 1986/7 more than expected and he set the tone in that first Test. He could still unnerve the Aussies – he would bowl them out in Melbourne operating at about 77 mph since he was not fully fit. 'Mike Gatting as captain led a relaxed regime,' he remembered. 'It was Micky Stewart's first tour as manager but he was on trial then and he was very much Gatt's subordinate. It was not like the rigid regime operated by Stewart and Gooch later on. And we were written off by the press of both sides before the series began yet we ended up winning everything, the Tests and two one-day competitions. There's nothing better than stuffing the Aussies in Australia and making fools of a few pressmen in the process.'

Of course from my far-west vantage point I quietly enjoyed

England's success in that series as well, putting a consoling arm around WA's returning Test players (Matthews played two matches while Marsh, Reid and Tim Zoehrer were ever-present). By the time England arrived in Sydney for the final Test they had retained the Ashes and there they lost a tight game by 55 runs. I wonder what would have happened in Australia if England had won that series 3–0 instead of 2–1. Allan Border, who always seemed a bit of a reluctant captain, would have resigned or maybe have been sacked and the landscape would have looked very different. Instead Border was still in charge in 1994 and Australia were on the rise. In the west they would have been promoting the virtues of Graeme Wood because he was leading his state side to the Shield.

WA won five and drew five of their matches, which ensured that the final would be played at the WACA and a draw would be sufficient to win the Shield. That final, played over five days, was not a great game. Victoria declared on 404–8; WA were bowled out for 654 with Mike Veletta scoring 262. On the final day Victoria hung on for the draw.

Before that WA had played some terrific cricket. The side, often weakened by Test calls, certainly maximized its potential. Compared to England far more attention was paid to the build-up before each game. There was more scope to practise seriously; the opposition would be discussed in more detail. We ran more frequently.

The cricket itself was more intense than in the County Championship, where, for example, Nottinghamshire might choose not to bowl Richard Hadlee on the final day because they calculated that it would be better to have him fresh the following morning when the next game started. There was no such let-up in the Sheffield Shield. But there were not as many great cricketers playing in the competition. Overseas players were a rarity – Richard Ellison was playing for Tasmania that year and I think we were the only two from outside Australia. So, unlike county cricket, there were no great West Indian cricketers to encounter.

But it was tough and combative and occasionally ridiculous. Generally the behaviour in state cricket was better than at grade level, where I happily resumed my link with Bayswater Morley CC when available. There were some crazy moments, but I had been around long enough not to be too distracted by them. For example, at the WACA I was once batting against Mike Whitney, the brisk, busy left-armer from New South Wales, who was no shrinking violet. It was the last half-hour of play and Whitney was charging in and when I got to the non-striker's end I received some very quiet, menacing threats about how his extreme pace was going to cause me considerable damage. I think the gist of the message was: 'I'm going to fucking kill you.'

I survived until stumps with my body and wicket intact and then, as was the custom, the batting team would go into the fielding side's dressing room for a beer after the close of play. In I went and there was Whitney. Immediately he broke into the broadest of smiles; there was an arm around my shoulder and a beer thrust into my hand. 'How's it going down at Bristol?' he asked since he had played some games for Gloucestershire the previous year and we chatted like long-lost friends. This is the Australian way but it can still be a bit puzzling: sworn enemies at 5.30 p.m.; best buddies half an hour later.

Later in the season when we played New South Wales in Sydney I had to walk past Whitney on the way to the crease. At the Sydney Cricket Ground they were justly proud of their electronic scoreboard, perhaps the first of its kind, so even for state games it was in full use. This allowed the spectators – and in Shield cricket the crowds were much smaller than in the Championship back home – to learn about the statistical background of the players involved. Up came my career record as a batsman as I made my way to the crease. By then I was nearing 10,000 runs at an average around 30, a phenomenal number of runs by Aussie standards since they do not play anywhere near as much first-class cricket. 'I don't bloody believe that,' said Whitney.

However my statistics looked pretty good by the end of the season at WA: there were 30 wickets at 31.83 from 456.4 overs and 370 runs at an average of 46.25 in a season when the state side was unbeaten in first-class cricket. And I had a Sheffield Shield winner's medal. I think that Tony Lock, who led WA to victory in 1967/8, is the only other Englishman to win one. As it happens Lock was still in Perth in 1986/7 and towards the end of the season I was asked to help him with a spin clinic. Of course it was a thrill to meet him – I managed to avoid the subject of Old Trafford in 1956 – and to watch him at work. He was then fifty-eight with a formidable stomach but off a couple of paces he could still fizz the ball down respectably when he was demonstrating what he wanted his pupils to do.

So this had been another rewarding visit to Perth. Once again we had received the warmest hospitality. This time the WACA rather than Bayswater Morley CC had been responsible for finding us a house and it was in South Perth, facing the city from the other side of the Swan River, a more salubrious spot. Nearby was South Perth Primary School, which welcomed Amy with open arms. Within two days she sounded like an Aussie; within a week she knew every word of 'Advance Australia Fair', which she had to sing every morning. Off she went happily with Sheridan, her new friend from just up the road. For the last thirty years whenever covering an Ashes tour I have called in on Sheridan's parents, Ian and Janine George, and every time it is as if we saw each other only last week. Ian and Janine epitomize the warmth of the welcome we have always received from West Aussies – even though both of them originally hail from Mildura in Victoria.

There was a buzz in the West that winter since it was hosting the America's Cup. Fremantle suddenly became the place to be and we all became yachting experts, though ultimately disappointed that the uncompromising American, Dennis Conner, and his boat, *Stars and Stripes*, defeated that nice Iain Murray in *Kookaburra*. Good old Alan Bond – 'Bondy' – Australian of the Year in 1978, had brought the America's Cup to Perth. In the nineties his empire collapsed and he spent four years in prison for fraud. On the one day we went out to watch the yachts in action there was a lull, which hardly ever happens in Perth, and racing was abandoned.

It may be that my West Country background accounts for my eagerness to be regarded as an honorary West Aussie when in Australia. I once interviewed John Inverarity, a benign godfather of WA cricket, who led the state team to four Shield victories in five years in the seventies, happily maximizing the prodigious talents of Lillee and Marsh in the process. He spoke of the bond of being out west.

'In Perth at that time there was a strong adolescent type of feeling in the community of 'us against the rest'. We were the outcasts in the West, who had been patronized and given short shrift by the Eastern states. As captain I was more than happy to exploit this feeling, which was a tremendous way to build harmony and close ranks against the rest.

I remember my first Eastern states tour vividly. In Sydney on a flat wicket we scored 424. New South Wales declared at 425–1. In the second innings we scored 269 and Richie Benaud, their captain, decided to send in their Nos 4 and 5 to open the batting and gain some practice. They won the match by nine wickets so in the whole game we had dismissed just two players. In Brisbane Queensland scored 600 and the same happened in Melbourne. We were the chopping blocks. Our captain, Barry Shepherd, kept saying. 'Soak every bit of this up, son. Our day will come.' When I became captain, with Ian Brayshaw as my deputy, at most of our meetings we'd remind our players of our experience. That coupled with Western Australia's isolation helped to foster unity within the team.

That atmosphere still prevailed in 1986/7 and has stayed with me. Even on the last Ashes tour in 2017/18 I found myself taking umbrage when I heard one of the Australian correspondents – from sophisticated Melbourne – complaining at the end of the day's play at the WACA that 'the one taxi in Perth had already been taken'. How dare he patronize the West Aussies like that? To a lesser extent it sometimes felt like that at Somerset as well. We could be easily riled by those metropolitan elitist bastards inside the M25 – except that there wasn't an M25 then.

So we left contentedly. I was so grateful to Anna, who had cajoled me into going in the first place and I was in proud possession of a bushman's hat that I still have, which was a gift from the team. Any suggestion that I might go back for a second season was scuppered since it soon became evident that Anna was going to give birth to Rosie the following November. In any case it was a cunning plan not to return. My stock in WA was really quite high when I left in 1987; it might have been a struggle to keep it there after another season. And WA won the Shield in the next two seasons anyway. The following year they defeated Queensland, who had their own Englishman in the side, at the WACA. I must show Ian Botham my Sheffield Shield winner's medal sometime.

Rod Marsh was also pleased at the way everything had panned out since he had stuck his neck out to sign me up in the first place. I had played well in an alien environment and won the respect of new teammates. By the same token I felt indebted to Rod since that season in WA was as fulfilling as any I experienced.

Please do not fall for the stereotype of Rod Marsh. He may seem the epitome of the rough, tough, beer-swilling Aussie, who formed a formidable triumvirate with Ian Chappell and Dennis Lillee in the good old bad old days. Well, he did like a beer and he was tough all right but that is only a fraction of the story.

Take Mike Brearley's word for this as well. Writing back in 1985 in *The Art of Captaincy*, he was keen to set the record straight about Marsh. 'For behind the abrasive front was a thoughtful, astute and humorous man, whose players when he led WA, were totally committed to him. The Australian Cricket Board, however, were not, but their prejudice was not based on technical consideration, such as having a wicketkeeper captain. For them he was tarred with the same brush as Ian Chappell, the brush of revolution and extremism. Greg Chappell with his dignified air they could stomach as captain, but they refused to swallow Marsh; this was a major mistake.'

Marsh played the game properly. Witness his recall of Derek Randall at a critical moment in the Centenary Test of 1977. Marsh knew, but nobody else did, that he had not taken the catch cleanly and he immediately summoned Randall back. Perhaps it was the obvious thing to do but I can think of many in that situation, before the cameras were so omniscient, who would have managed to convince themselves that the catch was probably legitimate. Witness too Marsh's genuine horror behind the stumps in February 1981 when he realized that Greg Chappell had instructed his younger brother, Trevor, to bowl the last ball of an ODI against New Zealand underarm to prevent the batsman hitting a six.

As Brearley suggests, Marsh knew the game inside out. He subsequently became a bit of a poacher turned gamekeeper as he ended up running the cricket Academies of Australia and then, after a brilliant coup by Hugh Morris, ECB's cricket director at the time, the ECB's National Academy. He knew how the larrikins operated and he enjoyed that little tussle as a coach, whether in Adelaide or Loughborough. He once tried to justify to me the odd bout of heavy drinking as a player for WA when he would frighten the life out of coach Foster on away trips. 'I reckoned that if I was a bit under the weather after a big night out I would be so desperate the following day not to let my mates down that I would try doubly hard in the field not to make any mistakes. Perhaps it made me a better player.' Well, that's not a bad effort, though I doubt whether Rodney, the academy chief, would have swallowed that theory from any of his charges.

Rod has always loved working with cricketers and improving them. He oversaw the young Ponting with Australia and the young Pietersen with England with the same enthusiasm. Once he had finished playing it did not matter so much where they came from. Thus he has the unique distinction of being a Test selector for England and, ultimately, a chairman of selectors for Australia – though even he was not capable of holding these posts simultaneously.

For a while I ended up ghosting his columns in the *Observer*, which was never a hardship since he always had something to say. Sometimes the relationship was unusual. Most ghosts are desperate to get their columnist to say something interesting. More often I found myself intervening with Rod along the lines of 'You can't possibly say that about Duncan Fletcher.' For some reason Fletcher and Marsh did not gel when they held key posts in English cricket and, as John Inverarity once pointed out to me, 'Rod has the most benign view of about 95 per cent of all the people he comes across, but if you happen to be in the other 5 per cent, watch out.'

It was always a pleasure to meet up with him to cobble together another column. Once in Melbourne he was like a little schoolboy with a new toy. His eyes were alight, buzzing with excitement, as he told me, 'I've just seen a young kid who reminds me of Thommo.' He had just been watching Brett Lee bowling at extraordinary pace for the first time and just in case I thought he was losing his marbles he ushered over some of the boys in the academy to verify this good news.

Towards the end of his time writing for the *Observer* he asked, almost sheepishly, 'Do you mind if I try writing the columns myself?' After a millisecond of contemplation I snapped, 'Not at all. Please do,' while restraining myself from asking why the devil he had not made this excellent suggestion earlier. And of course the pieces were very good, probably better than their predecessors.

So one plus of that Western Australian winter was getting to know Rodney Marsh a little better. Another was that it got me out of the West Country where there was a little civil war going on. I missed the extraordinary meeting of members of Somerset CCC at Shepton Mallet's showground when the fates of Ian Botham, Viv Richards, Joel Garner and Somerset CCC were finally sealed. I was bowling into the sea breeze at the WACA at the time.

ELEVEN

TROUBLE OVER BRIDGWATER

THE START OF THE 1987 season at Somerset had one similarity with my WA experience. It began with me wandering around a dressing room, introducing myself to several cricketers I barely knew. I recognized some of the names: Neil Mallender had always been a doughty opponent when he was playing for Northamptonshire while Adrian Jones had shown himself capable of the odd, devastating spell for Sussex. I was less familiar with Graham Rose from Middlesex and Neil Burns from Essex.

The exodus at Somerset had taken place and the new captain, Peter Roebuck, and Brian Rose had gone shopping in the winter. Viv Richards and Joel Garner had not been re-engaged and had been replaced by Martin Crowe. As a consequence of that Ian Botham had, predictably, left the club and joined Worcestershire. Moreover there had been other recent departures, less trumpeted but of some significance. Peter Denning had retired; Rose – who was briefly nicknamed 'Kenny' after Kenny Dalglish at Liverpool since he became a sort of player/manager – was still around though he did not play very often; Jerry Lloyds had moved to Gloucestershire; and Nigel Popplewell had retired prematurely to get a proper job in the legal profession just as he – and everyone else – realised that he was really rather a good batsman. Suddenly I felt a bit of a stranger in my old dressing room.

How had it all come to this? There had been plenty of optimism back in 1984, the first year in which Ian was the official captain of the club with me as his deputy, which meant, given Test calls, that I would end up captaining the side for about half the season. The West Indies were touring so we were denied the presence of Viv and Joel, but we had signed Crowe, who was twenty-one and who had inevitably impressed Ian and me on England's 1983/4 tour of New Zealand.

Martin obviously possessed rare gifts. He was desperate to learn and improve, and utterly determined to strain every sinew in his role as Viv's replacement throughout the summer of 1984. He sought perfection, which is usually a virtue though just occasionally we thought that this might be hampering his progress. There was a contradiction here. On the one hand Martin single-mindedly pursued technical excellence in a clinical, clear-sighted way, yet by his own admission he was an emotional cricketer who could not yet operate in isolation; he was, like most of us, affected by the mood around him. And when he just trusted his instincts he could be devastating.

In that summer he also took on the role of being a guide and mentor to other young players on the staff, most notably Ricky Bartlett and Nick Pringle. He was their age but in cricketing terms they were light years behind him. Martin was obviously more talented, but also more driven and more mature. He formed the Nags Club, comprising the youngsters on the staff, who also included Julian Wyatt, Richard Harden and Nigel Felton, and most of them would meet regularly in the Nags Head pub just outside Taunton and the talk (I think) was usually dominated by cricket. Martin wanted to help and inspire them, and most of them were eager to listen. It was beyond the call of duty but such was his zeal as our new overseas pro.

However, his first task was to score runs in the middle order for his new employers and in his first month he struggled to do that. Back in New Zealand the previous winter, once Martin had signed up, Ian had said, 'Come and live with me in Taunton,' which was not the sort of invitation that was easy to reject. Ian was not only the great, charismatic all-rounder, who had dominated the cricketing world for half a decade, he was also the club captain. So Martin had agreed to this arrangement. But after a few weeks he knew that it would not work. There was plenty of mutual respect but their lifestyles were different – and Ian's could be overpowering. But how was Martin going to break it to Ian he wanted to move out?

I recalled this situation when I last saw Martin at the World Cup final of 2015 in Melbourne, just under a year before he died from the lymphoma that had plagued him since 2012. Martin attended that match almost as a farewell to the cricketing world and this was triggered by the fact New Zealand were pitched against Australia in the final. I was a little nervous of meeting him after a long interlude in such unusual circumstances. Martin probably sensed that and somehow he made it easy. We talked briefly of his time at Somerset and I told him how much I admired how he had possessed the strength of mind as a twenty-one-year old, a long way from home, to tell Ian that living with him was not working and that he was moving out. 'How did you go about that?' I asked. 'Ah, I thought about that', he said, 'I decided to tell him when he was in the bath. He couldn't do much about it from there.'

For whatever reason everything clicked for Martin in the first weeks of June 1984 when Somerset decamped to Bath in the north of the county. There he scored his first two Championship centuries and he was on his way. One knock later that month at Taunton stood out; he hit 190 in Somerset's second innings against Leicestershire – and Andy Roberts – thereby masterminding a brilliant run-chase alongside Peter Roebuck (128). Together they added 319 out of the 341 required for victory. Crowe was imperious against Roberts and the rest of a fine Leicestershire attack. At the start of that game I had tossed up with Peter Willey, who greeted me with 'Now the prima donnas are out of the way [he was, I intuited, referring to Gower and Botham, who were playing in a Test match] we can have a proper game of cricket.'

In between scoring beautiful runs Martin bowled regularly and impressively for us with surprising pace, taking 39 wickets in the Championship season, but this did his back no favours at all. But in 1984 he was willing to do anything for the cause and it was a delight to have him in the side – not just for his runs – a fact noted by a few key men in the committee room. The situation would be tougher and tenser when he returned in 1987.

Crowe hit five Championship centuries for Somerset that summer; more surprisingly I hit three, which was remarkable since throughout my career I only managed a paltry five in total. They came in a rush between 9 and 25 August when batting suddenly became an unusually straightforward operation. During the third hundred at Worcester in a match we lost I had that rare and wondrous feeling that everything was happening in slow motion. I did not have to think or worry about the provenance of the next run. In my ultra-relaxed state I just watched the ball and everything slotted into place; the feet, the head, the bat and the ball were all magically in harmony. It was a pity that this did not happen more often.

The last match of the season saw Ian in his puppeteer role, pulling strings without scoring a run or taking a wicket. And it all worked out wonderfully. At Taunton we were playing Nottinghamshire who had to beat us to win the Championship ahead of Essex. Ian declined the option of batting Nottinghamshire out of the match. Instead he kept the game open by setting them 297 to win in what would be sixty overs, a decision that was not especially popular in Chelmsford.

All except eight overs in Nottinghamshire's second innings were delivered by spinners, with Stephen Booth, a young Yorkshireman, bowling even slower than me at the other end. Nottinghamshire kept chasing, wickets kept falling and it transpired that they needed 14 from the last over from Booth, with their last man, Mike Bore, not noted for his power as a batsman, on strike. Bore cracked two fours and a two; then he launched into another drive, which seemed to be going into the old Pavilion for a match-winning six until Richard Ollis, our substitute fieldsman, came into view to hold his second superb catch of the innings. So Somerset prevailed by three runs, the champagne corks popped in Chelmsford and Botham's reputation for conjuring unlikely victories – and brighter cricket – was enhanced.

At the end of the match he spoke optimistically of 1985 to those who assembled around the pavilion. Viv and Joel would be back so watch us storm up the table and dominate again in one-day cricket, was the gist of his message. But Botham could conjure no magic victories the following summer. Instead there were some embarrassing declarations that did not work out so wonderfully. At Old Trafford he declared ten minutes before the close of play on the second day, saying sagely, 'They'll chase 330 on the last day but not 340.' Thus proceedings for the day were brought to a close early and we soon understood why. Ian had an arrangement to go to watch Burnley with Lancashire's Jack Simmons that night and the extra ten minutes meant that they could get to Turf Moor on time. As Lancashire romped to victory on the final day Roebuck observed, 'Burnley 1, Somerset 0'. Another contrived declaration at Taunton saw Essex, driven brilliantly by Graham Gooch (173 not out), achieve their target with twenty-one overs to spare.

Somerset compiled more batting points than any team in the Championship in 1985 and finished bottom of the table with one victory. There were some prodigious innings but the side was hopelessly unbalanced. The bowling attack lacked bite. Joel, less than fully fit and restricted to 15 matches, took 31 wickets; Ian, who was busy for England against an ailing Australian side, took 11 wickets in 11 matches. I bowled 745 overs, about my usual quota in a season in that decade, while the next man (Mark Davis) bowled 298. The team had not evolved and had not been strengthened. There was the perception that players were reluctant to come to Somerset; the prospect of a dressing room containing Botham and Richards may have been too intimidating. Tony Pigott of Sussex, for example, curiously changed his mind, having signed a contract.

With the bat there were staggering contributions from Richards and Botham. Against Warwickshire Viv hit 322 in a day, facing 258 balls; I was batting with him when he was in the 290s and was suddenly nervous that I might run him out but he made sure there were no alarms. Likewise Botham hit stunning centuries against Hampshire and Essex at Taunton, both of which I witnessed from the other end. Every time he took a single there would be a minute's delay, while the man at deep mid-wicket would be relocated to second slip when I was on strike. He was decimating county attacks and finished the season with a Championship batting average over 100. But that did not mean we were capable of winning games.

Our solitary victory demands a mention since it coincided with my career-best figures. On a worn pitch at Bath I took 8–17; the ball spun a lot and I must have bowled well as Lancashire were dismissed for 89. Graeme Fowler was in the opposition and I remember him asking umpire David Constant – in all seriousness – to tell me to stop talking to him. Apparently I was making him laugh. That was a bit of a mystery to me though it was always a treat to play against those with whom you had toured. More obviously I recognized that the conditions were heavily in my favour and I managed to exploit them. It may be that earlier in the season an eager young local groundsman at Bath, where we created a cricket ground out of nothing each year, had inadvertently spread weedkiller rather than fertilizer on the square. It seems preposterous now but Somerset's two festivals at Bath and Weston were held on grounds that did not host any other serious cricket matches throughout the season.

England were playing a Test match at Headingley as I was scything through the Lancashire line-up. There the assembled press corps, with whom I had spent so much time during the previous winter tour to India, were obviously taken aback by these bowling figures and they very kindly sent me a postcard, acknowledging their surprise and offering their congratulations.

In my tour book *Marks Out of XI*, I had quoted John Woodcock on the subject of wives on tour. During England's tour of Australia in 1974/5 John had written, as ever memorably, 'Lord Hawke probably took the same view as I do about families on tour with the MCC players. It is no more a place for them than a trench on the Somme.' I had taken issue with Woodcock's view in the book, saying how essential it was that wives and families be allowed to join England's players on a long tour. Anyway, there on the post-card from Headingley, amid the congratulations from the nation's cricket correspondents, was the unmistakable handwriting of Woodcock, who had penned the words, 'Was Anna there?'

Apart from the 8–17 it had been a nightmarish season. I had been the solitary player to appear in every game; as vice-captain I was obviously despondent that our results had been so dire. But amid the never-ending flow of fixtures I don't suppose that I had given much thought to the future. It was clear that something had to change and, by the time I turned up to a committee meeting just after the last match of the season, it seemed likely that Ian's period as captain would come to an end.

At the committee meeting Ian and I were asked to leave the room. I had naively assumed that if Ian were dismissed or if he resigned then I would be invited to take over. Clearly I had not thought it through. Returning to the committee room it was estab-lished that Ian would not be captain in 1986. As with the England captaincy he resigned just before he was sacked. I've never quite understood his aversion to being sacked since in sport that is surely an honourable occupational hazard. Then they announced that Peter Roebuck would be the new captain. I was stunned, barely capable of speech, and just wanted to make an exit as swiftly as possible.

All through the eighties there had been the expectation that I would take over. That had been implicit and just occasionally explicit in discussions with the club. In my innocence I had just assumed that this was my time, albeit in wretched circumstances. Perhaps I had taken it for granted that the captaincy would just fall into my lap. I certainly had not contemplated manoeuvring quietly for the role.

I spoke to Pete Roebuck that evening. He said that he had tried to warn me of what was going to happen – since he was obviously aware of the committee's plans – but those messages had not come through. The perception, in part promoted by Ian, perhaps to safeguard his position, must have been that I was not tough enough to cope with the strong personalities in the dressing room. Perhaps he was right. We will never know but I would have accepted the opportunity to find out. Moreover as vice-captain I was part of the old, unsuccessful regime and was therefore regarded as a poor option.

I was surprised by how hurt I was by that decision. If there was a clear explanation at the time, which is not my recollection, it would have fallen on deaf ears. I was knocked back by the outcome of that meeting, which just confirms how at the end of a long season I had not considered all the various permutations. I had no divine right to be the new captain but stupidly I had just assumed that would be the case. In addition to the shock I felt gullible and, to an extent, exploited.

The permutation chosen by the club was that Peter Roebuck would take charge with Viv Richards as his vice-captain. The loss of the vice-captaincy was not hard to bear. I understood the logic of trying to ensure that Viv was on board and committed and, in any case, I was not the first sportsman to discover that being the vice-captain of any team is a position with far more pitfalls than prospects (not that this deterred me from accepting the role again before too long).

It transpired that the end of that 1985 season with Botham resigning the captaincy barely constituted a ripple compared to the waves created at the end of the 1986 season when the club announced that Viv and Joel would not be re-engaged and that they would be replaced by Martin Crowe, with the inevitable consequence of Ian's departure. This grabbed the attention a long way north and east of Bridgwater, which is where the originator of this plan, Michael Hill, the club's chairman, ran a thriving farm.

In 1986 the new regime had done little better than the old one. Somerset finished sixteenth in the Championship and there was a critical loss to Lancashire in the second round of the NatWest Trophy in July. Defeat in that competition at that stage of the season condemned a county side, which was struggling in the other competitions, to another trophy-less season. That was always when the mumbling started in the committee rooms.

Roebuck, as captain, was batting better than ever before; he was more assertive at the crease, providing another example of how the captaincy can enhance a player. Botham and Richards fired sporadically, though Ian's contributions were always far more likely to come from his batting rather than his bowling.

This was the summer when Ian was banned from the game for two months after admitting that he had smoked pot earlier in his career. The response of his relatively new and ill-conceived choice as manager, Tim Hudson, to Ian's admission, which was revealed on the front pages of the *Mail on Sunday* after a deal had been brokered between the two parties, raised the odd eyebrow. 'Doesn't everybody?' said a bemused Hudson. Ian's manager was a charmer but not the ideal man to be running his business affairs in the mid-eighties – or in any other decade. The notion of a career in Hollywood, promoted by Hudson, never quite came to pass though Ian did appear in pantomime half a dozen years later. Tony Brown and Ray Wright, the secretary and treasurer of Somerset at the time, used to delight in telling the story of turning up at Birtles Hall in Cheshire to negotiate Ian's next contract. They had a ceiling for his salary – not much more than £15,000 – and were thrilled that they could leave with a figure agreed that was considerably smaller than that.

In 1986 Ian's enforced absence from first-class cricket meant that he was obliged to play in Somerset's second team to get some practice for the first time in over a decade. Julian Wyatt was leading the team at the time and he was asked how tricky it was to captain Botham. 'It was very simple actually,' he replied. 'Ian told me when he wanted to bat and he told me when he wanted to bowl.' (For the record Ian scored 41 and took 2–47 from his fifteen overs.)

Another problem stemmed from the mediocre output of the newer members of the side. There were no new sources of wickets, while the likes of Nigel Felton and Jon Hardy struggled to have an impact as batsmen. In the wake of that defeat to Lancashire in the NatWest Trophy Viv had been in a foul mood, frustrated by another Somerset failure, and increasingly the argument surfaced that the younger players struggled to perform because of Viv's mighty, broody, overbearing presence. It was an argument that failed to convince me then, it does not convince me now nor did I find it vindicated soon after Viv had been sacked when the output of the players concerned was exactly the same. Even so the proposition that Viv somehow stifled the young players was widely promoted when the debate about the decision to get rid of him and Joel was raging.

In a curious way it was not really about Viv, who, like Joel, could be regarded as a victim in all this. Ian was more of a problem for the captain. In those petty yet important matters, such as when you turn up at the ground and how you go about practice,

Ian was far more likely to cut corners than Viv. But if Ian was going to turn up at 10.35 a.m. then Viv might feel entitled to do the same, even though he would hate himself for doing so since he had a far greater awareness of the basic disciplines required for the team to function properly.

In Ian's absence Viv was seldom a problem for a captain. In fact he was an obvious asset. He would be there, he would be supportive and he would score his runs. So Viv and Joel may have suffered from some of Ian's excesses when Somerset made their decision. It was obvious that when Viv joined Glamorgan in 1990 he was an inspiration to their younger players. No doubt having been rejected by Somerset, a decision that hurt the proudest of men, he was determined to demonstrate that he could fulfil that role as a mentor and a motivator as well as a runscorer. As for the genial Joel, the only issue for a captain was his fitness. Increasingly the body was rebelling but in one-day cricket he was still formidable.

The overhaul was not Peter Roebuck's brainwave. The idea stemmed from the chairman, Michael Hill, and the process was ignited when Martin Crowe, whose registration was still held by Somerset, asked permission to speak to Essex, which he assumed would be a routine request. The plans were kept secret and I was astonished when Pete told me about them. My immediate view, which did not change, was that 'In your shoes I would not do that.' However, Pete seldom shied from confrontation; I was always the conciliator.

There was another factor in all this that went beyond the cricketing ramifications. More than anything as captain, Pete craved a side that would, amid all his eccentricities, listen to him and follow him without too much questioning. His hero, if ever he had one, was Jack Meyer, captain of Somerset in 1947, and his headmaster at

197

Millfield School. Pete's interview there began with an orange tossed in his direction, which he caught (but he should have thrown it back) and it ended with Meyer not only offering him a scholarship but also employing both his parents on the staff. Meyer was known as 'Boss' by staff and pupils alike; he was obviously an unconventional, dictatorial, inspirational leader who founded Millfield out of a few Nissen huts in the countryside around Street and who persuaded princes and sheikhs to pay massive fees to allow him to offer places to able children without wealthy parents for free.

Peter's ideal was to be a similarly unconventional leader, dispatching wisdom along the way to a willing band of spellbound followers. This was wishful thinking with an ordinary professional cricket side; it was downright impossible in a team containing Ian and Viv. Holding complete sway in those circumstances could never be an option. In fact even after Viv and Ian had gone it was never possible for Pete to have that team of devoted disciples at Somerset. Curiously he got closer to that ideal when he captained Devon in the 1990s, winning four Minor County championships. He had in his Devon team an exceptional group of men and some fine cricketers like Nick Folland, Gareth Townsend, Julian Wyatt and briefly a young Chris Read, who were prepared to laugh off a few preposterous plans one moment but to lap up Roebuck's cricketing wisdom the next. I think that was when Pete was happiest as a cricketer; it was certainly his happiest time as a captain.

Towards the end of the season there was the final committee meeting. I saw Pete that evening, eager to know the outcome. 'I could have saved them,' he said – after all, he was the club captain – 'but I could not bring myself to do it.'

Now it became ugly, very ugly. Viv and Joel were stunned, especially Viv who had always had such an emotional tie with the club since 1974. Back then Pete and Viv had been close. Viv had called him 'The Professor' and had admired his guts as a batsman, while Pete had the highest aspirations for Viv that went beyond the cricket field. When Viv had a son he asked Pete to look out a name for him and both of them settled on the choice of Mali.

In the early years Pete and Ian had also enjoyed each other's company. Unbelievably a collaborative book by Pete with and about Ian, called *It Sort of Clicks*, would be published in November 1986. Well, this really was an elaborate way to boost sales. More relevantly here was a reminder that they had been able to work together well into the mid-eighties, even when Pete was despairing at the way Ian was captaining the club.

But now the gloves were off. A placard appeared, presumably via Ian, on Pete's peg in the dressing room bearing the word 'Judas'. Unsurprisingly Ian was fuming at the decision and threatening to leave – he had taken the precaution of signing just a one-year extension to his contract in 1985. Meanwhile Viv had long since stopped functioning as the vice-captain – how could he fulfil that role now? – and he was trying to make sense of it all.

At the end of August we arrived at Birmingham for a Sunday League game with a squad of at least fifteen players because no one could be sure that Viv and Joel would turn up (they did and between them took four cheap wickets in a six-wicket victory). After that Viv and Joel understandably withdrew for a while; Ian was steaming but obliged to play (after all, he had not been sacked); Pete was feeling the pressure too and, as ever, I was just about the only one talking to both parties, to no good effect.

Pete was not around to captain the last few matches. So they had to cast around for someone to take the team out. And of course, I was prevailed upon to do it. And of course I agreed to do so. Looking back perhaps they were right and I was too damn soft and gullible to be given the captaincy on an official basis. The most poignant occasion was in the last Sunday League game of the summer against Derbyshire at Taunton on 14 September. It was a privilege I could have done without and I can't quite recall what, if anything, I said beforehand but this was the last game played by Viv, Joel and Ian for Somerset. We won by three wickets; Joel took 1–27, Viv made 55 and Ian 32. It wasn't supposed to end like that.

There would follow meetings, talk of rebellions and vigorous expressions of no-confidence in the committee. Pete was under severe scrutiny but he was also stimulated by the controversy, revelling in the challenge of a forensic debate and a political battle to win. I'd seldom seen him so alive. There was an extraordinary members' meeting at the Shepton Mallet showground, by which time I was in West Australia in what seemed to be a remarkably uncomplicated and unified dressing room. At that meeting, in which Nigel Popplewell, a recent member of the dressing room, made a critical contribution, the club's position was ratified (oddly enough Nigel travelled to the meeting with Roy Kerslake, who was no longer involved with club – sadly – and who took the diametrically opposed stance to Nigel in favour of the retention of Richards and Garner).

So Somerset had seen off the rebels but there were no real victors in this outcome. The club had been torn asunder and it took a long time to recover. For Pete I think this was the seminal moment in his life and it stayed with him for years, longer than any of the other protagonists. I remained friends with him but there was always a tension on this issue. He always sought affirmation from me that he had taken the right course in 1986 and I was never able to give it to him.

Nonetheless it had been a brave move to sack Viv and Joel and there would obviously be nasty ramifications. It was the end of Pete's relationship with Ian, who never forgave him, and with Viv. Of course there is absolutely no guarantee that everything would have worked out rosily if the club had stuck with the two West Indians. Joel would have retired imminently; Viv might have kept going for a while but what would have become of Ian? Perhaps he would have left anyway. But there were other serious issues at the club, including a shortage of enough decent players. After the departure of Roy Kerslake – he had fallen out with the committee in 1983 – there was little foresight or constructive planning upstairs.

In fact the immediate upshot was that Ian joined Worcestershire, which proved to be a successful move for both parties. If nothing else the signing of Botham and Graham Dilley was an indication of that club's ambition. Even though Ian seldom dominated for Worcestershire as he did for Somerset his new employers would go on to win the Championship in 1988 and 1989. There was the odd suggestion, triggered by Ian, as to whether I wanted to join him there, which I never pursued; Viv next appeared in England playing for Rishton in the Lancashire League and he later joined Glamorgan, where they thought the world of him; in 1993 inspired by Richards they won the Sunday League. Joel retired from international cricket in March 1987.

A shrewder man would have renegotiated his contract with Somerset at this point. They would have been desperate to keep me, I think, after such an exodus. Pete must have been concerned by the possibility of my leaving as he was quick to suggest that I should leapfrog him as a beneficiary – he had been capped before me and was therefore entitled to a benefit sooner. And, of course, he asked me to be his vice-captain. And, of course, I bloody agreed, yet again.

Eventually the three titans were rehabilitated with the club. Either side of the Ian Botham Stand in front of the River Tone are the Viv Richards Gates and the Joel Garner Gates.

TWELVE

RETIRED HURT

IN 1987 AND 1988 Martin Crowe returned to Somerset and so did an uneasy tranquillity – except when we played Worcestershire.

Martin was a tougher, more self-contained cricketer now. He had been on the Test circuit for more than three years; he had been bombarded in the Caribbean by the West Indies' pace attack and had endured the burden of being the Kiwis' best batsman. He was still a fine influence in the dressing room and a wonderful player. But he also recognized that he now had a limited amount of energy to give. He could no longer bend over backwards to help every ailing young professional on the staff as he had done in 1984; he was, justifiably, less patient with those cruising or cutting corners, and his bowling days were just about over.

He played some brilliant innings for us in 1987, none better than an unbeaten 155 in the B&H Cup at Southampton when he seemed to be effortlessly drop-kicking the ball over the square-leg boundary in the last few overs. Through no fault of his own the spotlight was upon him. He had been catapulted into the unenviable position of being Viv's replacement – not to mention Joel. The club would have been desperate for him to vindicate their

1986 decision; likewise there would have been those eager for him to fail. Without question Martin fulfilled his part of the bargain throughout 1987, which would not, of course, mean that Somerset were suddenly challenging for trophies.

Peter Roebuck also maintained the higher standards set in 1986, though in this season and the next he would be beset by a variety of injuries, often to his hands, which meant that Somerset's perennial vice-captain would be busy. In the second half of the eighties Pete was a major county batsman, better than some of those summoned for England in this period. But there would always be some extra angst for him whenever we played Worcestershire.

The newshounds had inked into their diaries 15 July 1987 at Taunton, which was when Somerset were scheduled to entertain Worcestershire in the County Championship. Ian Botham was back. In fact the match, as a contest, was a non-event. There was a lot of rain around though this did not prevent abnormally high gate receipts of £4500. Worcestershire were put into bat but there would be only one innings in the game, and any drama hinged upon whether Botham would score a century upon his return to the County Ground. He had decided that this was what he was going to do.

I quite enjoyed the occasion but I don't think Pete did. Two bowlers, Graham Rose and Gary Palmer, pulled muscles and we had already picked a side packed with batting and short of bowling. So in between the showers I bowled all the time. *Wisden* records I operated at the River End throughout the second day, though there must have been a few stoppages for rain. With our captain fast running out of bowlers I could not resist feigning a pulled hamstring as I ran up to bowl at the start of proceedings. Later as I prepared to propel my first delivery to Ian in first-class cricket I managed to wobble melodramatically at the knees to suggest that I was completely overcome by such a monumental challenge. This cheered me up but I don't think it amused Peter greatly.

My recollection is that Ian decided to block me and my bowling figures in that innings bear that out: 40.1–15–74–2. Ian inevitably reached his century on the fourth day so his mission was accomplished. One of my victims was Graeme Hick, bowled for a duck. Young Hick did rather better at Taunton the following season when Worcestershire haunted us again. The same scenario applied when the two sides met – Roebuck was not talking to Botham and vice versa. I was talking to both of them, but not simultaneously. This was the summer when four-day cricket was introduced for a few games at the beginning and end of the season, and initially Somerset were not so impressed by this innovation.

In early May we reduced Worcestershire to 132–5 after Botham had been bowled by Graham Rose for seven. The door was ajar. A day later Worcestershire declared on 628–7, Hick 405 not out. At the start of their innings the ball had darted around. Then the pitch must have flattened out and Hick was remorseless; he averaged 75 runs per session – until he reached 300, whereupon he opened his shoulders a little. He dispatched every imperfect ball clinically to the boundary; he ran like the wind for himself and his partners as Steve Rhodes, who faced 275 balls for his 56, and Richard Illingworth offered passive support at the other end. At the declaration Hick had faced 469 balls in his nine and a half hours at the crease and he did not even have the decency to look tired at the end of it all.

David Foot, that wonderful West Country wordsmith, who wrote for the *Guardian* among many others, was there and watched Hick leave the field after Phil Neale had declared. 'He should be drained with traces of elation etching through his weariness. Instead he walks with a brisk step, the face offers not a flicker of emotion as the smallish crowd, belatedly sensing the proximity of cricketing history, converges to applaud. He passes not more than a yard away and there is not the merest evidence of perspiration on his cheeks and forehead. He could be out for a walk along Worcestershire's River Severn.' I think I looked rather more dishevelled as I left the field when I uncharitably mentioned to Hick that A. C. MacLaren had scored 424 at Taunton as recently as 1895.

Peter Roebuck recalled that innings in the following year's *Wisden* in an article entitled 'We Already Knew He Could Bat'. He remembered how Hick's first ball was hit in the air to square leg and that he had been thinking of stationing a fielder there as he took guard, but, unusually for Roebuck, he let bygones be bygones. The ball sped away for Hick's first boundary. 'There was never any sense of awesome personality in this awesome batting,' wrote Roebuck. 'Apart from its proportion it was not a masterpiece.' He added, 'Hick, I believe, will become a major force in Test cricket.' We all thought so. And we were all wrong.

A nasty pattern had been set since Botham's Worcestershire kept humiliating Somerset. Within a fortnight we were pitched against them again and fearing the worst at New Road. For a change the game exceeded expectations. This time Crowe hit a century; Hick made 11 and 8; Somerset won by nine wickets and poor Ian, who had just dismissed Pete for 8, fell awkwardly in the slips and damaged his back in the process. He required immediate surgery and did not play again that summer.

Hick could not stop scoring runs in the late eighties before he qualified for England in 1990. He was clinical rather than ruthless. Perhaps he was too mild-mannered to impose himself on Test attacks as he routinely did at domestic level in the gentler pastures of the County Championship. No doubt there were technical issues as well. He was the most decent and diligent of run-gatherers but as the Aussies sometimes say, 'Where's the mongrel?' – not that this dissuaded them from employing Hick as a batting coach in 2016.

The last time I played against him was in a Sunday League game at Worcester in 1989. I was leading an unsuccessful chase when he was bowling his off-breaks. A couple of times I hit him for straight sixes into the stand at the New Road End. 'I owe you thirty-seven more of those,' I said.

A more ruthless cricketer appeared at Taunton in August 1987 after Crowe had been summoned by New Zealand for a hastily arranged series against Sri Lanka. For a few games we managed to secure the services of Steve Waugh, who had been playing some league cricket in the Midlands, an arrangement that would be repeated on a longer-term basis in 1988 after Crowe had been laid low with back problems.

Waugh did not say much at the start. In fact he did not say much at any stage in his brief Somerset career but whenever he spoke we listened. He was only twenty-two when he turned up at Taunton in 1987 but he had already played Test cricket. He was eager to broaden his experience and his second match for Somerset against Surrey at the Oval most certainly achieved that goal.

In that era the prospect of a game against Surrey immediately brought to mind one man, Sylvester Clarke, the West Indian fast bowler, who seldom smiled or bowled slowly – or full in length. In some ways Clarke was an endearing character but he could also be a terrifying opponent, who could generate remarkable pace off a twelve-yard run-up with a whirlwind action, which made it devilishly hard to pick up the trajectory of the ball.

Clarke had been around the county circuit for a while. Back in 1984 he had been undermined by Botham at the Weston Festival in quite spectacular fashion. The plan, if ever one existed, was simple but effective. Botham cornered Clarke after the game and invited him along to the sponsor's tent for an hour or so, after which they went off drinking together somewhere in Weston-Super-Mare for the rest of the night. The following morning we could hear the Clarke groans through the wafer-thin walls of the Weston pavilion; meanwhile Botham seemed as fresh as a daisy.

Clarke was just about fit enough to come out to bat alongside Pat Pocock at the start of the day. Our left-arm spinner, Stephen Booth, was bowling and Pocock drove straight and in the air with all his might. The ball thudded into the elbow of Clarke, who was already nursing a monumental headache at the non-striker's end, and Booth deftly caught the rebound, which meant that the Surrey innings was over. Any doubts over whether Clarke would be fit enough to bowl in our second innings were now blown away. He spent the rest of the day sleeping or groaning under the table in the Surrey dressing room rather than terrorizing our batsmen.

That was a considerable relief and a job well done by Botham since we were all wary of facing Clarke, though in that era he always seemed to torment Brian Rose more than anyone. Our former captain always had a nightmare against him and on one occasion Clarke had broken several of his ribs. Rose would have preferred Holding, Roberts, Garner or Lillee, anybody rather than Clarke, as an opponent. Worse still, Clarke knew that Rose hated facing him.

Rose was at the Oval on the morning that Waugh made his second appearance for Somerset in 1987. In fact he was there in a coaching/managerial role but before the start he was out and about in his tracksuit participating in the morning stretches on the

outfield with the rest of us. Clarke obviously spotted him and glee-
fully registered another first-class wicket. Somerset started batting,
Clarke started bowling and Surrey were soon working their way
through our line-up. Clarke was still bowling when I appeared, by
which time he was sweating profusely and somewhat mystified by
my arrival. 'When's Rosie coming in?' he asked. 'I've been waiting
for he all day.'

In Somerset's second innings Waugh hit a superb hundred.
There had been mumbles that he was a bit windy against extreme
pace but he dispelled any such thoughts within a couple of games,
here against Clarke and soon after against Courtney Walsh at
Bristol, where he hit another gritty century. Waugh rarely looked
pretty against the pacemen or disdainfully in control. He might
jerk out of the way of a bouncer at the last minute, hinting at some
vulnerability in the process, but how he relished the contest. At
Somerset he sensed a golden opportunity to test himself against
West Indian pace bowlers, to assemble a method to play them, and
that is exactly what he did. He alone in the Somerset team would
be looking forward to duels with Clarke or Walsh. In 1989 Jimmy
Cook, eager and curious as he emerged from the bubble of South
African cricket, had the same approach. 'I just can't wait to face
[Malcolm] Marshall,' he said to a puzzled audience.

In Waugh's intimidatingly massive autobiography he says that
his first month with Somerset in 1987 'developed into one of the
most influential periods of my whole career' because of the experience gained against West Indian fast bowlers. 'Their pace was
something I hadn't confronted in a first-class match. This was
particularly true of Clarke, who bowled the most awkward and
nastiest spell I ever encountered in a match at the Oval. Pace and
bounce of the kind Clarke could muster is something you can't

prepare for; it's an assault both physically and mentally and the moment you weaken and think about what might happen, you're either out or injured. I think this was the first time I experienced a genuine awareness that if I didn't concentrate there would be serious implications.'

Waugh goes on to talk about 'good fear', which made him more alert and sharper in his movements, rather than 'bad fear' that brings only doubt and sluggishness, which he sensed, probably correctly, had invaded the Somerset dressing room. 'As the contest [at the Oval] drew nearer I could see the determination of the players disintegrating and by the time we pulled on the whites half the boys were already out,' he recalls.

So Waugh learnt fast against Clarke. His unbeaten century at the Oval meant that Surrey needed 217 to win in thirty-six overs, a target they were keen to chase and at several points they looked as if they would get there. Our fielding was far from flawless. Pete Roebuck had a nightmare, dropping three catches in quick succession, which prompted him to race off the field at the end of one over. Apparently he had the wrong trousers on. Obviously this was the reason the catches had gone to ground so he had to sprint back to the dressing room to put on his 'fielding trousers'. There were other blemishes as well at a time when Waugh had been summoned to bowl since he was our best bet of rescuing the situation. By now Waugh was becoming increasingly bewildered and exasperated by the efforts of his new colleagues in the field and he eventually spoke: 'Do you blokes want to save this game or not?' Once again everybody listened. In the end Surrey were six runs short with nine wickets down, mainly thanks to Waugh.

It was already clear that here was a special cricketer, who later achieved a remarkable modern distinction: he would become the most successful Australian captain – he won forty-one of his fifty-seven Test matches in charge – never to be scooped up by Channel Nine in Australia. Perhaps he was not interested in working on television; perhaps they never asked. He was certainly not the favourite of one of Channel Nine's doyens, Ian Chappell.

Over the years I've come to like and respect Ian Chappell a great deal. He became the least one-eyed of the Channel Nine team offering a broader, more objective view of Australian cricket than the rest; increasingly he became the last remaining commentator among the cheerleaders. Chappell was great fun to work with when he occasionally appeared on *TMS*; he had a deep reservoir of stories from the seventies and was never shy of dipping into them. Like so many Aussies of that generation he has the wonderful capacity to take people as he finds them; a whole raft of Test caps are not necessary to qualify for a conversation with Ian. Late one evening when he was working with *TMS* we somehow ended up on the topic of the elder Waugh twin.

Basically my thesis was that Steve was an exceptional cricketer and leader; Chappell, curiously, took the alternative view and, of course, despite the figures he could not be swayed. The words 'I've changed my mind about that; perhaps you were right all along' have rarely, if ever, escaped Ian's lips. I think his argument had something to do with the fact that Waugh always batted down the order, rather than at three (like Ian); that he had a lot of not outs batting at five and six when he seldom modified his way of batting when stranded with the tail; that anyone could have captained that Australian team; and that he wasn't Shane Warne. It was an amicable debate and neither of us shifted, which was no great surprise in Chappell's case.

*

THE FOLLOWING YEAR, 1988, was my benefit season. It was run by a cheerful, life-enhancing estate agent from Weston-Super-Mare (there cannot be so many of those) called Roy Main, who had also organized the benefits of Brian Rose, Peter Denning and Colin Dredge in the eighties. He seemed to specialize in the Somerset boys, for whom he worked tirelessly and with unquenchable good humour. Colin had had his benefit in 1987. I remember this partly because that was the year when Peter Roebuck, being a forward thinker, had invited a sports psychologist down to Taunton during pre-season training. We had a few meetings, all fairly constructive – though not as entertaining as the advent of an aerobics teacher – during which the inevitable goal-setting process was introduced.

We all sat down with our pencils and paper, and were required to write down general and specific targets for the season ahead. I have no idea what I wrote but have always remembered Colin's goal: 'To try to make as much money as I can in my benefit year.' Of course, this gives a false impression of Dredge. He was the most selfless and dedicated professional imaginable, and one of the most guileless – if we discount the slower ball he developed (though even that could have been so much better disguised). Colin would bowl all day if required, often when the flak was flying and the captain was running out of volunteers.

For all but a season or two of his career Colin trekked to Taunton from Frome, a journey that would take an hour and twenty minutes on a good day. On one occasion he was disturbingly late. Usually the formula applied that the further you lived from the ground the earlier you arrived – this was obviously the case when Ian was living around the corner – but on one damp day at Taunton there was no Colin. He was absent for the stretching exercises before play began; he missed the team talk, if there was one, and he was still nowhere to be seen when it was time for us to take to the field.

We began to become anxious about what might have happened to him – there were no mobile phones to deliver an instant explanation. The game proceeded and then after about an hour in the field we saw Colin ambling from the pavilion, seemingly unconcerned by his tardiness. We rushed towards him to check that all was well, which he confirmed was the case, and then we wondered why he was so late. 'Well,' he said, 'it's pissing down in Frome.' If ever anyone deserved a good benefit it was Colin.

Now the benefit season seems more of an anachronism since county cricketers are so much better paid in the modern era. It was heading very slowly in that direction in the late eighties. In my last season I think I was paid about £15,000, hardly a fortune. Nonetheless it felt a bit uncomfortable to be asking the supporters to dig deep into their pockets to contribute to my benefit fund. At least that was the feeling at the start of the year; towards the end with time running out such pangs of conscience did not hang around for so long.

Mine was an old-style benefit with matches against local clubs, including the one against the village team at Middle Chinnock where my brother was captain, as well as a game back at Blundell's School. There were a few dinners, which meant that I had to cobble together a speech that has changed a bit over the years but not perhaps as much as you might expect, and there were countless evenings at a pub somewhere for skittles and darts. One such evening was at the Three Pigeons in Bishop's Tawton, a small village up in North Devon, not too far from Barnstaple.

My old Oxford friend John Claughton was staying with us and we set off into the wilds towards Bishop's Tawton for a darts evening. Upon arrival there were seven people in the bar and there was no clear evidence that any of them had turned up specifically for this bumper benefit extravaganza. Anyway, there was no alternative but to plough on with the darts competition, which did not take too long. In the end the contest was won by the landlord of the pub and I therefore presented him with a bottle of whisky, a prize that he himself had donated in the first place. I don't think the pub exists any more and I'm not sure that the modern beneficiary has many darts evenings.

Towards the end of that season Pete Roebuck surprised me again. He had been hampered by finger injuries so I had often led the side, but then he told me that he was resigning from the captaincy immediately and that he wanted me to take over. He explained that the timing was such that the club would have no alternative but to make me the official club captain – for the first time.

So it was a curious and frantic last month or two of the season. I was busy being a beneficiary, I received a one-off recall to the England ODI side for a game against Sri Lanka and now I was made club captain. Maybe the injuries had worn Pete down; the captaincy had been a draining experience for him, too, and not quite as rewarding as he had anticipated while the relationship with the club's committees since the departure of Roy Kerslake was always a source of frustration, whoever was captain. Moreover, after the traumas of 1985 and 1986 I think he wanted me to have a go at the job before I retired.

There was quite a turnover at the club that year. Tony Brown, who had been the secretary for five stormy summers, left; so did Brian Rose, who went off to work in the paper industry, and Peter had resigned the captaincy. As captain I was part of the panel to appoint the new chief executive (rather than another secretary since we recognized the benefits of expanding the powers of the top employee at the club, thereby avoiding an overdependence on an unwieldy committee).

We offered the job to Peter Anderson. Many years earlier he had played for Devon, where he had been in the police force before heading out to use his expertise in Hong Kong. Peter was – and still is – a cheerful, ruddy-faced, straight-talking man who knows how to get things done. The night before his interview I had received a phone call from Rod Eddington, who had played cricket with Peter in Hong Kong, during which he mentioned some of his virtues. A coincidence? No. A good appointment? Yes. Peter held the reins at Somerset for sixteen years, during which he was still preparing the pitch at Seaton CC on the south coast of Devon. He took no nonsense but beyond the bluff exterior he looked after his players and had a good relationship with them. In the nineties after an appalling defeat to Middlesex in the NatWest Trophy he breezed into the dressing room the following day. 'My door is always open,' he announced. 'If anyone would like to pop in to discuss next year's contract, they are more than welcome.'

Increasingly the committee took a back seat as Anderson explored the limits of his power. Indeed the principal reason why Somerset finds itself more buoyant than most county clubs stems from the fact that they had three excellent, proactive chief executives in succession, which must be some kind of record: Anderson, Richard Gould, currently chief executive at Surrey, and Guy Lavender, now chief executive of the MCC.

Looking ahead I was clear that we needed more direction from the top – and more help for the captain – to improve our younger players and I had identified a man who was well equipped to provide that. Jack Birkenshaw must be a contender for the most cheerful cricketer ever to come out of Yorkshire. I had never encountered anyone so passionate about the game; even better he had the capacity to share that passion, along with his expertise, with succeeding generations.

Jack was an off-spinner who could bat breezily, and began his career at Yorkshire in 1958. But he soon left when he realized that his path into the first team was blocked by the mighty presence of Raymond Illingworth. So Jack moved to Leicestershire in 1962. And what happened in 1969? Illingworth also took refuge at Grace Road as Birky's new captain. In fact Illingworth and Birkenshaw usually played in the same team for Leicestershire though the legend, which probably possesses a grain of truth, is that Illy generally bowled on the turning pitches while Birky bowled on the flat ones.

By 1989 Jack had done most things in the game: he had played for England, he had umpired at first-class level and in a couple of Test matches, and he had coached the game all over the world – when we were negotiating he was doing that far away in Bunbury, south of Perth in WA. As a player I had always picked his brains when he was umpiring in county cricket, occasionally to my embarrassment.

I always liked bowling at his end and we would chatter away. At Cardiff one year I was in the middle of a long spell; I finally took a wicket and out came a young Matthew Maynard. I had not seen him play before but Jack had. So I made some enquiries. 'He's a very gifted young cricketer,' said Jack. 'He can hit the ball a long way but he can be a bit impetuous. If you give him a couple of flatter ones then toss one up in the air, anything could happen.'

I duly followed Jack's instructions and, lo and behold, Maynard was stumped by a mile. So far, so good. Now in my excitement I

Preparing to bowl against Sri Lanka in the World Cup
match at Taunton in 1983, a serious business.

Me and Pete Denning recline either side of Brian Rose, recuperating
after winning the 1983 NatWest final against Kent.

My main job for the majority of my three England tours:
net bowling – this time in Delhi, 1984.

Two members of the social committee (Cowdrey and Marks) prepare for Christmas festivities in Calcutta, 1984. (PETER BAXTER)

English tourists at the Taj Mahal, January 1985.

CMJ in position and on time. (ADRIAN MURRELL/ALLSPORT PHOTOGRAPHIC)

Masquerading as a teacher, 1985. (ALAIN LOCKYER)

My first summer in the press box in 1990. Note just a pen and paper, no laptop and a clunking Observer 'mobile' phone which I shared with the rugby correspondent, Clem Thomas. (PATRICK EAGAR/POPPERFOTO/GETTY IMAGES)

Another partnership with Viv who was making his debut for TMS, Antigua 1994.

TMS team photo 2007. L TO R: Peter Baxter, Henry Blofeld, Shilpa Patel, me, Mike Selvey, CMJ, Colin Croft, Tony Cozier, Jonathan Agnew and Bill Frindall.

At the Oval busking with Jonathan Agnew.

Giving Dom Bess his first England cap at Lord's
in 2018. Not sure who was more nervous.

A World Cup forum with Andy Caddick and Marcus Trescothick at
Taunton in 2019. The closest any of us came to touching the trophy.

My two lovely daughters:
Rosie (the bridesmaid) and Amy (the bride).

Three elegant hats upon Anna, her sister Charlotte and nephew Laurie. And me.

swivelled round and bellowed towards the umpire, 'Well done, Jack!' This was not such a good idea since Glamorgan's captain, Rodney Ontong, was at the non-striker's end at the time. Perhaps I should add that the following year at Weston, Maynard hit a magnificent 160 during which he kept straight driving my clever off-breaks into the massive white tarpaulin that served as a sightscreen there. Maynard was as gifted and dominant as any batsman in county cricket in that generation. Yet this never allowed him to succeed at Test level. Maybe he was not as sure of his ability as he seemed.

I was certain that Birkenshaw would be a terrific influence, – and for the next three years at Somerset he was just that. Then he was seduced back to Leicester, where the county side won the County Championship twice in 1996 and 1998. In his later years he joined the coaching staff of the England women's team and they enjoyed his wisdom as well as his company. I assume that at the age of seventy-eight he is still continuing the search for the perfect off-break.

It was also self-evident that the batting needed to be strengthened. Over the previous two years we had been overly dependent on Peter Roebuck and the overseas player, either Crowe or Waugh. The only one of our younger players to have advanced since the fall-out in 1986 was Richard Harden, a single-minded, middle-order batsman from Burnham-on-Sea, who made the most of his ability. When I last saw him he was prospering and he was the mayoress of Nelson in New Zealand (I think that is the correct term – his partner, Rachel Reese, was the mayor).

So to strengthen the batting I persuaded Chris Tavaré to join Somerset, which was not too difficult. He had captained Kent in 1983 and 1984, whereupon he had been sacked and replaced by

Chris Cowdrey. Both were excellent captains with completely different approaches to the job, but the manner of Tavaré's dismissal, no doubt prompted by Jim Swanton who headed up the Cowdrey faction in Canterbury, had rankled. This was a happy reunion for me. Meanwhile, with neither Crowe nor Waugh available, Anderson set to work upon the signing of Jimmy Cook from South Africa, who would score a phenomenal number of runs for Somerset over the next three years. Despite such brilliant signings there were no trophies in 1989.

The season started promisingly but on the morning of 16 May I was pole-axed. The phone rang at 5.00 a.m. and it was my brother. The brain works in mysterious ways and once he had announced himself at such an early hour I somehow knew what he was going to say. My father had died in the night from a sudden heart attack. He had not been ill though he had grown increasingly breathless as he continued farming at the age of sixty-nine. He had rebuffed attempts to get him to retire properly; it was almost as if that process was laden with too many difficulties and tricky decisions.

He had followed my cricketing career in the best possible way. He was inordinately proud on the good days though he would never say so; he didn't have to. My brother would sometimes explain that if I'd had a good day at Taunton he could crash the Land Rover and mislay a few cattle on the farm and still my father would be in a contented frame of mind, which was certainly not the case when my miserable figures with bat and/or ball appeared in the morning paper. He would come to watch sometimes, but never imposed or criticized.

The funeral took place just up the road from our farm when Somerset were playing Lancashire. The church was packed with relatives and the local farming community. The Revd Percy

Nichols, who had known my father for thirty years, spoke of his loyalty to the village and the farmworkers he had employed, which, he said, partially explained why he did not like change. 'I remember he kept a working horse far into the tractor era because his old carter, Joe Sansom, could not bear to see it go. And Joe was able to remain in the farm cottage after his retirement as long as he was able, without obligation.' The vicar also mentioned how 'he epitomized a true Somerset countryman' and he quoted a letter my mother had received: 'In all my long life,' it said, 'I have never met a nicer man.'

After the service everyone went back to the farm for refreshments, whereupon Ian Botham appeared for half an hour. He had long since left Somerset, of course, and was now based in Worcester during the summer. But he knew of my father's death because it had been mentioned in the press that this was the reason for my late withdrawal from Somerset's fixture against the touring Australians. And typically he had made the extra effort. I was taken aback by his arrival; more importantly my mother was both stunned and delighted that Ian should come all the way to Middle Chinnock to briefly pay his respects.

BACK AT SOMERSET our best chance of winning something was in the B&H Cup. We won all our early season zonal games, coming top of the group, and I soon realized that this could result in a home quarter-final against the Combined Universities, who had won two games under the leadership of Mike Atherton. That would be a bonus for us since the Combined Universities had never reached the knock-out stages before so we had to be favourites to beat them. Well, we did get drawn against them in our quarter-final and it was quite a game; the Combined Universities should have won and Atherton still winces at the memory of it.

His team possessed some gifted cricketers: Nasser Hussain, Martin Speight, Adrian Dale, Chris Tolley, Jonny Longley, James Boiling, Tim O'Gorman, Somerset's Jonathan Atkinson, and Steve James, who has since reminded me in several press boxes that the examiners at Cambridge refused him time off to play in that quarter-final. Somerset made an adequate 252 at Taunton with Roebuck hitting 102; Atherton, the leg-spinner, took 4–42 and was remarkably effective in the closing overs.

Hussain led the run chase with a superb century; he received support from Atherton (solidly) and Longley (audaciously), and any notion that Somerset would be able to breeze into the semi-final vanished rapidly. With six overs to go the Universities needed 30 to win with seven wickets in hand. It was time to play my joker.

Throughout our careers I had always rated Peter Roebuck's bowling potential and he had sometimes felt the same about my batting. For a few games back in 1986 he had asked me to open the batting and in my first outing I hit an impressive 65 against Courtney Walsh and Syd Lawrence. Now it was his turn to surprise everyone. In his youth Pete, who had big hands, bowled leg-breaks – he had even turned out for Somerset seconds as a thirteen-year-old in this role. At university he switched to conventional off-breaks. Now he was experimenting with quickish off-cutters, which he would bowl very frequently and effectively when leading Devon in the nineties.

In a desperate situation Roebuck was my only remaining option. In his favour was the fact that our opponents would not have known what he was going to bowl; moreover his lofty presence just might disturb them somehow. At the very least I knew that he would not be overawed by the challenge. In any case, by any normal standards the game was up.

Roebuck contrived to have Hussain caught on the boundary for 118 and Tolley stumped. He pretended that this was all part of the grand plan; these dismissals prompted panic in the student ranks. There was a run-out and at the start of the last over, which was to be bowled by Adrian Jones, the score was 244–6 with nine runs needed for a surprise victory. Another run-out plus two wickets for Jones and Somerset had somehow won the match by three runs. Atherton still can't quite fathom how that happened; James always assumes that the Universities would have won but for the blinkered outlook of the examiners, another indication of how Oxford and Cambridge increasingly set little store upon sporting success; meanwhile Hussain had announced himself to a wider audience in some style. Within a year Atherton and Hussain had begun their distinguished Test careers.

In the semi-final we lost to Essex by four runs despite a brilliant century from Tavaré. By then my new bowling sensation, Roebuck, was bowling his full quota of overs in several of our limited-overs games. However, we seldom threatened in the other competitions despite the runs from Cook, Roebuck and Tavaré.

At the beginning of July Micky Stewart, England's manager, was in touch with Jack Birkenshaw. The England side was in disarray (again); they had lost the first two Tests against Australia badly and, just before the third match at Edgbaston, Allan Lamb and Robin Smith (injured) and Mike Gatting (a family bereavement) were suddenly unavailable – all this chaos and the extent of the damage from the second rebel tour to South Africa had yet to come to light.

Micky's question was: 'Who should we take from you, Tavaré

or Roebuck?' Both Jack and I agreed that Roebuck was more likely to score runs. He had compiled a stubborn hundred for Somerset to save the match against the tourists earlier in the summer, and we both felt that Tavaré would not particularly welcome a recall five years after his last appearance. Who knows how Pete would have reacted to a first call-up at the age of thirty-three, but we thought he was playing better and that he could well be excited by the challenge. That judgement was passed on to Stewart. They picked Tavaré, who scored two in a wet draw. It was not a particularly happy ending to Chris's international career.

Soon, at the age of thirty-four, my professional career was going to end much more quickly than anticipated. In August the *Observer* invited me to become their cricket correspondent and after much agonizing I decided to accept their offer. So I had some explaining to do at Taunton once I had made up my mind. The key men all understood but this did not stop them from berating me for such a sudden departure, albeit with a twinkle in their eyes.

Peter Anderson reminded me how we had sat down together the previous autumn and had earnestly mapped out how we were going to transform the club, and yet now I was moving on. Jack Birkenshaw might well have said something similar, though I remember telling him that I knew it was time to go when I was meandering around the boundary at Weston and someone mistook me for him when asking for an autograph – Jack is fifteen years older than me. Chris Tavaré, who would succeed me as captain, recalled how I had outlined how much fun it would be to play together in the autumn of our careers, which he took to mean more than one season. Pete Roebuck hinted that he would miss me as well. I understood him and his sense of humour rather more easily than Tavaré or his new opening partner, Jimmy Cook. And who was he going to eat with on away trips? He even suggested that I should hang on until I had taken 1000 first-class wickets. Well, at the rate I was going that would take me three or four more seasons (1989 was my worst ever summer with the ball).

I went with a bang and a whimper and most definitely not in the grand manner. The penultimate match of the season was at Bristol. At tea on the first day after two long sessions in the field I was looking pretty grubby, but at the interval it was my job to go down the line introducing the Somerset team to the Patron of Gloucestershire, the Princess of Wales, without getting my Hardens and Hardys muddled up. That was probably the highlight of that match for most of the Somerset players.

On a grim, grey final afternoon I was batting with Roebuck, trying to save the game. In came Courtney Walsh; the ball leapt from nowhere and crushed my left knuckle. The pain was excruciating as I experienced the worst – and last – injury of my career. I retired hurt immediately. And so four days ahead of schedule I had withdrawn from the professional game after sixteen years on the Somerset staff. Obviously I missed the last match of the season at Taunton, which was, in hindsight, no hardship. It rained for the last two and a half days.

A few days later with my left hand in plaster I was driven up to Taunton for a little presentation. The players had had a whip round and they gave me a present. It was a rocking chair.

THIRTEEN

THE OBSERVER

IT WAS ON WEDNESDAY, 16 August 1989 that I first became a media tart. I was at Southampton for the semi-final of the Nat-West Trophy between Hampshire and Middlesex and I was there to work for BBC radio, which I would do frequently over the next three decades, and for BBC TV, which would be a very rare occurrence. More importantly I had arranged to meet the magnificently bearded David Hunn, who was, briefly, the sports editor of the *Observer*.

My clearest memory of that day is sitting alongside Richie Benaud in the commentary box. As a six-year-old I had watched him bowling in grainy black and white on the 1961 Ashes tour and I had listened to him frequently on television. I also remember some charity match at Lord's, which was being televised, and being so impressed when Benaud was bowling to Denis Compton. He was miked up and he informed his viewers, 'We're just about to go off air as it's time for the news. But before you go I'll let you have one last look at the famous Compton sweep shot,' whereupon he pitched the ball an inch or two outside leg-stump on the appropriate length and Compton duly swept as only Compton could.

I had met Benaud a few times but to broadcast with him felt very dreamy. Naturally I was open to any words of wisdom. I waited patiently and he did not disappoint. The microphones in the TV box were big, fluffy and yellow, a similar size, shape and colour to a tennis ball. Richie spoke: 'I think you'll find that if you have the tip of your nose just touching the microphone, you'll be in about the right place.' Obviously I've never forgotten that handy hint even though microphones have changed a bit over the years.

Beyond that I don't remember much. Middlesex won a close game by three runs and I left the ground having committed myself to working for the *Observer* as their cricket correspondent from 1 January 1990. This was reported in the paper at the weekend. Apparently I 'broke the news to stunned county colleagues' on the Saturday night. 'Marks, whose trenchant and witty column has captivated *Observer* readers for two seasons, has chosen to seek (and gained) release from his two-year captaincy contract with Somerset to take up one of the most prized jobs in journalism.' David Hunn introduced me as 'a man who is more Yorick than Prince' – I'm still trying to work out if that was a compliment. In other parts of the paper there were the words of legendary figures of Fleet Street like Peter Dobereiner, Hugh McIlvanney, Richard Baerlein and Peter Corrigan. I wrote a little piece myself: 'Up until now I have always regarded playing the game to be far more demanding than writing about it. I wonder how quickly I'll change my mind.'

So how did it come to this? The first time that I was paid for writing anything was on the Ashes tour of 1982/3 after I had been asked by Christopher Martin-Jenkins to write a column, 'From the Dressing Room', for *The Cricketer* magazine. This column continued on all three of my England tours and during the English summer I would contribute to the magazine whenever CMJ asked.

During the eighties I also cobbled together a cheery 'scrapbook' about Somerset when they were winning their trophies; a book on England's tour of India in 1984/5 entitled *Marks Out of XI*, a rather better title than the first suggestion, *View from the Balcony*; and I wrote a coaching guide for the TCCB which contained pencil drawings of promising teenagers Mike Atherton and Mark Ramprakash, demonstrating all the shots then known to cricketers (a few more have been added since then) as well as a many fine pictures of my interviewees in action.

Along with my long-standing friend Robin Drake, I also produced a game book (sadly just before the advent of computers taking over the world), in which the reader was the captain of England for the day at Lord's and confronted with choices that would determine the outcome of a match against the Rest of the World. More in the manner of Herodotus rather than Thucydides – according to my longstanding classics guru from Oxford days, John Claughton – I wrote an illustrated history of the game with vital statistics from Bill Frindall. Note how most of these publications shrewdly involved quite a lot of photographs. None of these undertakings made me very rich but they were obviously invaluable practice for the magnum opus you are currently holding – despite a little gap of about thirty years.

In 1988, when Scyld Berry had been the cricket correspondent of the *Observer* for a decade, I was asked to write a weekly player's column throughout the summer. Bob Low was the sports editor then and a constant source of encouragement, as was Scyld. The following year Scyld decided to leave the *Observer* to join the *Sunday Correspondent*, a new venture that created much fine copy but few sales. So there was a vacancy. I was told that CMJ, then the BBC's cricket correspondent, had expressed an interest but they thought him 'unsound on South Africa'. He soon ended up at the *Telegraph* instead. Hunn offered the job to me.

This had not been part of some grand plan, but the offer was flattering and hard to resist. I was only thirty-four and had had to wait a long time to become the proper captain of Somerset. Amid the usual exasperations I was still enjoying that challenge. I had asked Hunn whether it was possible to keep the post warm to allow me another year at Somerset. In the politest of ways – he was a very polite man – he explained that this was not an option.

It was clearly an appealing post. Moreover, I had been at Somerset long enough to recognize the perils of coming to the end of one's career in the county game. I have seen the most measured of men leave professional cricket feeling embittered, in part because the future seemed so much less exciting than the present. Too few county cricketers depart on their own terms, and not many of them are sound judges of their own worth at the end of their careers. By definition a professional sportsman tends to think, 'Of course I can still do it.'

I'm not really an Edith Piaf type. I like the song but don't go along with the sentiments. I've had a few regrets but I have never had any qualms about the decision to retire in 1989. I had been employed by Somerset for sixteen years. Would one or two more have made any difference? I was unlikely to get any better as a cricketer. Moreover there was every sign that the *Observer* was going to be a civilized, sympathetic employer, which turned out to be the case. And this writing business did not seem too difficult – it never does when it is little more than a hobby.

I understand now how much of a greenhorn I was and can appreciate how the odd career journalist might have resented my easy elevation. I had a few months at home to recover from the crushed knuckle from the last ball I received in first-class cricket from Courtney Walsh, and to prepare for the new career. I remember receiving a delightful letter from David Hunn in his spidery handwriting in which he tried to outline the basics of a match report. I'd never written one and the most taxing place to start would be in the Caribbean because of the time difference. The Queen's Park Oval in Trinidad was to be my first venue as a cricket correspondent and the first-edition piece would have to be delivered around lunchtime, while the last one would have to go the moment that play had finished for the day. 'It's probably a good idea to mention the score somewhere in the first two or three paragraphs,' wrote Hunn.

So I pitched up in Trinidad in February 1990 with my shorts, my floppy hat, a pad and a pencil and not much else, which provoked some knowing smiles from my new colleagues. There were a few portable computers around, known as Tandys, precursors to today's swish laptops, but at this stage one of those would only have complicated matters for such a novice.

I may not have looked like a zealous newshound yearning to make an impact on my first day in harness, and in any case the attire for cricket journalists in the Caribbean could never be described as business-like. The press box in Jamaica a decade later was a large tent with trestle tables and I meandered in for my first appearance of the tour, a little later than my colleagues, dressed in shorts, a straw hat and sunglasses. A proper, hard-nosed journalist, David Facey, deputizing for the *Mail*, looked over and blurted out, 'All right, who's going to tell this bloody wink [a not so affectionate term for the English cricket fan on tour] to get out of our press box?' This prompted me to adapt the Colin Cowdrey response to Jeff Thomson, in the Perth Test of 1974 when he had been sent out there as an emergency replacement. I thrust out my hand with a 'I don't believe we've met before. Vic Marks of the *Observer*.' Facey smiled but was not quite as crestfallen as I'd hoped.

The West Indies is not the simplest venue to start as a cricket correspondent. Just about the most hazardous of operations in the job is to report a one-day international in the Caribbean with the outcome impossible to predict as the match reaches its climax. I was cheerfully oblivious to this and a bit disappointed when it rained in Port of Spain on 17 February 1990, the day of the first ODI of the tour.

The following Saturday was the first day of the first Test at Sabina Park in Kingston, which, against all the odds, England would go on to win. The West Indies were cruising at the end of the first session with the surprising run-out of Gordon Greenidge by Devon Malcolm their only setback. So for the first edition at lunchtime I informed my reader about the same old story of West Indian domination and the folly of omitting Eddie Hemmings. Two editions later at the close of play West Indies were 164 all out and England were 80–2. So here was my first experience of frantic rewriting followed by the painstaking delivery of the copy via a telephone, shared with the *Daily Star*, upon which one had to dial about twenty-five numbers to get through to the unfortunate incredibly patient copytaker.

The bonus was that for the next four days of the Test, in between popping into the *TMS* box, I was essentially a spectator of a memorable game, an experience to be savoured alongside my fellow rookie, Tim de Lisle of the *Independent on Sunday*. In our innocence we defied the convention. When England took another wicket we leapt out of our seats cheering jubilantly – at least we did a couple of times before it was really quite bluntly explained to us by one or two of our senior colleagues that this was no way to behave in a press box.

Even so we were still very excited when England won by nine wickets on the final day. We trotted off to a press conference, where to my consternation I soon found myself listening to John Thicknesse, a doyen of the *Evening Standard*, asking Micky Stewart, the team's manager/coach, about the alignment of England's slip cordon. In the wake of such a brilliant victory this seemed such a ridiculous question and I soon heard myself remonstrating with Thicknesse (I had not understood that he was gathering material for distant columns). After such an epic victory how could he possibly be concerned by such minutiae as the composition of the bleeding slip cordon? 'If I'd wanted you to answer the question I would have addressed it to you, not Micky,' he pronounced frostily – and with a touch of venom. And I shut up. Another lesson learnt.

The following Saturday we were still in Jamaica and de Lisle and I, the novice 'fans' of the press corps, got our comeuppance. This was the day of the second ODI and this time it did not rain. England scored 214–8 from their fifty overs, surely not enough to prevail even in those days. In reply the West Indies at one point were 158–3 with Richie Richardson in control. So de Lisle and I were writing furiously to meet our final deadline and both of us were hailing – from the very first paragraph to the last – a West Indian victory.

While engrossed in composing our copy England rallied imperceptibly; a few wickets fell and, although Richardson remained, the West Indies' innings lost its momentum. So it transpired that when Angus Fraser was running up to bowl the last ball of the match to Ian Bishop the West Indies needed two runs to tie and three to win. If they failed to manage that England would record a famous victory and the flowing prose destined for the *Observer* and the *Independent on Sunday* would make no sense whatever. De Lisle and I watched, helpless and in horror. Fraser ran in and delivered; Bishop swung and the ball fizzed beyond the long-off boundary for four. Both of us leapt out of our seats and cheered with relief – at a West Indian victory this time. Our copy would make some sense after all and that was what really mattered to us.

It was an eventful Test series, in which England did much better than anticipated. They lost 2–1 but only after unexpected rain, West Indian time-wasting and a broken finger for Graham Gooch (mind you, we were assured it was only 'bruised' on the final afternoon) denied England a second victory in Trinidad. There was controversy in Barbados where Viv Richards' celebration of the dismissal of Rob Bailey – who was given out by umpire Lloyd Barker, caught down the leg-side – spilled over to the rest day in Antigua when Jim Lawton, then of the *Daily Express*, tracked Viv down and an ill-tempered conversation ensued. The following day, a Saturday and therefore the important one for a Sunday correspondent, Viv was so displeased when he discovered what Lawton had written that he marched into the cramped press box at the St John's Recreation Ground five minutes before the match was due to restart with the West Indies in the field.

Viv, sweating profusely, confronted Lawton. He spoke quietly but somehow this made his words all the more menacing. The rest of us were looking on silently at this unusual chain of events as Richards made his displeasure known. By now the umpires were out in the middle and they were followed by a somewhat bewildered West Indian team, who were also puzzled about the whereabouts of their captain. At this point Matthew Engel said to me, 'You know him. Say something.' I was never inclined to interrupt Viv when he was angry but I think I exclaimed, 'Viv, they're out there,' a reference to the umpires putting the bails on, which were also the words that often constituted a team talk at Somerset unless it was an especially important match. This did not appear to have any immediate effect. Even so Richards soon terminated his conversation, before rejoining his team in the field.

After he left the press box there was a sort of collective exhalation of breath and everyone suddenly found their tongues. About now I remembered it was Saturday. I was going to have to write about this. I turned around to Scyld Berry, so much more experienced if not much older, and obviously my eyes were pleading for some guidance. 'Don't lead on the cricket,' he said. I cannot remember what I wrote but I'm pretty sure it was less scathing about Richards, with whom I shared a dressing room for a decade or so, than the other contributions from the press box.

Somehow I survived that first tour despite my naivety. I would never cheer in a press box again; I seldom bowled in the nets again to the England players, which I did quite happily on that trip (not that it would have helped them greatly), and that incident in the press box in Antigua demonstrated that it might not always be possible to be the players' friend, even if that was my inclination.

My new colleagues were welcoming. The senior citizens at that time included John Woodcock, who was no longer the *Times* correspondent, but would pop up at vital moments of a tour to everyone's delight. He would often be found in a deckchair at one end of the ground under a straw hat with his notepad. He never succumbed to the pack mentality. He would watch the game and write about it, effortlessly plucking out a striking phrase and a historical reference beyond everyone else, and he never suffered from the insecurity that always seeks the opinion of others in the press box before committing to print.

I would also bump into Woodcock at board meetings of *The Cricketer* magazine since I had recently been invited, no doubt at the prompting of CMJ, to provide some 'fresh blood' on this august panel. The owner of *The Cricketer* at the time was Ben Brockle-hurst, an old amateur captain of Somerset in the early fifties (when they usually came bottom) and a noted bon viveur, who bought the magazine in 1972 and somehow managed to make it profitable. The board meetings were surreal and entertaining. When I joined, the members of that board not only included Woodcock but also Colin Cowdrey, Jim Swanton, Brian Johnston and Michael Mellu-ish. No one seemed to be too interested in the balance sheets and soon we might easily be discussing Frank Woolley batting at Can-terbury. Then came the realization that Swanton had actually seen Woolley batting at Canterbury and off they would all go down a wonderful cricketing cul-de-sac, which was always far more inter-esting than a comparison, usually from Ben's son, Tim, of the sales figures in Todmorden and Tonbridge.

Swanton was renowned (quite rightly) for his pomposity but by the time he had reached his eighties he was, I think, prepared to parody himself now and again. If pomposity was anticipated he was quite happy to deliver it but he was also encouraging to young writers. It was in this vein and with a twinkle in his eye that he said to me at the end of one meeting, 'Whatever are you doing writing for that pinko rag?' by which he meant the *Observer*.

Like Woodcock, Robin Marlar, the former Sussex captain, would dip into tours as the *Sunday Times* correspondent. Once a fine off-spinner for Sussex, he was famously dismissed as a night-watchman, stumped for 6 – off the second ball he faced. He did not think much of the invitation to fulfil that role and through-out his life he has never been a man who seems overburdened by self-doubt or inclined to keep his opinions to himself. Robin tended to commute to the West Indies in his latter days with the *Sunday Times*; indeed he often commuted to Lord's from his place in France during the English summer – 'By the way, who won that Test match last week?' he might ask on a Saturday morning.

He was incapable of writing a dull or unprovocative paragraph. A regular function of the Sunday paper correspondent in those days was to pontificate about the selection of the Test team, which would be announced on Sunday morning. Robin had a foolproof system of dealing with this undertaking. He did not sink to inform-ing his readers of a likely eleven; instead he shared the team that he would pick. Very often this included only three or four players who would actually be chosen by the selectors for the forthcoming match. Thus Robin's pontifications could never be proven wrong.

When he was president of the MCC in 2005/6 Marlar became agitated ,while watching a game at the Parks, at the volume of chat-ter and mindless encouragement on the field in between every delivery. So he strode out on to the pitch at the end of an over and told everyone to shut up. Perhaps more significantly in his MCC role Marlar did much to advance the rise of cricket in Afghani-stan and it was thanks to him that Hamid Hassan and Mohammed Nabi, early stalwarts of Afghan cricket, came over to England to enhance their game.

A fellow pupil alongside Marlar at Harrow in the 1940s was John Thicknesse, who had put me in my place so effortlessly at Sabina Park. He was seldom riddled with uncertainty either during his thirty years as the *Evening Standard*'s cricket correspondent. By the time I joined the pack he was an accomplished, canny tourist.

In India, for example, in the days when cigarette smoking was widespread in the press corps and everywhere else, John always took the precaution of buying a cheap local packet upon arrival; he would empty the contents and replace them with the treasured duty free cigarettes of much higher quality that he had purchased at Heathrow Airport. In those days it was appropriate to 'flash the ash' whenever lighting up but no one ever took any of John's 'Indian' cigarettes.

He was a keen golfer and on one tour of India he spent hours playing backgammon with Mike Gatting. In both pursuits he was extremely competitive and not averse to the odd argument. And he could be formidable at press conferences. Before England's tour to India in 1992 he challenged the chairman of selectors, Ted Dexter, about the controversial omission of David Gower. 'How is it, Ted, that you are setting off for India without a single Test-quality left-hander in your squad?' Dexter spotted a rare half-volley from Thicknesse and with a gentle, triumphant smile replied, 'Thickers, I think you'll find that Lancashire's Neil Fairbrother is in the squad,' which provoked a firm and immediate response from Thicknesse: 'I said "Test-quality", Ted.'

In the Caribbean Alan Lee was *The Times* correspondent, the most conscientious of newspapermen, who knew even more about racing, a sport to which he returned before his premature death in 2015. Lee formed the Pompous Dining Club, named in a moment of self-mockery, which met with great enthusiasm on Friday nights in the knowledge that the daily correspondents had their day off on the Saturday. Peter Deeley was the unlikely *Telegraph* correspondent, soon to be succeeded by CMJ. He could be grumpy and was, in my eyes at least, a hardened hack, even though he was the one mugged when walking across the Savannah in Port of Spain on that 1990 tour. He explained how at one point in his career he had worked in Vietnam during the war. 'Not that different really,' he said. 'You get on the bus in the morning; you're driven up to the front, take a few notes and then you're transported back to the hotel at the end of the day, where you write up before having a few beers.' I'm not entirely sure Swanton approved of him or his appointment, but he was an effective newsman with a sardonic sense of humour. The other daily broadsheet writers were Mike Selvey of the *Guardian* and Martin Johnson of the *Independent* and they will resurface later, probably on a golf course.

The *Mail* and the *Express* were in the capable hands of Peter Johnson and Pat Gibson, two old hands, elegant writers and endearing companions; both had a sense of humour that was drier than sawdust; they smiled rather than guffawed. There were certainly no guffaws from Johnson in Georgetown, Guyana, where the facilities were basic and unreliable. It was practically impossible to get a telephone line to the UK, which is the lifeblood of any journalist.

A working telephone was a prized possession on tour and it always seemed to be the case that when Allan Lamb wanted to borrow one to make a social call he would magically get a line, but when Peter Johnson needed a vital conversation with his office the line was always dead. Peter would dial and dial and nothing would happen. Then after days of frustration in Georgetown Johnson eventually got through to his sports desk. 'Peter Johnson,' he said with relief, whereupon the young tyro at the other end paused to check something with a colleague before blurting, 'No, he's not here; he's in the Caribbean at the moment,' and slammed the phone down. No further contact was possible, nor was a smile from Johnson.

Pat Gibson, despite the odd scowl, is a kindly, warm-hearted man, who was something of a mentor to new recruits to the press corps. When Mike Selvey began at the *Guardian* Pat was a ready source of sound guidance to a new correspondent. And the same applied when I joined the *Observer*, though that did not preclude him marching up and down hotel corridors late at night in Australia, where you had hours to file your copy, in search of the perfect intro, which he would eventually find.

Among the red-top correspondents there were Ian Todd and Chris Lander, two of the most engaging men imaginable, who had both cut their teeth as journalists in Bristol. Todd looked as if he must belong to the *Daily Telegraph* rather than the *Sun*. Meanwhile in the Caribbean Lander would inevitably find himself in a little swimming pool between the stands, which became a popular destination for the growing numbers of punters from the UK. Surrounded by skimpy bikinis and fortified by a rum punch he would write a distinctive colour piece from there. Both Todd and Lander had the capacity to be charming and ruthless simultaneously, which helped make them so good at their jobs.

The Sunday paper men – and there were quite a few of us then – were known as 'The Bucket and Spade boys' since there was not much for us to do – apart from polish the features (for the broadsheets) or dig out the exclusives (for the tabloids) – until Saturday came along. From the *News of the World* there was David Norrie and from the *Mail on Sunday* Peter Hayter, son of the famous Reg, who was once the agent of Denis Compton and Ian Botham as well as the founder of a press agency that spawned dozens of notable sports journalists. Both Norrie and the young Hayter had the capacity to get alongside the players. It used to amaze me how Graham Gooch, when captain of England, would be the one seeking out Norrie after play, asking, 'What are we up to tonight, Norrers?'

Likewise Peter, who was generally known as 'Reg', was well liked and trusted by the cricketers and he would end up ghosting books for some of them with great skill and sympathy, though not much tea. His work spawned the autobiographies of Botham, Phil Tufnell and Marcus Trescothick. Peter was – and still is – a gifted thespian and his flair would come to the fore at the end-of-tour parties that were usually organized by him and Norrie. Fortunately these were conducted amid a drunken haze so the details of the award ceremonies are impossible to recall. For Norrie and Hayter their job was well done if the rest of the Bucket and Spade boys late on a Saturday night were required to follow up the 'exclusives' that they had just revealed in their papers.

So I was on the road as a cricket correspondent though it still jarred a little whenever I wrote 'journalist' on immigration forms around the world. Any progress was achieved in a similar manner to my cricketing career, trusting more in trial and error rather than meticulous training and preparation. As a Sunday journalist there was ample scope to agonize interminably over a feature, though whether this did much good I'm not so sure. It was around this time that Gary Lineker joined the *Observer* with even less experience than me, and it was impressive to hear that during his brief time there he wrote every word of his columns and that it might take him up to ten hours to do so. Over the years I may not have got any better, but I certainly became quicker, which was a necessity when, around 2007, the role of *Observer* cricket correspondent had to be combined with writing on a daily basis for the *Guardian*. It was only then that I properly realized what a gloriously leisurely job being a pure Sunday correspondent had been. The one Bucket and Spade boy to survive is Simon Wilde of the *Sunday Times*, and ironically he was always the most industrious of the lot. Sometimes on tour we had to chastise him for opening his laptop on a Wednesday – though I noticed that on England's tour of Sri Lanka in 2018 he had been dragooned to write some pieces for *The Times*. The rest of us have long since been rumbled or have moved on.

At least I came to understand the basics soon enough, which are to get it there on time at about the right length. I soon concluded that this was not an easy profession for perfectionists (phew! That's OK, then) because when the appointed hour arrives you have to press 'Send' (having graduated to a laptop), despite the recognition that the prose or the opinions hastily assembled may be far from flawless. Of course, the great ones often touch perfection as well and they never rest. At the *Observer* Hugh McIlvanney was king when I joined and I would hear how he would sometimes ring the office after midnight on Saturday just as the last edition was leaving with a vital request to enhance his piece. 'Could you make sure to change "late spring" to "early summer"?'

McIlvanney was one of several grand characters who would sometimes inhabit the *Observer*'s office in those early days and attend boozy lunches to celebrate something, which I occasionally attended. Peter Dobereiner, I discovered, had been a regular contributor to *That Was The Week That Was*, the satirical programme of the sixties; Arthur Hopcraft, author of the *The Football Man*, also adapted John Le Carré's *Tinker Tailor Soldier Spy* for the BBC; and Colin Welland, an occasional contributor to the *Observer*, wrote the screenplay for the Oscar-winning *Chariots of Fire*. Today's journalists rarely have the time or space for such hinterlands.

Over the years I've seldom spent much time in the office on the sports desk so what they do there as they speed the paper on its way remains something of a mystery. Most of the communication with editors has been over the phone or, more recently, via email (not to mention Gchat) rather than face to face. But I've been fortunate to work for some excellent editors, who would sometimes take the time to try to improve the piece I had just sent them. Early on Simon Redfern, a cheery deputy sports editor at the *Observer*, had the good grace to point out that beginning a column with the words 'Last Wednesday' might not be the best way to draw the readers in. Occasionally a fruitful conversation with a good editor might begin with a 'I really enjoyed the piece on... but I was just wondering whether it might be even better if...' and he was nearly always right.

I remember Simon Kelner, one of my earlier sports editors who would go on to become editor of the *Independent*, taking the time to do that (this must be quite a long way back because I was writing a piece about Derek Pringle at the time). Kelner was always brimful of ideas and determined to ensure that he spent every penny of his budget plus a few more. Late one Tuesday evening in November 1991 he rang up telling me I should pack my bags for Calcutta. The hastily arranged return of South Africa to the international game after their twenty-two-year exile was about to take place there. This provoked mixed feelings in the Marks household; it coincided with the fourth birthday party of my youngest daughter, Rosie, and I knew such a trip at short notice would be beset by many logistical obstacles. I checked the dates and saw that the match in Calcutta was scheduled for Sunday not Saturday, which was hardly ideal for a Sunday paper, a fact I passed on to Kelner as dolefully as possible. 'That doesn't matter,' he said. 'Get out there and preview it and then write something about it for the following weekend.' And so off I went with very few other English journalists. Jonathan Agnew was there, so too Matthew Engel, I think.

After the first plane ever to fly from South Africa to India had landed in Calcutta, the streets from the airport to the hotel were lined with thousands of well-wishers waving banners celebrating the arrival of the South African cricket team, who had been pariahs just months before. On the Sunday, Eden Gardens was jam-packed and the president of the Bengal Cricket Association, Jagmohan Dalmiya, claimed that the largest crowd ever at a cricket match had gathered for this historic event. It was a grand, emotional spectacle, especially for the South African cricketers, who were understandably startled by the enormity of their sudden return to the fold. Maybe this, coupled with a 9 a.m. start on a smoggy Calcutta morning, contributed to a lacklustre display with the bat. Captained by Clive Rice and with my recent Somerset colleague, Jimmy Cook, as their opening batsman, South Africa limped to 177–8. They were all making their international debuts with the exception of Kepler Wessels, whose loyalties had by now switched back from Australia. India knocked off the runs with more than six overs to spare and their three-wicket margin of victory flattered South Africa.

It had been a forgettable match, but an unforgettable occasion. So it was bewildering and disappointing when returning to the bar of the Grand Hotel to hear several of the South African journalists agonising over their beers, 'If only so-and-so had held that catch we would have won that game.' Somehow on this particular day this did not seem to be the point of it all. And then South Africa's team manager, Ali Bacher, getting into the swing of the modern international game right from the start, made an 'informal protest' about the state of the ball when his team was batting since he believed it had been gouged to encourage swing, an odd intervention to make on the day South Africa had been offered the hand of friendship by India after their exile.

South Africans obviously took their sport very seriously and this was highlighted again three months later after their cricket team had been parachuted into the 1992 World Cup in Australasia, which added welcome spice to that tournament. In Auckland on 29 February I found myself at Eden Park covering the New Zealand–South Africa game. Alongside me was one of Kelner's enterprising, short-term signings, Donald Woods. This was *the* Donald Woods, the famous journalist, anti-apartheid activist and friend of Steve Biko, who was going to write a few pieces for the *Observer*. I was thrilled – and gobsmacked – to have him there, not exactly as my 'quotes man' but happy to sit beside me and write about the cricket.

It soon became apparent that he was both heroic campaigner and sports fanatic. Before long Woods rose from his chair in our lofty press box and pointed to a spot of turf at Eden Park. 'It was just there,' he bellowed. 'Just there. That's where that Welsh referee [Clive Norling] gave that terrible penalty against us.' The ensuing three points from Allan Hewson's kick in the ninth minute of extra time allowed the All Blacks victory in the epic series of 1981, which was stubbornly completed despite being punctuated by constant anti-apartheid demonstrations. I was surprised by this intervention from Woods, who proved to be a delightful, if fleeting, colleague. I don't suppose he was best pleased a month later when South Africa were denied a chance of making the final of the World Cup at the first attempt by the preposterous rain rule, dreamt up by Richie Benaud, which suddenly left Kepler Wessels' side needing 22 runs from one ball in their semi-final against England in Sydney.

A more regular new colleague was also a joy to work alongside. Around this time Kelner decided to enlist the services of Mike Brearley for home Test matches. He had been writing for the *Sunday Times* but Kelner offered him a handsome wage by the standards of 1993. As Mike has gently reminded me a few times over the years, that figure did not increase by a penny during the two decades that he embellished the *Observer*.

I had played against Mike several times, but had never been captained by him. We all knew he was clever 'with a degree in people' according to the Australian fast bowler, Rodney Hogg; I also recognized that he was a tough opponent. Batting against Middlesex I was inevitably aware of his presence at first slip. Once at Lord's I hit a delivery from Mike Gatting for four square of the wicket on the offside and I recall the Middlesex captain expressing his disgust: 'Oh come on, Gatt. You know he's only got one shot.' There were also times when I could hear him chastising Middlesex's West Indian fast bowler, Wayne Daniel, for bowling too full. Mike later explained to me how the *Sun* newspaper had put up a substantial prize for the bowler who hit the stumps most often throughout the season and Daniel decided he was going to win it. By and large this was good news for wary batsmen since Daniel kept pitching the ball up so that he could hit those stumps. This was a tactic that rarely pleased Brearley. He wanted more bouncers.

I would have loved to have played under his leadership. It was fascinating to sit beside him in the press box and witness him reading the game, querying a bowling change here or a fielding position there. Occasionally some of his old England colleagues might wander by – Ian Botham, David Gower, Geoff Miller, Bob Willis, Mike Hendrick or Derek Randall – and the warmth of their greetings was striking. Brearley may have been an unusual sportsman with his degrees and his subsequent profession as a psychoanalyst yet he always enjoyed the company of earthier cricketers – and the feeling was obviously mutual. He never patronized them and always sought and valued the opinions of a Botham or a Willis; sometimes he would even take their advice.

Contrary to what one might imagine, Brearley also had easy relationships with his old Aussie adversaries like Rod Marsh and Dennis Lillee, especially after retirement. I was present at one wonderful impromptu dinner in Perth on an Ashes tour with this trio plus John Inverarity comprising the old cricketers, and I marvelled how much they all enjoyed each other's company with just the odd smiling recollection of times past. At the end of the evening, brilliantly organized by Lillee, there were the two iconic old West Aussies in a minibus taking us back to the city centre singing innocent old songs together along the way. Brears and I, perhaps to our mild surprise, merrily joined in.

Mike had mellowed by the time he occupied his seat in the press box for half a dozen Saturdays a season. His views, while generously expressed, always carried weight – they still do – but he could still become animated. The Ashes Test at the Oval in 1997 was a case in point. It was one of those delicious low-scoring matches, which left Australia, who had already won the series, needing 124 to win, a target not so different to the one at Headingley sixteen years earlier. The game was racing to a conclusion on Saturday afternoon at about the time that the first edition of the *Observer* was going to press. Mike had already delivered his column – he liked to file early if possible – but it was now clear that his piece was rapidly becoming out of date.

So he picked up the phone in a state of some excitement (he still likes beating Australia). He rose out of his chair while staring at the drama unfolding out on the field and began to extemporize at ever-increasing volume down the phone to a startled copytaker. He attracted quite an audience in the press box at this epic performance, which must have produced some sparkling copy. England won by 19 runs – as opposed to 18 in 1981 – and against his instincts Mike Atherton was therefore persuaded to continue as captain for the winter tour to the Caribbean.

Fortunately Mike (Brearley, not Atherton, who is always there) still pops into the press box sporadically though sadly no longer writing for the *Observer* (perhaps he finally got that rise from *The Times*) and has become a frequent presence at Lord's, where he has been president of the MCC as well as chairman of the World Cricket Committee. He has mellowed so much that he does not even mind wearing a tie at Lord's now and again. I'm very grateful to Simon Kelner for enlisting him all those years ago.

Brian Oliver, who came to the *Observer* from the *Daily Telegraph* in 1998, was the sports editor for thirteen years. On the sports desk he was known as 'The Gaffer' but, as with Alec Stewart, I stuck to his Christian name since I was still an infrequent visitor to the office. There they clearly loved working with him; he had a curious, quirky mind, bags of experience and enthusiasm and an easy manner. It was hard to say 'No' whenever Brian or his deputy, and an old pupil of mine from Blundell's, Oliver 'Eggy' Owen, sent me off on non-cricketing jobs – though they never managed to persuade me, as was the case with Claire Tolley of the *Guardian*, to report upon Tom Daley at a diving competition at Plymouth ('I promise you, it's nothing to do with where you live'). Daley is bound to know more about cricket than I do about diving.

Geography may have played a part when Brian, an expert on non-league football among many other things, asked me to report on Yeovil Town just as they were about to get promoted to the Football League for the first time in 2003. I mentioned to Brian that I grew up in south Somerset and that as a kid I had very occasionally watched Yeovil play in the old Southern League. So off I went to Huish Park; I had a chat with their engaging manager, Gary Johnson, an enthusiastic cricketer I discovered, who had come across the young Gatting in his youth. And I duly filed my piece on the Saturday. On the Sunday I opened my *Observer* to check that all was well and was taken aback and amused at the byline: 'Lifelong Glovers' fan, Vic Marks, returns to Yeovil Town'.

Brian also enlisted me to do some rugby. I became quite a regular at the Millennium Stadium for a while, and in 2007 I went to Croke Park in Dublin to witness England's historic visit to the stadium where there had been a terrible massacre in 1920 by a detachment of 'Black and Tan' auxiliaries intent on exacting revenge upon the IRA. There was much nervous speculation about what would happen when the National Anthem was played. In fact there was a respectful silence after which the Irish thrashed England 43–13 at the traditional home of Gaelic games. On the walk back to the hotel Pat Collins of the *Mail on Sunday* gave me a wonderful history lesson via the bullet holes still visible on some of the buildings of central Dublin.

On that occasion I think I was there as Eddie Butler's quotes man, but there were also times when I would pitch up at an international with the task of giving marks out of ten – plus a few pithy observations – for all thirty players on the pitch. I was not well qualified for this role. How was I, a cowardly schoolboy scrum-half, supposed to assess the performance of an English prop forward, who, as far as I could see, did not touch the ball for half an hour? I sought advice from Butler, a Welsh captain, a British Lion and a back-row forward. 'Don't worry,' he said, ' I haven't got a bloody clue what they do up there either. As a rule of thumb I reckon if they're getting penalized they must be doing something right.' So the prop forwards usually got a minimum of 5/10 for their selfless, unseen industry.

I remain more reliable on cricket even though my news sense has always been as sharp as a marshmallow. Ali Martin, a proper newsman, who has been covering cricket at the *Guardian* since 2015, came up with a plan to cope with this problem when I took over from Mike Selvey as the correspondent. 'You tell me what's happening on the pitch. And I'll tell you what's happening off it,' he said. I approve of this system and am constantly grateful to Ali for putting it into operation.

By the way, Matthew Hancock, once the *Observer* sports editor but now performing that function for the *Guardian* as well, is also a civilized man to work for as are his colleagues, who often seem to eke out more words from me than had been my intention. I do not mention this purely out of duty or self-preservation; there is a grain of truth there as well. Matthew began his journalistic career working for *Wisden Almanack* when Matthew Engel was the editor. He discussed the possibility of taking up this post with Engel on the terraces of Hereford United football club, an even more unlikely venue than the old cricket ground in Southampton for a job interview.

FOURTEEN

TEST MATCH SPECIAL (THEN)

FOR THIRTY YEARS, WRITING for the *Observer* and more recently the *Guardian* has been my 'proper' job. Sometimes there is the assumption among that little chunk of the population unfamiliar with the *Observer* or the *Guardian* that the BBC has been my main employer because I have seemed more visible – or audible, to be more precise – when appearing on *TMS*. Working on radio has been a delight and a wonderful bonus, but it has always been a freelance activity, which my main employers have been happy for me to pursue. It has never been my main job and on most days it does not feel like a job at all.

I first appeared on the programme in Delhi on 17 December 1984 as an emergency replacement. England were playing the second Test match against India and, as ever, I was in the touring party but not in the team. On the fifth day the match was bubbling up nicely. India collapsed dramatically in their second innings, leaving England with a modest victory target of 125 and an unexpected chance to level the series on the final afternoon.

It was at this point that Peter Baxter, the producer of *TMS*, popped his head into the England dressing room. In those days

– and on that tour in particular – it was still possible for a member of the media to be welcomed into the dressing room during a match. I was there alongside our assistant manager, Norman Gifford, who had just filled his pipe in anticipation of the climax of the Test (another thing that would not be possible today). 'I need a summarizer now,' said Baxter. 'Anyone will do.' So I happily volunteered.

Baxter became used to dealing with crises in the sub-continent but these usually related to the loss of the line rather than the loss of his summarizers. Over the years I occasionally saw his serene nature severely challenged in India. In Calcutta on a subsequent tour there was a commentary box populated with delightful women, designated to provide much-needed technical assistance to the BBC. Unfortunately none of them spoke a word of English and I retain the picture of Peter's face rapidly acquiring the hue of a beetroot as he bellowed hopelessly in their direction, 'London. Get me London.' Eventually after much exasperation we somehow got London and Peter was soon relaxed again. Later, with everything going mysteriously well he pointed to a solitary, frayed, seemingly random bit of wire on the floor, which looked as if it could snap at any moment. 'See that wire,' he explained. 'That's our connection to London.'

But on this occasion in Delhi Baxter's problem stemmed from a shortage of manpower. Neither of his summarizers was available. Before the match Abbas Ali Baig, the most urbane of former Indian cricketers, who had also played for Oxford University and Somerset, casually announced that he had to attend a wedding during the match. However, he may have omitted to mention to Peter that Indian weddings can last for two or three days. He was nowhere to be seen. The other summarizer was Mike Selvey, not yet the *Guardian*'s correspondent, who was in India as a free-lance journalist, having just retired as a professional cricketer the previous September. He had suddenly been afflicted by stomach cramps, which left him no option but to exit sharply, groaning, and to head for the sanctuary of his hotel room.

So I sat alongside Tony Lewis, a former England captain in India on the 1972/3 tour, and Mike Carey of the *Daily Telegraph* in the commentary box as they described the action in the final session of the Test when England knocked off the runs, losing just two wickets along the way. It was not a bad place to witness a famous victory. I didn't even have to resort to a 'David [Gower]will be a little disappointed with that shot.' Our captain was not even required to bat.

Three of us in the England squad must have made an impression on Baxter on that tour, possibly the last one when the media and the players were happily living in one another's pockets: Graeme Fowler, who played in all the Tests and hit that double century in Madras in his penultimate match for England; Jonathan Agnew, who came out in the middle of the tour as a replacement for the injured Paul Allott, and me. We would all spend many happy hours in Baxter's commentary boxes in the years to come. While we were still playing Peter enlisted us for 'County Talk', a recorded half-hour of chat that was broadcast in one of the intervals during a Test match. We would assemble at the appointed hour at various county grounds with our COOBEs – a box that somehow allows you to broadcast; plug it in at some clandestine point known only to the BBC and, hey presto, one could record a conversation with the others (on a good day). Once we were all in place with the machinery working Peter would host a discussion about burning issues of the day in county cricket.

In 1992 Baxter persuaded his bosses to appoint Agnew as the new BBC cricket correspondent, replacing Christopher Martin-Jenkins, who had just joined the *Daily Telegraph*. Jonathan was probably the least experienced candidate – though David Gower, who was also interested in the post, had not done much broadcasting at the time – but undoubtedly the best one as the years have proven. At the time Agnew's appointment, which seems so obviously a good idea now, was a bold decision. Baxter used Graeme Fowler as a summarizer after his retirement from first-class cricket in 1994 when his commitments coaching at Durham University and broadcasting with Sky allowed. And, from 1990 onwards, he employed me, almost always as a summarizer (I did have one Caribbean tour in 1994 as a commentator but was seldom asked to fulfil that role again, and I guess there may have been a reason for that). And for that I'm extremely grateful.

Apart from those rare occasions when the connection was down or his commentators had not turned up on time, Bartex, as he was known, oversaw a most relaxed and civilized commentary box. Requests to work on *TMS* sounded more like an invitation to supper. 'Would you care to join us at Trent Bridge?' No one declined. Why would you unless far more lucrative offers came from the TV broadcasters? Bartex did not overwhelm a new recruit with an avalanche of advice and it was a very rare occasion when he said anything into your earphones when on air. He wanted his broadcasters to be relaxed and his summarizers to engage in an easy conversation with the commentators. So he trusted them to get on with it. It was an excellent formula and one that Adam Mountford, his successor, has tried to maintain (and it is fair to say that Geoffrey Boycott, for example, does not invite too much production). *TMS* works better when it is off the cuff and sounds as if it is coming from a country pub rather than a pulpit or a comedy club.

If problems arose Peter would conclude, 'Ah well, we'll have to busk it' and since he had so many experienced broadcasters at his disposal that usually worked rather well. Whenever a fuse blew (a metaphorical one, that is) he recovered his appearance of calm and composure remarkably quickly. Like a cricket coach beyond the boundary watching his team in action it does not help if the producer is having a tantrum on the sidelines. This seldom happened but there was the odd occasion – like the morning of the epic Australia–South Africa World Cup semi-final at Birmingham in 1999 – when his patience was stretched.

There was a horrible snarl-up around Edgbaston (at least that's our story), which meant that there was no one in his commentary box to start the programme. Bartex was fuming and understandably eager to vent his anger, but this was not possible since he had to begin broadcasting himself, which he was perfectly capable of doing in the most urbane manner. When we arrived, panting and apologetic, I sensed he wanted to let rip at some length, but since we had to start broadcasting immediately he willed himself to exercise restraint. But we could tell he was none too happy.

But for the vast majority of the time we were all very happy in Baxter's commentary box. He produced *TMS* for thirty-four years until his retirement in June 2007. He still pops in occasionally and has not aged a jot since giving up, which may not have been the case if he had kept going for much longer. In his era I would usually spend most of the day in the box, chewing the fat with the others not on air (and occasionally being instructed not to make so much noise), but since then I have been working for the *Guardian* as well as the *Observer* so I tend to go back to the press box in between stints. Moreover, space can become ever more restricted as more people are engaged to work on a Test match.

I had listened to the programme as a kid when Brian Johnston and John Arlott were in their pomp, though my favourite commentator was Alan Gibson, whose career on *TMS* came to an abrupt end at Headingley in 1975. Gibson was a brilliant man with a first in History at Oxford, where he was elected president of the Union. He became, very briefly, a Liberal candidate in the 1959 election and, more permanently, a writer and broadcaster supreme. There were one or two flaws as well, I suppose.

Alan must have possessed a rebellious streak. Like Arlott he liked a drink during the day; unlike Arlott he was not always able to disguise this fact successfully. He received a warning from the BBC hierarchy during the Headingley Test of 1975, which came to a conclusion in unusual circumstances with the pitch being sabotaged by those campaigning to free George Davis, an armed robber from East London – in the end it rained anyway. Gibson's response to this warning was to fill his flask with whisky and water rather than tea and to drink it. This did not go down well and he was never invited to work for *TMS* again.

He continued writing for *The Times* for another decade. As ever, John Woodcock, *The Times* cricket correspondent, explained the situation the best: 'I wrote about the cricket, Alan wrote about a day at the cricket.' On one occasion Woodcock and Gibson somehow turned up at the same ground after an administrative hiccup and Gibson, of course, wrote a wonderful piece about this.

He could sense a character from a distance of a hundred yards, whether it was Colin Dredge, Robin Jackman, Brian Close (obviously) or the GRIP (the Glorious Red-headed Imperturbable Pamela running the bar at Bristol) and, like several other characters, they appeared frequently in his reports. He wrote beautifully and was both funny and insightful.

Fortunately the Parks at Oxford was one of his regular haunts when I was playing there back in the seventies. Towards the end of play he could be heard sending his copy, occasionally irascibly, from the solitary phone available in the pavilion and then once this task was achieved he might cut quite a forlorn figure in one of the smallest beer tents on the first-class cricket circuit. So I would see him there sporadically from 1975 onwards. Sometimes – from my second season at Oxford onwards when I had my battered old VW Beetle there – I would give him a lift to Oxford Station ahead of his tortuous journey home via Didcot (of course), which may explain why he wrote so sympathetically about me thereafter. A decade later when his health was failing he moved to Taunton and in a winter when I was teaching in the town we would meet in the pub run by Roy Marshall (the great Bajan opener who played for Hampshire) for a Friday lunchtime beer. Somehow in this instance meeting a hero was not so disappointing, even though Alan's life had had its fair share of pain and torment.

Over the years I have broadcast with Anthony Gibson, Alan's son, who has a similar facility with words. After working for the National Farmers' Union when he seemed to be the only man making sense during the foot and mouth epidemic, he now commentates – in his so-called retirement – for the BBC on Somerset cricket in between writing erudite books on a variety of subjects. For the cricket lover his collection of Alan's writing, mostly for *The Times*, titled *From Didcot to The Demon*, is a gem.

When I reappeared on *TMS* in 1990 Brian Johnston was the kingpin. It was odd to find myself sitting alongside a man whose commentaries I had listened to when wearing shorts on the farm.

The bonhomie was almost overwhelming. I was welcomed into the box by Johnston as a long-lost friend, albeit a young one, even though I had barely met him before. Alongside him I might find Bill Frindall, Fred Trueman and Trevor Bailey plus the more familiar Christopher Martin-Jenkins. This was surreal.

For all the japes and cakes Johnston was a true pro. He was meticulously prompt, and, unlike some of his earlier colleagues, always sober. Even though he made it sound so effortless he would prepare more conscientiously than he let on – either for his commentaries or his lunchtime interviews with a wide variety of guests. He was also mischievous.

With the advent of Radio 5 Live Jonathan Agnew decided that it would be good fun to get Johnston to do some trails (bogus, of course) for this exciting new station about the summer's Ashes coverage. There would be constant jingles in the background; ten seconds precisely was the requirement and it had to be catchy and quick in a manner far removed from Johnston's Radio 4 style. Peter Baxter did his best to demand several retakes but the ruse fell a little flat because Johnston, the old pro, did it all so brilliantly, fulfilling every demand to the letter. Ten seconds meant ten seconds and Johnson knew exactly when to stop.

Now seeking revenge, Johnston, with assistance from Baxter, set up Jonathan Agnew at Edgbaston in 1993 quite brilliantly by organizing a spoof interview with Fred Trueman and Jack Bannister, supposedly for the prime time Saturday afternoon TV programme, *Grandstand*. At the top of the pavilion Agnew unwittingly did an excellent impersonation of Alan Partridge as Trueman and Bannister were either wonderfully uncooperative or rambling away about Agnew's limitations as a fast bowler. Agnew suspected a set-up but he couldn't be sure so he ploughed on with ever increasing exasperation. Check it all out – including Jonathan's carefully coiffured hair for this special occasion – on YouTube.

While John Arlott had welcomed the *TMS* scorer, Bill Frindall, as his driver many years before, Johnston used him as his straight man, a role that Bill was very happy to perform. Frindall was an aggressive fast bowler in his youth and later an enthusiastic amateur thespian – as was Malcolm Ashton, who succeeded him. So Johnston created the character of 'The Bearded Wonder', who became an integral part of the set-up for four decades.

Bill could not abide inaccuracies, which occasionally annoyed Henry Blofeld in particular, and he had his own microphone constantly available to correct any mistakes made by the rest of us. At Headingley in 2003 when England were playing against a South African side that included the two black fast bowlers, Makhaya Ntini and Monde Zondeki, Henry was blithely commentating away during England's innings. 'And the ball is glanced down to the long-leg boundary,' Henry informed his listeners, 'and there it is picked up and thrown back to the keeper by... I think that's Ntini...' Bill grabbed his microphone earnestly. 'No, no Henry,' he blurted. 'It's the other one.' An avalanche of angry letters and emails was anticipated, yet mysteriously not one was received.

In contrast to Frindall, Trueman and Bailey, neither of whom could be considered bastions of political correctness either, were already national treasures among the cricketing fraternity when they were enlisted to *TMS*. Both of them were surprisingly hospitable to intruders. They were fifty-nine and sixty-six years of age respectively by the time I appeared on the scene, alongside a quorum of relatively new summarizers like Mike Selvey and David Lloyd. I am around that age now and often surrounded by younger ex-players, who are much in demand, a stark reminder of the rapid passage of time. For years Trueman and Bailey had been the constant summarizers yet neither seemed to resent the arrival of these newcomers, which impressed me then and even more now. I'm doing my best to be equally sanguine at the appearance of so many young, gifted broadcasters in the box.

By the end Fred was happy to parody himself with an 'I don't know what's going off out there' and sometimes he was all too easily prodded by his commentator. Neville Oliver from Australia was especially adept at winding him up. Neville would wait until the last minute of his stint before singing the praises of, say, Darren Gough, tossing out the notion that he must be the fastest bowler England have produced since... then there would be a little pause... Harold Larwood perhaps or Frank Tyson? Neville would then hand over the microphone to the next commentator with Fred swallowing his pipe (metaphorical or real) at such an assertion before launching a counterblast to such a ridiculous suggestion. The new, innocent commentator was left to pick up the pieces.

Fred always tried to help me out on Saturdays, my busy day for the *Observer*. For a new, young hack juggling the writing and the broadcasting on the same day could be a trial – nowadays I'm more accustomed to that – so Fred, having pointed out that he had his column for the *People* to do, would always say, 'Don't worry, sunshine, if you can't get back in time for your next stint. I'll fill in for you.'

Trevor, with his staccato, Mr Jingle assessments of the players out there, cared deeply about the programme. He played for Essex and England as an amateur but has there ever been a more pragmatic, single-minded, uncavalier amateur? I was fascinated to hear him talk of his time as an England cricketer under the first professional captain, Len Hutton. Take the Headingley Test of the

1953 Ashes series, which reflects how the game has changed a bit. Throughout the match England mustered 448 runs in their two innings; they faced 287.1 overs to get them. In the second innings Bailey scored 38 in 261 minutes. There was still a chance that Australia might sprint to their victory target of 177 runs as they set off aggressively. This prompted Bailey to go up to his captain and say, 'Len, do you want to save this game? If so, give me the ball.' Bailey, despite a dodgy knee, came off his longest run since he wanted to waste as much time as possible and then proceeded to bowl nine inches outside leg-stump to a packed onside field; Australia ended up 30 runs short. Jardine would have been proud of him; Hutton was, no doubt, grateful. Bailey, like most of us, was less dour in the box.

Fred and Trevor both finished – after twenty-six years – in 1999. By then I was a regular and was supposed to know what I was doing. Actually it is a simple enough operation. The commentator is the one at the helm. He – or she (I was lucky enough to be alongside Donna Symonds from Barbados when she became *TMS*'s first female commentator on the Caribbean tour of 1997/8, an introduction welcomed enthusiastically by the summarizers since she knew the game inside out) – describes the action, leads the conversation and is in charge of proceedings. This requires real expertise, which includes the ability to listen to instructions in your ear while saying something comprehensible with your tongue. The commentator is the one who requires the broadcasting skills.

However, some attributes are required to be a summarizer. The most difficult, although this is not written in any statute book anywhere, is that you probably need to have represented your country to get regular work. It also helps to have been a contestant on *Strictly Come Dancing*. If you can achieve one or both of those goals then everything else is a doddle. In fact, the trickiest task for any summarizer is to know when to keep quiet. That sounds simple enough but how many sporting broadcasters are there who have not been enamoured by the sound of their own voice? In cricket Richie Benaud, Tony Cozier, Jonathan Agnew and Simon Mann might be exceptions while my recollection of a distant Dan Maskell at Wimbledon is that he only ever said, 'Ooh, I say.'

The golden rule, usually passed on to all newcomers in the summarizer's seat and sometimes necessarily repeated to old-timers, is to shut up when the bowler is running in. It does not matter whether you are in the middle of some incredibly illuminating insight or a hilariously funny joke you have to stop, sometimes in mid-sentence, and let the commentator describe the action. After all that is the purpose of radio commentary; first and foremost the listeners have to know exactly what's happening out there – and they quite like to know the score as well.

There are other times when it is best to keep quiet or risk the ire of your commentator. At landmark moments – when a boundary delivers a century, at the fall of a vital wicket and most certainly at the end of the game – it is best to be quiet. Those clips played on the news bulletins will sound better to the rest of the world – and the commentator – without interruptions from the 'expert'. Agnew has often spoken glowingly of the Australian summarizer Kerry O'Keeffe, normally a loquacious soul, who was on air alongside him when Steve Waugh reached a memorable hundred in the last over of the day in Sydney in 2003. What had O'Keeffe done to win Agnew's admiration? He had stayed quiet.

I learnt to acclimatise to the different approaches of the various commentators. Brian Johnston might easily commentate through the entire over without interruption if nothing startling had happened. He might finish with a score and then he would pause in anticipation of his summarizer making his contribution before the start of the next over. The patterns of Henry Blofeld were harder to predict except for the advent of pigeons, cranes and buses, many of them 'pensive', but he would often operate in a similar manner.

At the opposite end of the scale is Agnew, whose style has always been conversational, and the same applies with Simon Mann. They describe the action and then there is always some interplay between commentator and summarizer. It is tempting to regard this as 'the modern way' until noting that both of them have been doing their jobs for well over two decades. The wondrous trio of CMJ, Tony Cozier and Jim Maxwell could do it either way. It was a privilege just to sail along in their wake. What a box of broadcasters they made. Two of them, CMJ and Cozier, are no longer with us.

CMJ often gave the impression that he was only in complete control of his life when he was behind a microphone, even if he had only just burst into the commentary box seconds before. Those clipped, precise tones became synonymous with the English summer, as were some of his impromptu similes, whose end could be so hard to predict – often he was none too sure where they were heading himself. He was the consummate broadcaster but even when he wrote – for the *Telegraph* and then *The Times* – you could hear his voice.

He was an incredibly polite man, often an underrated virtue. On tour he would often be spotted by doting readers and listeners following the England cricket team, and he would always give them the time of day or night while some of his grumpier colleagues were fleeing for cover. And he would also be the first to welcome strangers, visitors or nervous teenagers on work experience into the commentary box. Here was the epitome of an English gentle-man. And yet we all know that's not quite the complete picture.

CMJ was a source not only of great affection – as Mike Selvey memorably wrote after his death on 1 January 2013, 'cricket has lost its greatest friend' – but also much hilarity. He was a catalyst for laughter, both wittingly and, perhaps not as often as we first thought, unwittingly. He was a superb speaker after dinner and a fine mimic. A slightly scurrilous story in the hands – or on the lips – of the perfectly polite, God-fearing gentleman, educated at Marlborough College and Cambridge University, somehow had an added piquancy. It was like hearing the vicar swear.

As with Brian Close, with whom CMJ does not share many similarities, there are countless anecdotes about him and they are usually true. While cricket followers loved him, computers hated him and rebelled in his presence. It was a frequent occurrence for his employers to have to ship reinforcement laptops to some distant corner of the globe. Those computers were sometimes disobedient at home as well. When walking down Cardiff's High Street on the way to Sophia Gardens on the morning of the first ever day of Test cricket in Wales, he announced on the spur of the moment that he was just going to pop into Marks and Spencer's to buy another laptop.

Golf was an important part of CMJ's life at home and away. In Cape Town we played on New Year's Eve and found ourselves locked inside the course and having to clamber over a flat roof to extricate ourselves, which we somehow managed to do without triggering any alarms. It was on a golf course in Jamaica that he famously tried to ring his office with the TV remote control he had picked up on his way out of his hotel room. Even when he recog-nized his mistake he still seemed betrayed that the device did not get him through to London. Then there was the incident in Barbados when he borrowed a rather fine set of clubs from a generous host. He duly propped them up on the back of a Mini Moke and, encouraged by his erratic driving, they fell one by one out of the bag and onto the streets of Bridgetown. The following day on air he delivered a forlorn appeal for anyone who happened to come across some stray golf clubs on the city's streets to return them to him at the Kensington Oval. As he noted in his autobiography, 'I started having senior moments at the age of seven.' He once turned up at Lord's unusually promptly, only to discover that he was first on the rota for the *TMS* broadcast – at the Oval.

Latterly golf was almost as important as cricket to CMJ. He revelled in the challenges that the game presents. He could hit the ball a long way after intense and deliberate preparation. He was great fun to play with and against partly because he was so competitive (it's not much fun trying to beat someone who doesn't care). He was known to play a second or even third provisional ball. A disappointing drive, chip or putt would trigger a rich and individual vocabulary. CMJ hated to swear. So when the ball decided to remain at the bottom of a deep, deep bunker another invisible swish of the club would be followed by a yelp of 'Fishcakes' or 'Fotheringay-Thomas'.

There was often a problem getting him to the tee on time. CMJ did not like to be early for anything since that would inevitably mean that time was being wasted. And he hated to waste a second; he was always busy, writing articles, books and postcards to demanding deadlines. His fear of being early had one predictable consequence: he was often late, usually with a cast-iron explanation. He once described to me how he would set off for London in his car from West Sussex with no time to spare and a bowl of cornflakes, liberally sprinkled with milk, pinioned between his knees. He readily understood the agonies of the John Cleese character in *Clockwork*.

Naturally CMJ followed his son Robin's career at Sussex as intensely as any father. How stoically and professionally he disguised his angst when Sussex had the impudence to make his son twelfth man for the Lord's final of 2009, and how proud he was of Robin's stalwart service for the county for over a decade. A few years earlier at a Lord's final, which took place just before the announcement of the tour parties for the winter, we were discussing what the selectors might do and what we might write. 'I'd like to put him [Robin] in my England ODI squad in *The Times*,' he confided. 'I really can't do that, I suppose.' I nodded in agreement and then he paused for a moment before adding, 'But you could put him in yours.'

The last time I saw him he was weak and dying, angry that his semi-retirement plans had been thwarted. Like several of my colleagues I was keen to visit him before a long tour of India – just in case. As arranged he was on his own at home and it took an age for him to answer the door because he was moving so slowly. He asked me for a mundane favour. As Christmas was approaching he had procured some special tea for his wife, Judy, and he sent me up to his study above the garage to hide it there in a chest of drawers.

The cricket still dominated his thoughts. 'They must play Panesar as well as Swann in the first Test. But they won't!' he declared. (They didn't; England lost in Ahmedabad but had the sense to rectify their error for the next match.) By then he was riddled with cancer but he still cared passionately about the game. It is amazing how frequently in both press and commentary boxes we recall him, always with a smile. The same applies with Tony Cozier.

Quite often I'm asked who has been my favourite commentator.

Well, it's a tricky question that has to be sidestepped somehow because I have never wanted to upset Jonathan, CMJ, Blowers or Simon Mann by choosing just one of them. So my usual response (unless I'm in Australia when I naturally mention the marvellous Jim Maxwell) is to say 'Tony Cozier'. This may be another of my convenient compromises, but it is also true. It was always a delight to sit alongside Tony, which I did whenever England played the West Indies from 1990 onwards.

He had already reached veteran status by then, given that he came over to England as a cub reporter on a shoestring on the West Indies tour of 1963. Despite being a lone novice he did have the advantage of knowing all the Bajans in the team very well; he would have played against Frank Worrell, Garry Sobers, Wes Hall and Charlie Griffith at club level in Barbados, where he opened the batting for The Wanderers, a club he joined after resigning from Carlton CC when they had rejected a potential black member. 'A lot of them were my age and I virtually became part of the team,' he once recalled.

Tony was recognized by cricket followers all around the world more by his voice than his appearance. A surprising number of devotees did not realize that he was a white Bajan – a native of Barbados – yet all were captivated by the unmistakable lilting tones of his commentary, and they trusted his clear and forthright analysis of West Indies cricket through thick and thin. To see Tony at work at a Test match was an education. He would glide between the TV commentary box to the much smaller radio box to the press room, where he would write a couple of pieces for *The Nation* newspaper of Barbados, then perhaps another for the *Independent* in the UK in between his broadcasting duties. It seemed such an effortless process, leisurely even, yet he never wasted a minute.

His knowledge of the game was encyclopaedic and not restricted to the Caribbean. He knew better than his English counterparts that Bloggs of Leicestershire had scored 37 in his last county match. But he did not broadcast to impress listeners with his knowledge. It was never about him but the game unfolding in front of him, which he would describe with an objectivity that is beyond many modern broadcasters. His soothing voice allied to a sense of mischief whenever the occasion allowed brought a distant game to life, the swaying palm trees as well as the cover drives. He had a light touch on the tiller but he could take charge of the broadcast whenever he wanted. Just occasionally if his summarizer, who might be Fitzwilliam born, was becoming a little overwrought or tiresome, Tony would demonstrate his prowess by continuing to talk for over after over without allowing any interruption whatsoever, and there was every chance that the broadcast would be enhanced as a consequence.

While he adhered to the traditional demand for objectivity in *TMS's* broadcasts, he remained forever passionate about West Indian cricket. As the dominance of the West Indies faded at the beginning of this century it was a common occurrence to see Tony joining Viv Richards and Michael Holding in a corner of the bar for a drink at the end of a day's Test cricket to thrash out the latest setback. The conversation was animated and gained in speed dramatically as three proud West Indians, Bajan, Antiguan and Jamaican, poured out their souls. As the discussion grew ever more intense it was hard for bystanders not to listen, but they could not understand much except that this trio clearly cared passionately about whatever the topic of conversation was.

Tony also knew how to relax, have fun and add a little sunshine. His beach parties, to which all visiting journalists were invited, were legendary provided you managed to find the shack on the east coast of Barbados. This meant negotiating an impenetrable cobweb of little roads in the middle of the island; if successful there was beach cricket, cricket talk, a few drinks, music and dancing. And somehow the journey back to Bridgetown seemed so much easier.

He last worked in England in 2013; his body was frail, but his love of life intact. One precious memory is of a meal in the basement of an Italian restaurant in Cardiff, where the voice of Elvis Presley could suddenly be heard in the background. Tony pricked up his ears and started to sing. The diners on the next table were South Africans following the cricket – and, it turned out, just as keen on Elvis. And then there was Tony, to the delight of everyone there, delicately dancing around the tables with one of the wives, a smile on his face and a sparkle in his eye. That impressed me even more than his recollection of Bloggs's 37 at Grace Road. Moreover he was a shrewd old operator. In fifty years of marriage to Jillian I don't think he ever forgot their anniversary; he took the precaution of getting married on his birthday.

FIFTEEN

TEST MATCH SPECIAL (NOW)

THE METTLE OF ANY broadcaster, journalist – or indeed cricketer – is properly tested when the unexpected happens. If there is no trusted routine to rely upon, the way ahead can be both exciting and intimidating. In the media this is especially true for the live broadcaster; if you are writing about a sudden, controversial turn of events at least the delete button is readily available even though time may be running out as the deadline approaches. There is no such luxury with a live microphone.

It is here that I have to doff my cap to Jonathan Agnew. I have been alongside Jonathan in the commentary box on countless occasions when he must have been rattled by the unexpected. Suddenly there is far too much going on yet to the listener, or even the casual visitor to the box, he manages to appear totally relaxed and in control.

Sometimes, perhaps in a rain break during a *TMS* broadcast, I can just detect that little moment of horror in Jonathan's eyes when a guest has been wheeled in beside him and he has absolutely no idea who he or she is. At these moments he usually manages to retain his swan-like appearance, all serenity to the unknowing eye while paddling furiously below the surface. In such circumstances CMJ was occasionally reduced to offering his hand to a new arrival to the microphone saying, 'Christopher Martin-Jenkins, delighted to meet you,' and then hoping that the person next to him responded with a name. But it can get more serious than that.

For example at Edgbaston on 1 June 2002 when England were in the process of defeating Sri Lanka in a Test match, reports were filtering through that Hansie Cronje had died. There were rumours of a plane crash. Suddenly Jonathan had to adopt the discipline of a news reporter. After all, this was the BBC so the appropriate rules applied about needing at least two independent, verifiable sources. He could not just recycle the latest rumour until reliable confirmation was available. So the tone and content of the broadcast had to change while those beyond the microphone were scurrying around for more detail; in the meantime the match had to be covered as well. In these circumstances as a summarizer the job was to fill time while Jonathan took off his earphones to consult and establish what we could broadcast.

At least we knew the facts on another sad day in the commentary box in July 2006 when we were at Headingley for an ODI against Sri Lanka. Mid-morning we learnt that Fred Trueman had died. So the task for Jonathan and whoever was at his side was to conjure up a tribute to our old colleague – and one of England's greatest cricketers – on the spur of the moment. That is when it seems important to get it right, albeit with the minimum of preparation, and it was another occasion when Jonathan undoubtedly earned his corn.

Upon my return to the press box at Headingley that day I learnt that Yorkshire CCC had offered to help us all out by bringing Brian Close in to share a few memories of his old teammate. 'He'll come in and talk about Fred for about ten minutes,' we were told. 'Oh no he won't,' I retorted to anyone listening. There was no way old Closey would talk for ten minutes about Fred; as anticipated, fifty minutes, with barely any need for a second question, was the absolute minimum and his input was much appreciated by all the cricket correspondents. Meanwhile, upstairs in the radio box Peter Baxter and his assistant, Shilpa Patel, were frantically pulling together half an hour on Fred for the interval. No doubt there would have been an 'I don't know what's going off out there' from the archive, which somehow seemed appropriate as Sri Lanka would go on to knock off the 322 runs they needed for victory inside thirty-eight overs after the interval.

I was also alongside Jonathan, who once again remained both composed and informative amid the chaos in the Caribbean when two Tests were abandoned on the first morning of the match. In Jamaica in 1998 the pitch was dangerous and the Test was abandoned with England on 17–3. Alec Stewart apparently greeted Nasser Hussain to the middle with the observation, 'It's Saturday; it's eight o'clock; it's the lottery.' At that time of my career (*Observer* correspondent only) it was a source of angst when these major events happened on a Saturday. I'm ashamed to admit that my first reaction to the news of Don Bradman's death in February 2001 while on tour in Sri Lanka was a deplorably selfish 'Thank goodness it's Sunday.' Back in Jamaica the match referee, the old Australian wicketkeeper Barry Jarman, who was ultimately responsible for calling the game off, memorably described his situation: 'I had an unplayable lie.' Even so he made the correct decision. Meanwhile Jonathan and the team were busking furiously as they tried to make sense of such a rare occurrence.

That Test at Sabina Park lasted 62 balls; in 2009 the match in Antigua against England lasted just ten. This time the game at the newly built Viv Richards Stadium was abandoned because the outfield was like quicksand. Running up to bowl was a perilous process. Viv was on air on *TMS* as the impossibility of carrying on with the match became apparent. 'It's like an arrow through the heart,' he said to Agnew as we all sensed Viv's horror at what had happened. Once again Aggers and co. had to busk it.

In fact that Test was rescheduled for two days later at the old Recreation Ground in the middle of St John's, the capital of Antigua, and this proved to be an uplifting occasion. There was the heroic scramble to get the ground ready; on the eve of the match paint brushes sloshed, hammers hammered and the biggest of heavy rollers went up and down the new playing surface for hours. In the end the Test was far better attended than it would have been out in the Antiguan countryside and we did not know the outcome until the last over (it was a riveting draw). All of which highlighted the risks of sticking up a brand new, remote stadium funded from overseas in the Caribbean – the same mistake has been made in Guyana. In fact the blunt truth is that the big out-of-town stadia do not really work in England either, despite all the honest ambition at Hampshire and Durham. It helps so much when a large proportion of spectators can walk up if the sun is shining and the match perfectly poised.

Soon after his appointment as the BBC's cricket correspondent it became apparent that Jonathan had the capacity to make any guest – or summariser – relaxed at the microphone. I still look forward to him taking the seat next to me. When he conducts his interviews he is obviously interested in his guests and has the vital capacity to listen to them and to have a conversation rather than spout a string of predetermined questions. The guests are soon comfortable and are therefore more interesting and, in certain instances, likelier to reveal a bit more than intended. At the conclusion of a successful Agnew interview there is a little tap on the knee for his guest and heartfelt thanks. And we have usually learnt something and been entertained.

In recent times it has been striking, not to say alarming, how eager politicians have become to appear on the programme. It got to the point when David Cameron was prime minister that his office might ring up to alert *TMS* to his presence in anticipation of an interview. Theresa May's hero is apparently Geoffrey Boycott, which is not entirely reassuring since he has been more than ready to offer her tips on how and why to Brexit vigorously. Ed Miliband is another boyhood fan of Boycott (though less keen on Brexit than Geoffrey, I imagine). Jonathan clearly enjoys these encounters but increasingly he gives the impression that they are now merely part of his routine – 'Oh, what shall I talk to Cameron about this time?' Perhaps the oddest meeting of minds sporting and political was when Henry Blofeld interviewed Dennis Skinner in the 'View from the Boundary' slot. Their backgrounds had little in common but from the outset they revelled in one another's company.

But the whole point of the programme is the cricket, which can reach a peak of excitement when the Ashes are at stake. So it was always special to be sent out on to the field after an Ashes victory as Agnew's sidekick, his 'friend', to act as a back-up filling in while he awaited jubilant Ashes-winning England cricketers coming to his microphone – as was the case at the Oval in 2009 and at Melbourne in 2010.

A more bizarre occasion out in the middle was the post-match expedition at Lord's in 2017 to monitor the celebrations of Henry Blofeld's last appearance on *TMS*. Even though I was not working for *TMS* on that match the producer, Adam Mountford, asked me to accompany Jonathan while Henry crowned his extraordinary departure with an impromptu lap of honour in front of thousands of adoring fans. The original plan was for Henry to be whisked around the ground in a golf buggy during the tea interval but the sudden conclusion to the Test changed all that, much to the disappointment of the buggy driver. However, the new arrangement, which had Henry strolling around the boundary, suited him much better since all time restrictions were now removed. He was in his pastels again as he set off on his lap of honour, waving to his fans and kissing one or two of the good-looking ones. I later learnt that he was perfectly happy to be described by me as 'a cross between Winston Churchill and Dame Edna Everage'. He was in seventh heaven throughout that circuit and was genuinely taken aback by his reception, especially when the England players came out onto the balcony to cheer him on his way. They seemed to recognize him rather more easily than he had recognized some of them in the past. To no one's surprise, once Henry saw the reaction he was getting he was more than happy to milk it with his customary expertise.

It was a shock when Henry announced that he was leaving *TMS* in 2017. My assumption had always been they would have to carry him out in a coffin. However it was his own decision to go rather than a result of long and tortuous discussions with the BBC. It was a surprise to the production team when the news broke in a Blofeld exclusive in the *Daily Mail*. In fact the manner of his departure was a masterstroke. His eyesight had been in decline and he confided that he was not enjoying it as much as in the past, but he oversaw his withdrawal brilliantly amid a blaze of publicity and with his stock as a national treasure higher than it had ever been. And he was not about to disappear into a monastery. His agent was being inundated with offers and those theatre gigs were multiplying by the minute.

Henry adorned the *TMS* box for forty-five years with a few interruptions (like the good freelance he had a go with Sky TV for a while before returning to the BBC after the death of Brian Johnston). Over the years I marvelled at his energy and his preposterous ability to spot butterflies and buses as well as his intimate knowledge of the game. While Henry sometimes struggled to identify the exact name of the bloke fielding under a sunhat at long leg, he could give you every detail of the England team that won the Ashes in 1953 or 1981 when he was commentating at *that* match at Headingley.

His zest for life is remarkable – in fact, in the box we often thought it remarkable that he was still alive. In the 1960s this was reflected by his decision to drive to India in a vintage Rolls-Royce to cover an England tour with John Woodcock as one of his travelling companions. On one distant tour there he almost played for England as sickness hit the dressing room. At the time he was easily the best qualified among the press corps to do so since he had been a prodigious young batsman and wicketkeeper at Eton and Cambridge University, who went on to play frequently for Norfolk. My impression is that he probably played a few shots. He would have been even better if he had not been run over by a bus in his last year at Eton. Thereafter he kept an eagle eye out for buses wherever he was.

That zest sometimes triggered the odd early departure from a cricket ground. Henry wrote about cricket for the *Guardian* regularly in the 1980s. Once at a routine county match at Chelmsford he left a little early for a pressing engagement having dutifully filed his copy, which focused upon Essex's innings of 287 with the end of the last sentence reading, 'and at the close Surrey were — for—'. The problem was that Surrey were bowled out for 14 by Norbert Phillip and Neil Foster in the last hour. Fortunately a young Matthew Engel was on the desk at the *Guardian* and he did a little more than simply add the numbers 14 and 10 to Henry's copy.

Henry has written for just about every newspaper, adjusting to fresh demands and equipment along the way. The sight of him in the commentary box meticulously counting the words of a piece he had just composed on a newly acquired laptop was too good to be true, and it seemed to us all that it would spoil the fun to inform him that there was something called a word count on his laptop.

Henry has been a prolific writer of newspaper reports and books. Yet his most memorable work has been for the BBC. I've witnessed many epic broadcasts, although I was not present in Zimbabwe in 1996 when England drew a Test there with the scores tied. The climax was thrilling and it was covered for *TMS* by a relatively inexperienced team – with the exception of Henry and Trevor Bailey. Simon Mann was on his first tour and, famously, the rota constructed by Peter Baxter was tossed aside. Such was the excitement of the game that Henry decided that he would not be relinquishing the microphone in the final hour. This episode has now passed into *TMS* folklore and parlance. 'Doing A Bulawayo' is when the commentator decides to completely disregard all previous plans laid out by the producer and to carry on commentating himself. You are not supposed to do that. No doubt Henry reported the drama on the field brilliantly.

Yet some of his finest moments came when there was no cricket going on at all. In Brisbane in 1998 there was a storm of biblical proportions on the final afternoon, which enabled England to draw the Test match. Henry was on air and his instincts kicked in.

This was something exceptional and off he went on an extraordinarily vivid monologue. When he eventually drew breath I began to mention what seemed to me to be a weird phenomenon. I explained how there were great streaks of lightning visible all over the ground 'and yet we can't hear any—', whereupon there was a great crack of thunder on cue, which momentarily drowned out the conversation. Henry continued his wonderful description of the storm, which soon became compulsory listening on Radio 4's *Pick of the Week*.

He had his stock phrases that were easily interpreted. 'My dear old thing' came about because he could not remember names. 'You're absolutely right' actually meant 'I haven't been listening to a word you've been saying for the last few minutes but it's my turn now'. Somehow at the age of seventy-seven the lovable old rogue managed to walk away from the box at Lord's in 2017 leaving them (well, most of them) wanting more – once he had extricated himself from a tangle of wires, the only unseen hiccup in a brilliant exit.

Women and children were special fans of Henry and among the women was one of the hidden stalwarts of *TMS*, Shilpa Patel, Peter Baxter's assistant producer for over twenty years and a heartbeat of the programme during that time. Shilpa did so much more than all the admin. She could be a newshound when necessary and her capacity to find A-grade guests and persuade them to come on the programme was without parallel.

At the Oval in 2006 when Pakistan refused to take the field because of the suggestion of ball-tampering she was in the pavilion in a flash with Simon Mann alongside her. Within minutes she had not only found the chairman of the Pakistan Board, Shahryar Khan, but had persuaded him to give a live interview to Simon for *TMS*. Somehow they never said no to Shilpa.

Sometimes she is not beyond a little subterfuge. When India had achieved a famous win against Australia in Adelaide in 2003 the BBC were keen to speak to one of the heroes of that victory, Rahul Dravid. After much grafting Shilpa discovered which hotel the Indian team was staying in but the receptionist, presumably following instructions, would not transfer her call to Dravid's room. Ten minutes later she tried again. 'Hello, Mrs Dravid here. Could you put me through to my husband, please?' The receptionist obliged immediately and once Shilpa was able to engage in conversation with him, beginning with a swift apology for her little white lie, Dravid was very happy to give an interview to the BBC.

In 2009 Shilpa learnt that Daniel Radcliffe, the star of the Harry Potter films, was attending the Lord's Test so, with binoculars in hand, she put him under surveillance for a few days. This was a tricky operation since he was not sitting in the posh seats. Eventually she tracked him down to the Compton Stand and persuaded him to do an interview with Agnew at lunchtime from the MCC box. 'We've got a little magic for you in the interval,' said Jonathan, who was always eager to challenge Shilpa's powers of persuasion. ('You've failed me,' he once chided her. 'You told me you'd get Russell Crowe but where is he?' And within the hour she duly got him.) Once the interview with Radcliffe was broadcast Shilpa was inundated with requests from the England dressing room – from the likes of Andrew Strauss and Paul Collingwood – and from John Major ('for my grandchild, of course') to get Daniel's autograph. And, of course, he obliged.

Shilpa knows how to speak her mind. Occasionally she was capable of telling Henry Blofeld to sharpen up if he had not done his homework on visiting teams – no one else could do that – and she also had a winning way with the overseas summarizers.

If necessary she could resort to the colourful language that Jeff Thomson or Ian Chappell readily understood. Even they learnt not to mess with her in the knowledge that she would look after them royally when they were on *TMS* duty. She even managed to improve I. V. A. Richards' punctuality. Likewise she made sure that everything was right for the overseas commentators such as Tony Cozier, Bryan Waddle from New Zealand and Australia's Jim Maxwell.

Maxwell is a wonderful broadcaster, who reports the action in an even-handed, crisp manner without ever quite concealing the fact that he is very keen for Australia to win. That, after all, reinforces the established order in his eyes. He loves the game and this may explain why he got married on the outfield of his beloved Sydney Cricket Ground. He can be identified immediately on the airwaves by his delivery of a solitary surname. Hear the sound of his gravelly Antipodean voice lingering on the syllables of Khawaja or McGrath and you know it's Jim.

Watch him, or Agnew – or Tony Cozier or CMJ in days gone by – introducing the programme out on the field and you witness masters at work. They often go off on a solitary stroll with their microphone as the transmission starts but they are somehow talking to one person tucked away in a kitchen, in a car or up a mountain. They do not need a visible audience to speak to. In a world of their own with their imaginary listener they offer a warm welcome and the promise of a brand new day to one and all.

Maxwell, like all good *TMS* broadcasters, can be totally objective. At the end of a Test there is a little tradition on *TMS* that the commentator from the country about to win the game is given the microphone to describe the final moments. At the epic Ashes Test at Edgbaston in 2005 Maxwell was duly ushered into the commentator's chair with half a dozen runs required by Australia. Almost immediately Mike Kasprowicz was caught down the leg side off Steve Harmison so that amid excruciating tension England won the match by two runs. Maxwell may well have been disappointed – in fact we can be absolutely certain that this was the case – but he conveyed the drama, elation and despair of that climax quite brilliantly.

Ten years on there was another vignette of Maxwell mastery. At the World Cup in Australasia in 2015 *TMS* had engaged Kevin Pietersen to work on a few games. Soon it transpired that Pietersen himself was the 'story' because of the discussion about England's future prospects, which at the time were looking incredibly bleak after dire performances in that tournament. The ECB's chairman, Colin Graves, not for the first or last time, had stuck his foot in his mouth by suggesting – without prior consultation with his cricketing experts – that there might be a way back into the England team for Pietersen. This was news and a reaction from Pietersen was sought on a day when he was appearing on the programme in Melbourne. Henry Moeran, Adam Mountford's resourceful assistant producer, asked Pietersen if he would give a five-minute interview to *TMS* to clarify the situation. Pietersen, understandably perhaps, declined. 'Don't worry,' said Jim. 'Just stick him on the rota with me and I'll get you what you want.'

Jim took to the microphone for his twenty-minute session and engaged Pietersen in conversation, winning his confidence with some shared experiences of Sydney and then towards the end of his stint he gently guided the conversation to Pietersen's future intentions. By now Maxwell was another of KP's buddies and Pietersen answered every question about his future plans clearly and to nobody's detriment. (The odd thing is that Pietersen is far more capable of being measured on air than Graves could ever be.) Maxwell, his stint over, popped down the microphone and headed off towards the Australian commentary box. On his way he gave me a wink before receiving some heartfelt thanks from Henry Moeran.

Maxwell is as Maxwell sounds and that applies to just about every broadcaster you have heard on *TMS*. You are on air for so long that it would be pointless as well as impossible to sustain an act as a clown or a curmudgeon throughout an entire Test match. It is the same with captaincy. You spend so long in a dressing room that your colleagues soon see through any pretence.

Geoff Miller once outlined to me the perils of trying to do that. Many years ago he took over from the South African all-rounder, Eddie Barlow, as captain of Derbyshire. Barlow always bristled with energy and aggression. A larger than life figure, he was forever bellowing encouragement and chastisements out on the field. He could be a strict disciplinarian and always in your ear but such was his innate, unquenchable enthusiasm that people were happy to follow him – though they also feared him a bit. So when Miller took over at Derby he tried to emulate Barlow at the start of his time in charge, yelling instructions and doing his best to be a bustler. But Miller is no fool. He soon realized that his teammates were seeing right through him; this was not the real Dusty. Miller regained his credibility when he reverted to being true to himself. The same applies in broadcasting, I think.

For example, it would be daft for my good friend Simon Mann to adopt some Johnstonian/Blofeldian persona when he is on air. Simon has a drier sense of humour than some of the others; he knows the game intimately and he knows how to describe it without any contrived frills. The listeners trust him. Simon is also an excellent interviewer. He has a journalistic nose and he does not shirk from the difficult question, albeit one decorously asked in traditional *TMS* style. Occasionally he has flummoxed the odd player with his enquiries. In a quick end-of-day interview with Kevin Pietersen he once asked, 'How good do you think you can be?' It's an interesting question, but one which on this occasion elicited no more than a bewildered stare. Whether it is Simon, Jonathan or any of the newer recruits I still marvel at the quick-wittedness they routinely show when delivering a coherent, impromptu interview. It is not as easy as it sounds.

Those newer recruits are not so new or young any more. Charlie Dagnall was once a pony-tailed paceman for Warwickshire and Leicestershire (though I should add that I opted for 'paceman' mainly for alliterative purposes), but now his voice and his face – he keeps popping up on Sky TV as well – are familiar to the cricketing fraternity. Daniel Norcross's route to *TMS* was unconventional, which may not be a total surprise to those who know him. He was once depicted as an ogre in parts of the ECB and the BBC, since he founded and became the figurehead of *Test Match Sofa*, an operation that provoked considerable angst from Jonathan Agnew and others. They broadcast cricket off the TV, initially from Daniel's own sofa, in an alternative, irreverent manner that developed a cult following with fewer cakes and listeners but more lager (I always presumed) than the traditional *TMS*. Regrettably I seldom had time to listen.

Eventually and surprisingly Daniel sold *Test Match Sofa* to *The Cricketer* magazine, which was once considered a bastion of the establishment; he wrote to *TMS* producer Adam Mountford, seeking work; hatchets were buried and before long the Sofa on his CV was replaced by something Special, a situation, I suspect, that he had always secretly craved. It is hardly surprising that he does not appear to be intimidated by a microphone since he had been busking it for years on a sofa with the most basic of resources.

Daniel is engaging and exhausting company. He became another of my classics gurus, once I made the startling discovery that we had shared the same tutor at St John's College, Oxford, though he was there more than a decade later. He captained the college cricket team and delights in reminding me of his chats with the old groundsman at St John's about the days when Marks and Tavaré played the odd game for the college – 'They never scored a run between them.' Daniel has plenty of opinions and is not so shy about sharing them. He is seldom dull, not a bad attribute for a broadcaster.

Norcross is one of several new voices introduced by Adam Mountford, who took over from Peter Baxter in 2007. This was a formidable undertaking for Adam. Peter had been the producer for so long that we were all comfortably set in our ways. How could Adam feel anything other than an intruder? Moreover the demands upon the cricket producer were changing and expanding with the advent of Radio 5 Live Sports Extra and a whole host of digital outlets, most of which remain a mystery to me.

So Adam faced a tough balancing act. He had to meet all the additional requirements; he wanted to put his own mark on the programme and he had to try to keep the old lags happy. It was almost impossible to do all of that simultaneously. He was keen to introduce some fresh personnel and to do that he had to downgrade or remove someone. The victim was Mike Selvey, who had been working on the programme for over twenty years. It might easily have been me; it was bound to be one of us.

Mike was a long-term colleague of mine – he had been the *Guardian* cricket correspondent since 1985 – and as a summarizer he had a fertile, independent mind that would always offer the listeners an unusual insight. He knows the game inside out. Understandably Mike was embittered by this decision, just as I would have been. Initially I was uncomfortable that I had survived the change of regime while Mike had not but here I underestimated the man. A natural reaction might have been for him to feel some resentment towards me since I was still being invited to contribute to *TMS* and he wasn't. Yet never, not for one millisecond, did Mike ever suggest that was what he felt. He might have had an argument with Adam, but not me. In fact over the years Mike has often been a supporter of my remaining on the programme. This is because he's a big man (and a very sound judge).

So Adam introduced some fresh faces of a higher profile than the Angus Fraser, Graeme Fowler, Selvey, Marks era. The status of *TMS* was obviously sufficient to attract them and most of them, I presume, acquired contracts with the BBC rather than working as freelances like their predecessors. Phil Tufnell was a natural and a bit of a fraud in that he is much cleverer than he makes out. I'm just young enough to have played against him but far more often I watched him as a Test cricketer from the press box.

In fact in Visakhapatnam on the 1992/3 India tour he caused me – and himself – some embarrassment. After an emphatic defeat in the first Test in Calcutta, in which England's solitary specialist spinner was, amazingly, Ian Salisbury, I wrote a long feature for the *Observer* explaining why Tufnell must play in the next Test. On the Saturday I reported on England's fixture against the Rest of India in Visakhapatnam and, after a missed stumping, Tufnell lost his rag with the umpire, England keeper Richard Blakey and anyone else within range. *Wisden* reminds me that he was subsequently fined £500 by the team management for ungentlemanly conduct towards an umpire and that he had a meeting with the Revd Andrew Wing-field Digby, who is described as 'the team's pastoral counsellor'. So the *Observer* ended up with two articles from me in their pages: the considered piece explaining why Tufnell must play in the next Test, and the match report outlining why Tufnell can't play in it. (In fact he did play in the next Test in Madras.)

Tuffers played his cricket on the edge; he could be a bag of nerves when waiting to bat, which was understandable, but he might well be the same when bearing the burden of being the solitary spinner in the England team, even though he had a special talent as a classical left-armer. For him playing cricket could often be a traumatic experience but when broadcasting he is naturally relaxed and in control of the situation. It looks a far easier experience than representing England – and it is. Even so it is wonderful that after his retirement from cricket Tuffers found his métier, a word he would not dream of using – but he knows what it means. I believe it was CMJ who first recognized that he would be an ideal fit for *TMS*. More recently Jonathan has marvelled how Tuffers lights up on stage when they are doing their shows together.

Soon we were to be joined by England's most successful cricket captain, Michael Vaughan, whose ambition was to become the next Gary Lineker (not as a goalscorer, but a broadcaster). Angus Fraser, when a much-respected correspondent for the *Independent*, acquired the nickname 'Martini' since he was willing to dispense his wisdom 'anytime, anyplace, anywhere'. However, Gus wasn't as ubiquitous as Michael, who has appeared on every major broadcasting outlet over the last few years in between delivering – via Nick Hoult – his columns for the *Telegraph*.

Then came Graeme Swann, along with all the other characters he brings with him into the box. He is our best answer to Rory

Bremner – amid modest competition. More importantly this pair added immense, contemporary cricketing knowledge and nous. But what impressed me as much as anything about Graeme were reports from a West Indies tour, which I did not go on in 2015. It transpired that he immediately built up a rapport with Tony Cozier, whose body, rather than mind, was then in a desperately fragile state. Apparently Swann acted as Cozier's devoted bagman as they travelled around the Caribbean, carrying his bags, finding that taxi, sharing that drink. I liked the fact that Graeme understood the wonders of Cozier so rapidly.

These were all high-calibre, high-profile signings, which suggested that the BBC meant business in their cricket coverage. They were prepared to go out into the marketplace to acquire such big names. But sadly the resources no longer appear to stretch to winning the rights for most of England's overseas tours. As a consequence, all the big names have an ever-diminishing stage on which to perform. The rights to broadcast the England tours of 2018/19 and beyond, namely those to Sri Lanka, West Indies, South Africa and India, have all been won by TalkSport. For many cricket lovers it is a minor consolation that the BBC has bought the rights to show a handful of games in the new short-form competition that begins in 2020 on television.

A less exalted – and less expensive – addition has been the scorer Andrew Samson. Actually the description 'scorer' nowhere near does Andrew justice. He is an amazing source of information from his own unique database. It remains a constant challenge to frame a cricketing question that Andrew cannot answer. I keep trying doggedly without much success. Like his predecessors Andrew has some thespian skills that he usually keeps well-hidden. Listen to Agnew winding Boycott up with the notion that his hundredth hundred was in fact hit in Faisalabad rather than Headingley, and you will find that Andrew's contribution is perfectly credible and convincing. For the ODIs we now have a comedian, a real one, in the scorer's seat, Andy Zaltzman, another unlikely choice but a good one.

In the last decade the pursuit of quality has gone hand in hand with the pursuit of equality, especially at the BBC, and here *TMS* has been lucky since several gifted female broadcasters have come to the fore. Alison Mitchell's excellence as a broadcaster and pre-senter is such that she was snapped up by Channel Seven in Australia to join the team that replaced the old soldiers of Channel Nine, the station that had retained the TV rights for Test cricket in Australia since the days of Kerry Packer. Adam Mountford also helped to launch the broadcasting careers of Ebony Rainford-Brent and Isa Guha, two former England players. I joined them in the old potting shed on the roof at Taunton, which once masqueraded as a commentary box, when they made their first appearance on *TMS* and it was obvious then that they would both make excellent broadcasters if that was the path they wished to take.

You can hear the smile on the face of Ebony when she speaks on the radio. She knows the game and she is also relentlessly posi-tive and cheerful on and off air, as she displayed in the T20 World Cup in India in 2016 when she covered thousands of miles around the sub-continent, usually alongside Charlie Dagnall and Henry Moeran, and often in the back of a bumpy minibus. She was in Dharamsala one day, Mohali the next, not to mention Nagpur. What a glorious way to discover the country as Jonathan and I uncomplainingly followed England despite being restricted to our familiar hotels in Mumbai, Delhi and Kolkata. Meanwhile Isa, polished and conscientious, has become a regular presence at the

IPL and with Sky TV as well as appearing sporadically on *TMS*. Unsurprisingly both of them are now in great demand.

However it would be inaccurate to regard this trio as the trail-blazers. In the 1990s Peter Baxter enlisted Donna Symonds, a lawyer from Barbados, to commentate on Test cricket in the West Indies and to be a regular contributor throughout the World Cup in 1999, and she proved herself to be a consummate broadcaster. He also signed up Clare Connor, the former England captain, who is now the head of women's cricket at the ECB, for that World Cup. In both instances the fact that they happened to be women soon faded away. Both of them knew their stuff and informed and entertained the listeners. The same applies to Ebony and Isa.

Some of the 'newcomers' have already moved on. At the time of writing Ed Smith is England's chief selector – and I'm confident that at the time of publication he will still be in that position. It could be a challenge sitting next to him in the commentary box since his brain was forever buzzing so that one never quite knew what question he might toss out next. Like any good selector he would have an abundance of theories fermenting in his head. Occasionally this might have hindered his commentary because he was so eager to continue the debate rather than describe the action. He would have been an excellent summarizer though this was not necessarily a suggestion I was keen to promote – there are only a limited number of slots.

Ed now has first-hand experience of the difference between being a pundit and a real decision-maker. And there are a lot of dif-ferences. His mistakes are now remembered; as a correspondent or a broadcaster any daft prognostications or theories that prove to be totally wrong soon fade from the memory. Our mistakes do not matter and, in any case, they probably result in a wonderfully spicy headline for twenty-four hours. This is not the lot of a selector or a captain. It is all too easy for the pundits on TV, radio and in print to forget the comfort of their position. We have varying degrees of exposure but no responsibility; in this sense it is the cosiest of existences.

Recently I bumped into Alan Wilkins, once a bowler for Glamorgan and Gloucestershire, but for the last four decades a sports broadcaster, majoring in cricket. He is now a household name, not necessarily in the UK, but in India and beyond. He explained that he had just written a book that focuses mostly on his broadcasting career, entitled *Easier Said Than Done*. I congratulated him on the title; I was almost envious of it since it provided such a neat reminder. It still remains the case that players, coaches and selectors are at the sharp end. The rest of us cruise along in their wake, only alerting our readers or listeners to the times when we got it right.

SIXTEEN

LOOSE ENDS

ON SATURDAY, 12 NOVEMBER 2011 Anna and I returned home at around midnight from a party somewhere in the middle of Devon to see our phone flashing. There was a brief message from the *Observer* sports desk saying, 'Peter Roebuck has died in Cape Town after being questioned by police earlier in the day.' We looked at one another and barely needed to speak; both of us had the same thought buzzing around our heads.

We had grown apart from Pete since he had become a permanent resident of Sydney in 2001. After that he only ever returned to England when Australia were playing in an Ashes series here, and the impression was that he came out of duty as a cricket writer for the *Sydney Morning Herald* rather than because of any enthusiasm to revisit the country of his birth. He had long been uncomfortable in England and after a court case in Taunton in 2001, in which he had pleaded guilty to a charge of common assault (a decision he subsequently regretted and which he regarded as a consequence of his eagerness to fly out to Australia as swiftly as possible), he cut his ties. He admitted caning three South African teenagers who had been staying with him at his house in Taunton and he set off for

Sydney the following day. He confided to Anna, who had attended every day of his trial, that he never wanted to go through that again.

Pete had been part of our lives for more than two decades. He was there on that first day at Somerset when we looked at one another in awe as we had our first sight of Viv Richards striking a cricket ball. He was best man at our wedding. He and I had shared countless meals, journeys (usually much longer than they should have been), hotels, dressing rooms and, latterly, press boxes. Now he was gone. And I was angry with him. It did not have to be like this. This was such a waste. He could have opened up more; he could have reached out for help; and along the way I could have offered more support.

But we had drifted apart once he had established himself in Australia. Ostensibly he flourished there. His work for the *Sydney Morning Herald* was essential reading for the cricketing community and beyond. He preferred writing the quick-fire, off-the-cuff commentaries of a day of Test cricket to the considered, polished feature pieces that would be sought from the *Sunday Times* in England, though those articles were also must-reads. Before settling in Australia Pete had worked for the *Sunday Times* for over a decade and he had an odd relationship with them. There was one summer when I'm sure that Pete and Robin Marlar were both convinced that they were the paper's cricket correspondent and so they carried on regardless. After about six years in their employment Pete announced that he was meeting his sports editor for the first time and he realized that he had absolutely no idea what he looked like. Perhaps the feeling was mutual. I offered to buy him a red rose to put in his lapel.

In his early days in the press box he would start to scribble animatedly around five o'clock in handwriting sometimes illegible even to himself before phoning his copy through. Eventually he acquired a laptop and a mobile phone, useful pieces of machinery but never ones he treasured. Yet his system worked all right. He could draw telling conclusions about a cricketer just by observing him from a distance rather than after any intricate research; his pen-pictures were nearly always accurate and insightful even though he may never have exchanged a word with his subject. Beyond that he could rail at injustices, perceived or real, with fearless venom. And, especially in his early books (like *Slices of Cricket* and *It Never Rains*), he could be funny.

In Australia everyone read Roebuck and soon they listened to him as well. Jim Maxwell of the ABC saw something special and opted to use him on the radio as a summarizer during Test matches, which proved a masterstroke. Pete spoke quickly in an accent that became ever harder to pin down as it hovered somewhere between English and Australian. Some Australian friends thought he had a 'beautiful accent', which was a surprise, but there is no doubt that the content was never dull or predictable and it was often provocative.

His work in his adopted country was automatically appreciated as an important, independent part of the cricketing landscape. It mattered to Pete what people thought of him more than he ever let on and it irked him that he was not so highly regarded in England, which contributed to his increasing Anglophobia. At least he *thought* that he was not so highly regarded in England; in fact he had many admirers here, more than he could imagine, but he never seemed to realize that. After his death there was a remarkable outpouring from the cricket writers in England as well as Australia, and just about all of them were fulsome in their praise of his writing and the gutsiness of his career as a cricketer years before. Pete would have enjoyed reading those pieces. Many of them hinted at what a tortured, distant soul he had become when I wanted to remember the early days when Pete laughed quite often at himself and the absurdity of the profession we had both decided to pursue as teenagers.

He described some of those absurdities in *It Never Rains*, his diary of the 1983 season: how he sought me out at Old Trafford and we meandered round the boundary during a rain break; he was at a low ebb explaining how ridiculous it was to keep putting himself through the agony of playing this stupid, impossible game; perhaps he should find a proper job. He was rather hoping I might talk him out of such a hare-brained notion but after a couple of laps I think I had come to the conclusion that he might be right; perhaps we should both retire.

Pete often kept everyone guessing at Somerset and I was supposed to be the one who knew how his mind worked. 'How's Pete?' they would ask in hushed tones. 'Why don't you ask him?' Sometimes explanations were not so easy. There was the car journey that went awry when returning from a terrible Somerset performance against Sussex at Hove in that dangerous time of the season for cricketers as August approaches. Pete was driving his car with Nigel Popplewell and me as passengers. He stopped at a traffic light near Worthing and suddenly tossed the keys to Nigel, declaring that he was going to walk home from there. And off he marched. Nigel took the wheel and we tried to persuade Pete to rejoin us on the journey home, a request he kept refusing. We tried again and again but he was adamant that he was walking home. In the end we shrugged our shoulders and drove on. It took Pete forty-eight hours and a bed and breakfast somewhere around

Salisbury to make it back to Taunton. By then his feet were badly blistered and a source of considerable pain, which he did his best to disguise before the next match. This episode was not a good sign but even then Pete could see the funny side of him having to disguise the reason why he was not moving quite as freely as usual in the field in the following game. Those massive feet were still hurting.

Then there were the meals over the years at our house, which would often end so abruptly. They may have been convivial and noisy – they usually were – but Pete retained the habit of suddenly rising from his chair and heading out of the front door with no expression of farewell or thanks. This mode of departure was commonplace when he was with many of his friends and it usually provoked no more than a smile and a shrug of the shoulders.

Pete played for Somerset for two more years after my retirement and then soon resurfaced as a cricketer for Devon, where he became a bowler of fast off-breaks, a belligerent middle-order batsman and the captain. The Devon team possessed some talented cricketers who were all happy to draw upon Roebuck's experience and to laugh at his eccentricities. This was a fertile union: a band of players who wanted to enjoy themselves and to improve allied to Pete's eagerness to be a purveyor of wisdom, cricketing or otherwise. Moreover, he had become a very handy bowler (oddly enough at various stages of our captaincy careers Pete made me open the batting and I made him bowl).

But sometimes his yearning to be a mentor of young cricketers became a problem, which was highlighted in that 2001 court case and his use of corporal punishment. Echoing the eccentricity of his old school headmaster, Jack Meyer, Pete would eventually seek to justify his abnormal behaviour; his punishing of his 'pupils' was part of the house rules and somehow it was in pursuit of the greater good. But this could never really tally.

So our relationship became more strained and distant after his departure to Australia. When we met up we could still talk about cricket easily enough and some of the good old days provided we did not settle on the topic of Botham for too long – on that score Pete kept seeking my seal of approval for the upheavals of 1986, without success. But beyond that it was trickier and he would sometimes be uneasy when Anna and I appeared in Australia on Ashes tours; it was as if we were uncomfortable reminders of times past that he wanted to banish from his memory. Maybe we knew him too well. And we were uncomfortable with the concept and values of the Straw Hat Farm in Pietermaritzburg that Pete had set up at great personal cost, despite his goal of aiding the education of so many young Zimbabweans.

Yet it was still a terrible shock, if not a complete one, when we heard about his death in Cape Town in a bleak hotel near the famous Newlands cricket ground that sits below Table Mountain. Since then I have walked by that hotel on the way to international matches with no inclination to enter. No one knows exactly what happened in the end but the words 'I never want to go through this again' keep resounding.

Pete's death stunned his Australian colleagues staying in the same hotel. Greg Baum of *The Age* was one of them and he wrote about Pete the following day.

The second last person to see him alive was the ABC's man, Jim Maxwell, who had grown as close to him as any-one did. The last person was a policeman. In these glimpses were clues to Roebuck, cricketer, writer, broadcaster, coach, philanthropist, educator but above all mystery. Clues must do; it is doubtful if anyone on Earth knew him intimately. He chose it to be that way. It is possible to say where he came from but not where he belonged. He kept houses in England's West Country, Bondi and Pietermaritzburg. He lived in three worlds because it suited him not to be tied down in one.

So Pete, like too many of the cricketers who were there when I pitched up at Taunton in 1974 for my first day as a professional cricketer – Brian Close, Tom Cartwright and Peter Denning – is no longer around. Meanwhile two of those who also started that season are now knighted, an outcome well beyond all reasonable expectation. Sir Vivian Richards still possesses that triangular torso; he looks as if he could stroll out and smash a hundred at the age of sixty-six. Instead he has become the keenest of golfers, whose handicap is still falling. He pops up somewhere at fairly regular intervals, maybe doing some commentary for *TMS*, and occasionally we speak of those early days and his unstinting admiration of our wonderfully mad first county captain, Close.

Ian is not quite so fit. But he has more than survived even if his back has been in rebellion recently. In the summer of 2018 he was compelled to use some crutches in between his commentary stints with Sky, which was an unnerving sight. 'It's all catching up with me,' he joked. So extraordinary were the cricketing careers of Richards and Botham that they were presented with dilemmas that most of us never have to encounter. If he had ever stopped to rationalize, Ian – Sir Ian from 2007 onwards – was bound to acknowledge that he could never touch the heights of 1978–81 again and that he was only twenty-five years of age when he was tormenting the Australians at Headingley and beyond. He was an astounding cricketer during that period and the foremost sporting personality in the country. It was impossible that he could ever do anything better than play cricket as he did in those four years, yet his life had barely begun. Where do you go from there? It seems that he has found a way. Raising millions for leukaemia research from all those walks was an inspired undertaking for the charity – and for himself. After his retirement he became a Sky pundit and still has a few business ventures, the latest of which involves wine, in between the shooting and fishing and the grandkids.

There may have been the odd moment when it was debatable whether Ian would ever get this far but he has always paid a little more attention to his advisors than he lets on. Even so, I do remember listening to him with mild astonishment on his fiftieth birthday, which he celebrated in a Lahore golf club in November 2005. George Best had just died of alcohol-related causes and I promise I heard a well-lubricated Ian chastising Best on that evening. 'I mean, what was he doing? They say he was drinking four bottles a night!' I started an intervention involving pots and kettles but in the end did not bother to proceed.

Naturally enough Ian and Viv never played cricket after their retirement. What would be the point? I played only sporadically. Unlike Pete I resisted a gentle enquiry from Devon after leaving Somerset. I played a few press matches on tour, often with modest results and amid much hilarity in a side that was usually led with great sensitivity by John Etheridge, a batsman who played with the no-nonsense aggression we expect from the *Sun* correspondent. And I was a regular in the *Observer* XI's annual fixture at Hinton Charterhouse in north Somerset, where Scyld Berry, who would produce delicious chilli con carne afterwards, still plays his cricket with unbridled enthusiasm.

I was persuaded to play a few serious games for Tiverton Heathcoat CC in the Devon League in the mid-nineties – for a couple of years I was able to turn out when they had league matches on a Sunday with my *Observer* duties done. This was a good standard of club cricket. Gareth Townsend, who was on Somerset's books for a while and who is now the academy director at Surrey, captained the side. Gareth's brother, Graeme, managed the side impeccably and another Somerset old boy, Julian Wyatt, who would later become an excellent coach, was in the team. But mostly I remember bowling alongside two larger-than-life leg-spinners.

First there was David Halfyard, once of Kent and Nottinghamshire, who often slept in his old campervan and kept playing well into his sixties, initially for Cornwall and then for Tiverton Heathcoat. I remember him bowling out Somerset's second XI in Truro in 1974 as most of us failed to decipher his googly. In my first game alongside him on a very windy day in the West Country about twenty years later Gareth asked me which end I would like to bowl. I looked over to David, twenty-five years my senior and now compelled to limp and lumber up to the crease, and I realized that I had better bowl into the wind (it is a myth, by the way, that spinners revel bowling into a strong breeze). This was the right decision on several counts since David was never slow to express an opinion. And he was about sixty-three. David was on the umpires' list when I was at Somerset and once when bowling at his end in helpful conditions he exclaimed as I tossed him my sweater: 'I don't know what you're doing out here. I would have bowled them all out by now.'

The other leg-spinner is better known. In early May I pitched up for a game at Budleigh Salterton and I watched this young Australian fizz down a leg-break that spun a mile, defeating the batsman, the wicketkeeper and an admiring first slip. This was Stuart MacGill, who would end up taking 208 Test wickets for Australia despite being a contemporary of Shane Warne. Very few Devonian batsmen could pick his googly and sadly that was often the case with our gallant wicketkeeper as well. In his first league match MacGill had to wait for about ten overs to come on to bowl. Thereafter he was never out of the attack when playing for Tiverton Heathcoat – until the disciplinary panel handed him a two-game ban before the end of the season. Stuart could be a charmer but he had a remarkably short and erratic fuse – he barely lasted a month up in the Lancashire League. But he bowled some of the most unplayable deliveries under 60 mph that I've ever witnessed at first hand.

Those Devon League matches aside, playing cricket became an occasional social activity. My last game was in 2012, the year of the London Olympics. It was for the Old Blundellians against France and it took place at Tiverton. This match was inspired by the Paris Olympics of 1900, the only Olympiad in which cricket has featured (so far). A band of cricketers named the 'Devon County Wanderers', which contained four old Blundellians and five players from Castle Cary CC in Somerset, happened to be in France and some matches were hastily arranged under the Olympic banner. According to the official report of those Olympics, Grande Bretagne '*gagne par 157 points*' against France and won the gold medal.

In Tiverton over a century later we celebrated that occasion. I stood at slip, bowled three overs, batted at number ten and cunningly led the home side to victory. According to francecricket. com there was compensation in defeat for one of their cricketers, Christopher Bartlett, '*qui ajoute un troisième "Test player" à la liste de ses victims au lancer, le guichet de Vic Marks s'ajoute à ceux de Hashim Amla et John Edrich*' (I know my readership needs no translation). At least I was in good company. Amid the post-match festivities I announced my retirement from international cricket, the nearest I had come to a scoop for a while. And I have not played a game of cricket since.

But I have played a few rounds of golf. Now this usually happens just below a few Dartmoor tors at Okehampton on one of the shortest and friendliest courses in Devon, where there is nothing so boring as a flat lie or a straight putt. I am also a Gibbon. Back in 1994 I was invited to join this 'honourable' society (I think inverted commas may be applicable here), which was formed by cricket hacks Mike Selvey, Martin Johnson, David Lloyd (not Bumble but Toff, the former Press Association and *Evening Standard* correspondent) and Graham Otway back in the eighties along with David Norman, a cricket lover who once helped Selvey and many other Middlesex cricketers by setting up lucrative benefit matches in his home town of Bury St Edmunds. 'Norms' would organize everything brilliantly on our annual trips to East Anglia in between cackling away in the corner of the bar often about his cricket tours to Devon in the sixties. Once the all-powerful (some might say tyrannical) committee decided to permit an expansion of the Gibbons, CMJ, Derek Pringle and I became regular participants on what was a week-long jaunt at the end of the cricket season (well, four and a half days of golf, which worked out at 162 holes that seemed to get longer and longer by the day). Recently this has dwindled to two and a half days and then to zero in 2018. Other Gibbons include Ian Todd, Chris Lander, Mark Baldwin, Reggie Hayter and Kevin Mitchell from the press box, from broadcasting John Rawling and Louise Ringer and a few ex-cricketers such as Paul Downton, Bill Merry, Angus Fraser, Paul Allott and

David Saker. Then there were a few of Selve's mates and a lot of Norms' mates when we suddenly found ourselves short for the afternoon foursomes.

I was going to offer some detailed descriptions of hilarious moments in Gibbons history such as CMJ's ill-tempered 13 on the eighth at Hunstanton; that fighting half in nine in the foursomes; the seventeen clubs discovered in Todd's bag; the time when the buggy hired by Norms only went backwards; being asked to get a move on by a septuagenarian with a wooden leg at Brancaster. But before the editor strikes I'll acknowledge that these moments may only be of interest to a Gibbon and there are not many of those around – it being such an exclusive society.

Suffice it to say that over the twenty-five years I kept trekking east at the beginning of October (I always won the longest drive), we played a lot of terrible golf on glorious courses especially at Hunstanton and Brancaster and there was an interminable stream of garbage spoken in the evening after a few pints of Wherry. There is a website, for which we must thank Martin Johnson, which is a bit of a surprise. In his capacity as a journalist of rare quality, mostly for the *Leicester Mercury*, the *Independent* and the *Telegraph* – it is one hell of a burden to make your reader laugh every day, which was the standard he set – Martin always gave the impression that his prime goal was to avoid work by any means possible. Yet over the years he has volunteered many thousands of words to the website which he has created with some assistance from David Lloyd, a resource that future golf historians may puzzle over.

The prospect of the Gibbons week used to keep Mike Selvey going towards the end of a long season. Mike was the *Guardian*'s cricket correspondent for thirty years and in the last period I was working alongside him. Selve did it his own way. Sometimes he would be rung up by some brave soul in the office who was planning the pages and therefore wanted to find out what he intended to write about. Selve would invariably answer, 'I don't know' though not out of bloody-mindedness. He genuinely would not know. He would create a file on his laptop with a distinctive lemon-yellow background; he would write 'from selve' at the top of the page and off he would go with only a vague idea of his final destination.

He always got there. Others would make more meticulous preparations before they started but Selve, even though he might have made some notes, scarcely looked at them. He would tap away and if he was writing a match report he could be guaranteed to finish within ten minutes of the last ball being bowled; then he would shut his laptop, off he would go and it would all make sense in the morning. There is no right way to do our jobs. Since taking over from Selve at the *Guardian* I wear an imaginary wrist band upon which are carved the letters WWSD. This is designed to be an encouragement and a source of comfort when life is getting tricky in the press box. 'What Would Selve Do?'

AFTER LEAVING SOMERSET at the end of the 1989 season I kept an amicable distance from the club for almost a decade. I followed their progress closely and popped in occasionally but felt uncomfortable about returning to the dressing room. This was not my territory now. In 1998 I had a call from Peter Anderson, the chief executive, asking whether I would become cricket chairman. Brian Rose had been in that post but needed to devote more time to his proper job in the paper industry. I agreed and remained until 2015.

It was not really an arduous post, especially after the appointment of a director of cricket beyond the first-team coach. The
cricket chairman watched as much cricket as possible, liaised
with the coaches, offered encouragement and attended committee
meetings, which was the most laborious of his commitments. And
the position came with a very convenient car parking space. The
post also involved saying 'I think you're all doing frightfully well'
quite a lot though inevitably there was some angst when we kept
losing.

At the County Ground Anderson answered to 'Chief' and
always gave the impression of being a benign, ruddy-faced dicta-
tor. He would sometimes berate his players with gusto but usually
with a smile as well and beyond the bluster he would look after
them. Peter Trego, while still in his teens, once managed to silence
him after seeking a meeting in his office. 'Chief, there is something
I've been meaning to ask you. Is it all right if I get married?' But
Anderson was not struck dumb very often.

By now he had been chief executive for ten years and he had kept
the club a vibrant place even though the lack of any trophies was a
continual source of frustration. Along with Rose he had recently
taken the bold step of signing Dermot Reeve, whom Anderson had
known as a youngster in Hong Kong, as the coach. Dermot has
always been a fertile, lateral thinker and he soon announced that
he wanted to sign Jamie Cox, an opening batsman from Tasmania,
as Somerset's overseas batsman. This sounded like a good idea. He
then said that he would also like Jamie to be captain before adding
that he had never actually met him. He had scoured lists of overseas cricketers and come to his conclusion. We cautiously agreed
with him. That winter Anderson came to Australia while England
were touring there and we met Jamie in Melbourne to seal the

deal but also to gain an impression of whether Dermot's scheme would work.

From the start Cox, a calm, self-contained man, impressed. More importantly, after arriving in Taunton he scored runs as well and Dermot's hunch worked a treat. Cox stayed at the club for six years and became the first Somerset captain to raise a trophy in eighteen years when his side won the Lord's final in 2001. He now shares something with James Hildreth, being one of the finest batsmen never to play international cricket.

Cox lasted longer at the club than Reeve. In part this is because Dermot with his bags of enthusiasm and ideas was a whirlwind, which finally blows out. At one point he decided Marcus Trescothick should bat at seven and develop his bowling and he wanted to sign Tim Zoehrer, a wicketkeeper and teammate of mine at WA, as a forty-year-old wrist-spinner. After a while everyone needed a breather from his cascade of theories but at the outset he had the invaluable capacity to enthuse the players. Then Dermot was increasingly in demand as a commentator for Channel 4, who now held the rights for international cricket in England, and it was impossible to combine the two roles. Kevin Shine took over Reeve's position in 2001.

Soon Brian Rose returned as an employee of the club when appointed cricket director, which meant that the cricket chairman could take even more of a back seat. By then Somerset had dropped to the second division but they won the T20 trophy in 2005 with a very young side, under the fleeting leadership of Graeme Smith from South Africa. Rose then recruited Justin Langer as captain and Somerset were promoted in 2007 and have been in the first division ever since, the longest stay by any county.

But the Championship has still eluded them. They have finished second four times in the last nine years. The most agonizing season was probably 2010 when Somerset played their last match against Durham and were still leading the table with half an hour of the season to go – the trophy had been delivered by helicopter to Chester-le-Street – but too many Lancashire wickets fell at Old Trafford and with points level Nottinghamshire won the pennant by virtue of more wins. It was a fraught, compelling few days for me since I was wearing too many hats: talking on the radio for the BBC, writing for the *Guardian* and as cricket chairman willing Somerset over the line – to no avail

The outcome of the 2016 season was almost as exasperating as Somerset had most points with one day to go but the negotiations at Lord's in the game between Yorkshire and Middlesex meant that the required draw would never come about on the last day. So Middlesex topped the table. No one could begrudge Marcus Trescothick, who loves playing cricket more than any man I know – with the possible exception of Scyld Berry – a Championship medal. The 2019 season is his twenty-seventh with the club. Despite everything the Championship remains the trophy that everyone, the players, the supporters really want to win even though most of the games now have to be played at the cold extremities of the season. I have two cricketing cravings to be satisfied in my lifetime: that Somerset should win the Championship and that the Championship should still be worth winning. In 2020 the plan is to have ten sides in the first division and eight in the second, and I approve of this change since it better reflects the strength of the counties. But I'm far less enthused by most of the other changes to the domestic schedule proposed for that summer.

Off the field Somerset's financial stability has been the envy of many other clubs in recent times, which was never the case when

I joined as a young player. Their latest appointment as chief executive, Andrew Cornish, has made an impressive start in continuing the excellent stewardship of his predecessors over the last three decades – especially when pointing out that he is not interested in any 'vanity' projects, the likes of which can undermine counties so rapidly.

In 2002 Peter Anderson, frustrated at the difficulty of acquiring sponsorship from the limited commercial sector in the West Country, hit upon the idea of asking headhunters to find candidates from the business community who would be interested in becoming a 'commercial' chairman of the club in the hope that their contacts would enhance income. The headhunters set to work and delivered their names. Among them were Giles Clarke, who they said would be 'the brave choice', and Andy Nash. So Somerset took the plunge and Clarke became the chairman of the club in 2003 while Nash was invited onto the committee as well and would eventually be appointed chairman.

It was indeed a brave choice to appoint Clarke and in many ways Anderson's plan worked well though not quite as he had anticipated. Old committee members had not encountered anyone like Clarke before. He breezed in and brooked no arguments. Clarke was a formidable, ruthless, wealthy businessman, who lived in a mansion in the north of the county. It was said (probably by him) that he had financed his time at Oxford University by playing backgammon and there he took a degree in Persian with Arabic – apparently in between the odd net with Imran Khan.

Clarke brought his boundless energy and impervious self-belief to the club. He knew how to get things done and his presence undoubtedly enhanced and speeded up the development of the ground at Taunton, which is now one of the best beyond the Test arenas. He did not appear to know how to sit on a fence, a skill at which most Somerset chairmen, being farmers, were adept. When Richard Gould was chief executive and hit a snag on some issue or another he would refer to Clarke as his 'nuclear option' to be used only as a last resort. Alongside Roy Kerslake, who had by now returned to the club as a hands-on president with invaluable experience of how everything worked, Clarke was also influential in bringing Brian Rose back, a move that undoubtedly improved Somerset's cricket.

The irony for Anderson was the realization that he and Clarke were increasingly incompatible. Both were used to running their own fiefdoms without opposition. Anderson had created and re-cruited someone with whom he found it extremely difficult to work. So he left, slightly prematurely, in 2005 after seventeen years of sterling service. Peter's departure was handled in an adult manner and he has been a regular visitor since. His successors have had the good sense to tap into his knowledge of the club.

Clarke's time as Somerset chairman should be viewed as one of significant progress. He was undoubtedly a positive influence. The stands went up on the edge of the outfield; the club went up the tables. From Somerset he progressed to being elected the chairman of the ECB in 2007 – he soon outmanoeuvred the establish-ment candidate, Mike Soper of Surrey. Before that he had rapidly become chairman of the ECB's marketing committee in 2004 and was therefore responsible for the vital TV deals, which are the lifeblood of the game. It is not so easy to be so positive about his contributions there.

Clarke's tenure of the ECB chairmanship, which lasted for a remarkable nine years, will be forever haunted by the 2008 photo-graph of him and Allen Stanford at Lord's standing in front of a cabinet supposedly containing twenty million dollars in cash. Stanford was the promoter of the winner-take-all T20 fixture in Antigua between his West Indian team and an England side up for hire. Everyone in that photo, except Stanford, looks very uncomfortable and that includes Clarke, Ian Botham, Viv Richards, David Collier, who was the chief executive of the ECB, and the England coach at the time, Peter Moores. If only Clarke had remembered the words given to Laocoön by Virgil in the Aeneid, 'Timeo Danaos et dona ferentes'. Even though he studied more distant foreign languages at university (he used to point out that he could understand – and therefore undermine – the cricketing bigwigs from the sub-continent when they were speaking their native language), he is bound to know what they mean. Whether it's Greeks or Texans bearing gifts one should beware.

It transpired that this was an almighty humiliation since Stanford would soon be proven to be a fraud. Yet even this was not the most critical moment in Clarke's time at the ECB. Far from it. That came before his election as chairman. It was in December 2004 under the guidance of Clarke that the ECB awarded the TV rights for all live cricket in England to Sky. It was a lucrative deal that no entrepreneur could turn down. At the time there were assurances that everyone's way of viewing sport was about to change radically. Ignoring terrestrial television would not matter much in the brave new world. Those assurances were wrong. In 2018 the ECB were bending over backwards in the most inelegant fashion to find a way to bring some live cricket back on terrestrial TV. In the meantime Alastair Cook had scored 12,472 Test runs and not one of them had been seen live on TV by those without a Sky dish. We never saw Graeme Swann take a wicket on live terrestrial TV, but we have seen him dance. Is that the best possible deal?

Clarke is an entrepreneur, brilliant at making money, and those instincts inevitably prevail when confronted by a decision. Such men are bound to be risk-takers and in recent times they have been drawn to cricket. The entrepreneur gambles in the knowledge that not all of his ventures will succeed but that does not matter provided some of them do. That may work in business; it is less effective for those governing one of our national sports. First and foremost the ECB should be the guardians of the game. The broadcasters do not fulfil that role; their priorities are to make money and grab ratings. Protecting the game can only be the ECB's duty. For a cricket board a failed venture really does matter as the losses – of income or interest – cannot be retrieved; for the entrepreneur it is just a mild setback. For all the money from Sky, whose broadcasting of cricket has been of the highest quality – arguably the best in the world – that decision back in 2004 has had a negative impact on the game, a fact acknowledged by the ECB's recent desperate attempts to restore some cricket to terrestrial TV. This was accentuated by the fact that the Ashes series of 2005, the last to be available on free-to-air television, was probably the best ever.

There was no easy way of turning the broadcasting juggernaut around after 2005. The terrestrial broadcasters were fast losing interest partly because cricket was so tricky to schedule. In 2015 Clarke was succeeded as chairman of the ECB by another entrepreneur, Colin Graves, previously the chairman of Yorkshire and a significant benefactor to the club when it was desperate for an infusion of cash. He is not risk averse either, which helps to explain the eagerness of the ECB to launch their new short-form tournament in 2020.

The ECB think I'm a curmudgeon because of my attitude to the 'Hundred', the short-form tournament proposed for 2020. It is true that I do not like the idea at all. On my list of pet hates it joins the tattoo and the referendum. The format is a patronizing gimmick rather than a radical change. The games will be 20 balls shorter than a T20 match and will be contested by eight urban sides, which will have no identities or fan-bases at the outset. They will have to be conjured up by the marketing men and women, who believe they can achieve anything with the right budget. Initially Sky and the BBC signed the lucrative contracts to televise these matches on the basis that they would be T20 games but the BBC, in particular, prefer the format subsequently dreamt up in the offices of the ECB: it is new, it is short, it might be deemed sexier and it is easier to fit into the schedules. It gets ever closer to 'Strictly Come Slogging' – perhaps Craig Revel Horwood could become one of the umpires. A reminder: the priority of the broadcasters is not to be the guardians of the game; that is the role of the ECB.

If I have become curmudgeonly on this – and I have tried hard not to morph into a press box dinosaur who constantly wonders what's going on out there – I'm not alone. Beyond those with a vested interest, like employees of the ECB or Sky, I have yet to meet anyone who greets this change with genuine enthusiasm. The fans feel alienated but because they are fans they may turn up if they happen to live within a twenty-mile radius of the city grounds, which still excludes hundreds of thousands of them beyond the seven urban centres. Meanwhile the counties not involved with the new competition are keeping their heads down, welcoming the promise of extra money, which was what persuaded most of them to give the nod to the proposals in the first place, and hoping that the current T20 tournament continues to thrive whatever happens to the Hundred.

I can be optimistic about English cricket – in fact more so than those at the ECB. The changes envisaged are predicated by their low opinion of the domestic game. Colin Graves once described our domestic T20 competition as 'mediocre', since when it has, of course, gained significantly in momentum. The ECB seem to regard the situation as being so bleak that they are prepared to gamble wildly. The English game – and the T20 format – is stronger than that.

However the format of the new competition is not my biggest bugbear. Of greater concern is the impact on a domestic schedule, which is already riddled with problems. In 2020 the likelihood is that most of the months of June, July and August will be given over to short-form cricket, the current T20 competition and the new one. No other cricketing nation has two short-format competitions in one season. A young English cricketer of talent will probably end up playing twenty-five to thirty of these games in the middle of the summer; hence the evolution of an all-round cricketer will be diminished even further. For him a long innings lasts an hour, a long spell is 20 balls. Meanwhile in the shires where cricket and cricket-watching still thrives, the only matches to be seen on our county grounds throughout the prime month of August are likely to be fifty-over games contested by a mix of first and second XI cricketers. The best players will be seconded to the city teams during the school holidays or they will be playing Test matches. All this is a massive sacrifice to get a little bit of cricket on terrestrial TV – and some more money in the ECB coffers.

In 2018 my *Guardian* colleague Ali Martin put forward an ingenious plan to solve the absence of any live cricket on terrestrial TV. At first sight it was beautifully simple. In his plan the Lord's Test each year would be broadcast by both BBC and Sky at the end of June. The BBC would give it the Wimbledon works, the full

Monty incorporating all their familiar programmes and personalities on radio and TV. The non-dish owning public would actually get to see Joe Root and Jos Buttler bat in one of the great sporting occasions of the summer. In this brave new world the casual viewers, which terrestrial TV attracts, would be intrigued and some of them would go on to purchase Sky packages so that they could continue to watch England play.

It is an excellent idea admired by many but, of course, it prompts much shaking of heads and a fair amount of doom-mongering. 'Yes, it would invigorate the game but along the way the ECB would have to take a substantial cut in income because Sky would never tolerate their exclusivity being threatened.' Another reminder: it is not the role of the broadcasters to safeguard and enhance the game. If that were the case Sky would be heroically open to plans to multiply the cricket-watching audience for one week every year. No, that responsibility lies with the ECB.

Cricket remains a damn good game capable of captivating the sporting public and that applies to all its current formats. I have watched two T20 World Cup finals that have provided stunning drama. In fact the format of the ICC's T20 World Cup is the most satisfactory of the lot. In Colombo in 2012 the West Indies were 32–2 after ten overs in the final against Sri Lanka and won. Marlon Samuels somehow propelled them to 137, enough to win by 36 runs. In 2016 in Kolkata it was Samuels again along with Carlos Braithwaite who conjured another astonishing West Indies victory – over England – with the latter hitting four sixes in the final over of the match from Ben Stokes. The T20 format works fine; it was not too difficult to understand what was happening out in Colombo and Kolkata; it was just harder to believe.

Yet nothing beats the prolonged drama of a great Test series and the best I have witnessed was, of course, in 2005. There have been other memorable contests, often in India, where England were almost mesmerizingly poor on the 1993 tour and really quite brilliant in 2012 when the unlikely triumvirate of Alastair Cook, Kevin Pietersen and Monty Panesar combined so well. The recent series in England against India in 2018 had its moments too, and the win in Barbados with Alec Stewart hitting two centuries in 1994 after England had just been bowled out for 46 in Trinidad had us all gasping in disbelief.

But 2005 trumps all these. That series also outstrips 1981 since the Australian side, led by Ricky Ponting, was the best in the world, not an accolade that could be attached to the team of Kim Hughes. Each Test match in 2005 was a mini-epic and by the end of August the nation was transfixed. Here we saw Michael Vaughan, the England captain, at his best. His greatest achievement – alongside Duncan Fletcher – was that he somehow managed to convince his players that they could beat those mighty Australians. They were mortal, after all. I don't suppose Vaughan adapted the words of Shylock for his team – 'if you hit them do they not bleed?' – but the blood of Justin Langer and Ponting was spilt during England's defeat at Lord's when Steve Harmison was bowling. In the following game at Edgbaston – with Glenn McGrath's suddenly out of the game with his ankle in ice – England were bowled out for 407 inside eighty overs on the first day. Traditional English caginess was put to one side and we were off on a wonderful roller-coaster ride. Even two-eyed Aussies recognize that this was the greatest modern series. For over two years – in 2005 and in the preceding eighteen months when England kept winning, most notably in South Africa – Vaughan's captaincy rivalled that of Mike Brearley and Ray Illingworth of distant memory. But after that triumph the team disintegrated with remarkable speed and Vaughan was reduced to rushing around frantically trying to pull rabbits out of his hat.

Bodies and minds started to creak and in 2006/7 England were ruthlessly crushed in Australia as if 2005 had been a pipedream, all of which made the 2010/11 series more pleasurable for an Englishman in Australia. I realize with mild alarm that I have been lucky enough to be in Australia for the last ten Ashes series, once as a member of the England touring party, once while playing for WA and eight times as a journalist. During that time they have won just twice, in 1986/7 under Mike Gatting and in 2010/11 under Andrew Strauss.

So we grew accustomed to the ritual humiliations that were all too frequently highlighted in the Australian papers. At one point in the nineties they kept asking, 'Why are we bothering to play the Poms in a five-Test series?' – a question that would have horrified the commercial department of Cricket Australia. Or there would be a photo of the Australian A side above the caption 'Is this the second best team in the world?' (Another '*Nonne*' question.) The English journalists can't help approaching an Ashes series differently. By and large the English press, while retaining their famous objectivity, always want their team do to well but this may not be their highest priority (the copy needs to hold up as well). But they are desperate for England to win against Australia come what may, especially in Australia.

By contrast the Aussie press, although they can be as critical of their own team as anyone, are always pretty desperate for their side to prevail against anyone – if only to confirm their idea of the world order. This helps to explain the extraordinary shock and horror in Australia that Steve Smith, David Warner and Cameron Bancroft had been tampering with a cricket ball in Cape Town in 2018 before being economical with the truth in the press conference thereafter. It was as if this trio had betrayed the entire nation. This was an act that required a prime ministerial intervention. In other parts of world it would have been a pinprick. All this contributes to the delight of the English journalist on the rare occasions that their Test team prevails in Australia. In Adelaide on that 2010/11 tour there were two separate press boxes. With the odd intruder the Aussies occupied one room, the Poms the other. Out in the middle the England side played superbly in Adelaide; the Aussies didn't and their journos were not happy. Their press room soon became known as 'The Library'.

Australia remains the best of tours. The cricket seems to matter; the hospitality is wonderful. One downside of today's schedules is that the chance to explore beyond the major cities is diminished. On our last trip Anna and I met up in Melbourne with some English friends, Rob and Nicki, who had been touring the country. They had decided that for a couple of days they wanted to try to glimpse something of the old outback beyond the glamour of the big cities and the beaches, and they took themselves to Broken Hill and beyond. There on a veranda outside a solitary pub an old local sat on his chair with a weathered face under his bushman's hat. 'Have you lived here all your life?' The old man stared at these rare visitors, paused for a while presumably to consider the question and then he drawled, 'Not yet.' Unfortunately that part of the country is beyond the scope of the cricket hack on a modern tour.

THERE ARE NOT many loose ends left. For nine years I chaired the MCC/Cricket Society Book of the Year award. The company and erudition of the judges and the chairman of the Cricket

313

Society and administrator of the award, Nigel Hancock, were always a delight. So too were some of the books, but not all of them. And I'm increasingly conscious that I'm now adding to the pile. Congratulations to any of the judges who have got this far. One of my traits is that I don't move on very quickly once I have links with an organization. As I explained when I withdrew from that judging role with the MCC and the Cricket Society, I almost felt I had to write a book so that I could justify stepping away.

My association with *TMS* remains and I guess it will continue to do so until they stop inviting me. They have a galaxy of fresh new experts so the invitations may not be quite so frequent now. But I have been lucky to stay on for so long and I keep telling myself that. I say to anyone who asks that it won't matter a bit if those invitations dry up since I've been so fortunate to be involved with the programme for the last three decades. Obviously it *will* matter but it seems the right thing to say. I have enjoyed being part of it too much to be so sanguine about the prospect of leaving.

Meanwhile the organization of my work as a journalist has been appalling. For nearly two-thirds of my career I worked only for the UK's oldest Sunday paper, the wonderful *Observer*, which, you may have spotted, comes out once a week. Then having reached my sixth decade, around about the time that some people start to wind down a little, I found myself also working for the *Guardian*, which comes out six times a week. Actually, despite the massively increased time commitment I have enjoyed it. It is a civilized place to work although I seldom actually go in to the office unless my laptop or phone is malfunctioning. It was always fun to work alongside Mike Selvey, David Hopps, who was usually fashionably late, and Andy Wilson. The same now applies with Ali Martin, Andy Bull and Barney Ronay plus all those in the office trying to make sense of what we send them. I have welcomed the challenge of writing on a daily basis. In one sense – just one – it is less taxing doing that simply because there is no longer the time to agonize. And there is always tomorrow.

I may be regarded as something of a throwback at the *Guardian* and in the press box. The importance of digital platforms and social media may have passed me by, though I do understand Twitter and I have therefore kept my resolve to shun it. I still cannot fathom why so many are keen to expose themselves by tweeting all the time. By the same token the magic of staring at one's phone for the vast majority of the day has also eluded me. This can mean I am a bit slower than some of my colleagues at catching up on the latest cricketing development.

But I still seem to be a bit obsessed by it all. Another cricket season comes around and I'm asked the inevitable question, sometimes by close family members: 'After all these years aren't you fed up with this stupid game?' And all I can do is echo the old boy on the veranda not so far from Broken Hill.

Not yet.

ACKNOWLEDGEMENTS

DEREK WYATT'S UNQUENCHABLE ENTHUSIASM set the ball rolling. He suggested that I write this book a mere 34 years after publishing *Marks Out of XI*. In London Clare Drysdale, the Editorial Director of Allen and Unwin, offered wisdom and encouragement in equal measure and she made the project seem like fun. In Devon Anna Marks has been a constant source of inspiration and good advice, who left no stone unturned in her determination to rid this work of clichés. Many thanks to all of you.

INDEX